BEWARE: THIS BOOK
DRY AND BORING!
IT WILL DRAIN ALL ENERGY AND
SLOWLY
MAKE
YOUR
EYELIDS
HEAVY
ENOUGH
TO PUT
YOU INTO
A DEEP
SLEEP
EVEN IF
WHEN
YOU PICKED UP THE BOOK, YOU
WERE WIDE AWAKE.

This is the completely revised and updated version of the immensely successful *Sociology of the Third World*. It is about the division of the world into rich and poor countries, and the disparities between rich and poor people, especially in poor countries. Chapters on world population trends and on the colonial episode set the historical scene for a detailed analysis of economic conditions and living standards in poor countries. Droughts, famines and environmental concerns are fully discussed, along with questions about limits to growth and sustainable development. Theoretical perspectives on development and underdevelopment are reviewed. Later chapters summarize the findings of the different social sciences on the growth of towns, language, culture and communications; the psychology of modernization; religious movements, sects, cults and fundamentalism; post-colonial politics, including ethnicity, military rule and recent democratization; and the issues involved in aid.

Some of my own comments: (Abridged)

This book is poorly written.
Some sentences are either incomplete
or incomprehensible - Sometimes both.

If this is a book on post-colonial
societies, why does it talk more about
Europe than the societies that are
under its control?

Who is this Guy anyway. I studied
Indians (American) last semester and
based upon my professor & the books
we read, he has included what
seems to me to be unacceptably
ignorant misinformation. But then, who am I
to judge? I wasn't there. But ..

I definitely reserve the right to question all that I read & hear and not to believe anything that has not been justly & thoroughly proved, or that conflicts with my common sense and previously-acquired, tested knowledge.

Warning to future Readers
   of this Book:

   Read Carefully & Question
   What you find herein!

If someone (you) is reading this book, it means that when came the time to sell this book back, I needed the money so, that I was unable to do to this book what I would have enjoyed - BURN IT!!

THE SOCIOLOGY OF POST-COLONIAL SOCIETIES

Economic disparity, cultural diversity, and development

THE SOCIOLOGY OF POST-COLONIAL SOCIETIES

Economic disparity, cultural diversity, and development

J. E. GOLDTHORPE
Senior Lecturer in Sociology, University of Leeds (retired)

CAMBRIDGE
UNIVERSITY PRESS

Published by the Press Syndicate of the University of Cambridge
The Pitt Building, Trumpington Street, Cambridge CB2 1RP
40 West 20th Street, New York, NY 10011-4211, USA
10 Stamford Road, Oakleigh, Melbourne 3166, Australia

The sociology of post-colonial societies: economic disparity, cultural diversity and development (first published 1996) succeeds and replaces *The sociology of the third world: disparity and development* (0 521 20521 2 hardback; 0 521 09924 2 paperback) first published in 1975 (second edition 1984), of which it is a revised and updated edition.

Printed in Great Britain at the University Press, Cambridge

A catalogue record for this book is available from the British Library

Library of Congress cataloguing in publication data
Goldthorpe, J. E. (John Ernest)
The sociology of post-colonial societies: economic disparity,
cultural diversity, and development / J. E. Goldthorpe
    p. cm.
Rev. edn of: The sociology of the Third World.
Includes index.
ISBN 0 521 57097 2 (hard). – ISBN 0 521 57800 0 (pbk.)
1. Social history – 20th century. 2. Developing countries –
Social conditions. I. Title.
HN16.G65 1996
306'.09172'4–dc20   95–26762   CIP

ISBN 0 521 57097 2 hardback
ISBN 0 521 57800 0 paperback

Contents

Preface

It was during my war service as a naval radar officer in 1942–5 in such places as Mombasa, Durban, Colombo, and Trincomalee, and through seeing at first hand the economic disparities and cultural diversities of peoples with widely different preoccupations and ways of life, that I finally decided to try to carry over the scientific attitude with which I had been imbued as a student of the natural sciences, especially at Cambridge, into the study of human society. After the war, then, I did not go back to Cambridge but went instead to the London School of Economics and Political Science to graduate afresh in economics and sociology, including social anthropology. As it had been what I saw in East Africa that had first and most strongly awakened my interest, in 1951 I eagerly accepted a post at Makerere College in Uganda (later Makerere University). There I pioneered the teaching of sociology as a degree subject, and in the process learned much and wrote something about East African society in general and the educated African elite in particular.

So it was with a somewhat narrowly East African focus that I came to Leeds in 1962, yet with a growing awareness that despite their profound diversities traditional societies throughout the world were subject to common forces making for change. Leeds proved to be a good place to seek a wider vision, with a consistently lively interest in development studies at all levels and in many departments throughout the University.

The idea of writing this book originated about the end of 1967, and the first edition was written during a 'semi-sabbatical' session in 1971–2. It was completely revised and largely rewritten just ten years later, my first task on taking early retirement from University teaching in 1981.

Revising it again in 1993–5 under a new and more appropriate title has sometimes felt like bringing out the third edition of a decennial newspaper. Some stories run and run, such as the continuing tension between Bretton Woods and Dumbarton Oaks institutions; some new stories demand inclusion, such as the Brundtland report and 'sustainable development'; yet others, such as famines, elbow earlier ecological concerns off the page. The UN Development Programme's adoption of a human development index as a counterpart to the World Bank's GNP per head has signalled an important shift in policy and thinking involving the dethronement of industrialization, once thought of as the main difference between rich and poor countries, and the main means for improving the human condition in the latter. Moreover, to an increasing extent the issues that demand attention are world issues, not only 'Third World' issues. Minimum wage laws afford one example; another is religious fundamentalism.

Successive revisions during two decades of rapid change have, I hope, given increased historical depth to the analysis, and taught me to write more in the past tense. Especially to one with a scientific background, propositions and statements about continuing tendencies are naturally expressed in the present. But strictly speaking we have knowledge only of past events; and if that is true in astronomy about receding galaxies, it has immediate practical importance for a social scientist writing in 1993–5 for whom the latest available demographic and economic statistics are for 1991 or 1992 while many recent research reports are of studies carried out in the 1980s. I hope, though, that a sense of immediacy has not been lost as the processes and problems of yesterday's world continue to affect today's.

I am grateful to those who taught me, including my tutors: at Cambridge, C. P. Snow; at LSE, Jean Floud. At Leeds the late Harry Hanson, professor of politics, encouraged me to start this whole project, while the late Lord Boyle, our vice-chancellor, was actively interested in development studies and honoured me with a foreword to the first edition. I am grateful to family and friends for tolerating my preoccupation with 'the book', and giving me their affectionate support. And I acknowledge with thanks the kindly help and guidance of the staff of Cambridge University Press at all stages.

J.E.G.
October 1995

Acknowledgements

Acknowledgement is made to:
Princeton University Press, for permission to reproduce from Kingsley Davis, *The Population of India and Pakistan* (1951) the figure showing birth- and death-rates in India, 1881–1946, as part of my fig. 4 on p. 38. Professor Michael Lipton, for permission to quote on my pp. 136–7 passages from his *Why Poor People Stay Poor* (1977).

Oxford University Press Inc., New York, for permission to quote a passage from the United Nations Development Programme *Human Development Report* on my p. 244.

1

Introduction and argument

Disparity and development

The transformation of human life through the application of science has been an uneven process, revolutionizing some societies and some aspects of human activity before others. From the outset we may distinguish the application of science to *health*, notably to public health and preventive medicine as well as to individual curative medicine; and to *production*, notably including agriculture as well as mining, construction, transport, manufacturing, etc., which we generally class together as 'industry'. Development, widely understood, refers to the whole process of transition, in which there has been a tendency in the past to over-emphasize the growth of modern industry (industrialization, the Industrial Revolution). As Ernest Gellner well said, the language of economic growth 'is misleading in as far as it suggests that what is at stake is something quantitative, a rate or speed or quantity of accumulation of goods. Ultimately, what is at stake is something qualitative – a transition between two fundamentally different forms of life.'[1]

Nonetheless, it is the transformation of production that has been associated with the wide and increasing disparity among rich and poor countries, and among rich and poor people in the world as a whole, that constitutes a central theme of this book. The disparities are especially stark within poor countries, where a few wealthy families can emulate the affluent life-styles of the well-to-do in rich countries, while the great majority live at or near a bare subsistence. But disparities have widened within rich countries too, for example the USA and Britain in the 1980s, with big increases in poverty and homelessness.[2] In the world as a whole, according to the United Nations Development Programme's estimates for 1988, the richest 20 per cent of the world's population received at least 140 times more than the poorest 20 per cent, and the disparity had increased sharply since 1960.[3]

Such disparities are often discussed in terms such as 'a divided world' and 'the ever-widening gap', but these are misleading expressions. Ours is not a divided world; on the contrary, the world is one. Economic disparities have certainly been 'ever-widening', but some other disparities could better be described as 'ever-narrowing'. Due notably to the application of science to public health and preventive medicine (rather than individual curative medicine), mortality rates in poor countries have converged on those in the West. So have fertility rates in major regions except Africa, and there has been convergence too in other aspects of development such as schooling and literacy.

Anthropologists of an earlier generation used to write monographs about societies which, if not strictly 'untouched', had been affected by outside influences to only a limited extent. In that golden age, social anthropologists could analyse a society as a unique form of human association with its own distinctive structure and culture to be explained mainly in its own terms. Now that is clearly no longer possible. The world has broken in. International politics and the world economic system have intruded into those 'untouched societies' in the form of institutions such as mines, factories, political parties, armies, and schools, that now have to be considered as integral parts of the whole which it is the business of the social scientist to study and comprehend. Yet the pre-existing diversity of cultures, and their continuing significance, has certainly not vanished overnight, as we are reminded every day when we open the newspaper and read of cultural diversity associated with nationalist, tribal, or ethnic conflicts the world over, not only in the 'Third World'. While the heritage and perspectives of social anthropology are necessary for the study of 'Third World' societies they are not sufficient, and while there is certainly material for the consideration of the more specialized social sciences such as economics and political science these can lead to partial and misleading conclusions unless they are informed by a constant awareness of the whole whose parts they are studying. We need social anthropologists to ascertain, and to remind us of, what actually goes on at the 'grass-roots', and to indicate scepticism about official statistics and policies based on them. We need, too, the synoptic vision of the sociologist.

Units of analysis

For many purposes, the unit we have to consider is the *country*, that is, a defined geographical area with a human population and a *government*. Often, indeed, we have little choice in the matter, since it is the governments of countries that collect and publish statistics. Thus when we compare birth- and death-rates, GNP per capita, or school enrolments, the statistics we find in the appropriate sources are for units such as India, Kenya, and Brazil.

Governments collect and issue statistics because they wield legitimate power. They use that power also to issue currency, collect taxes, regulate banking, impose tariffs, borrow at home and abroad, and in countless other ways that affect the economic life carried on within their boundaries. So each country comes to have its own *economy*: a natural unit for analysis, even though no country's economy is isolated from the rest of the world and each is to a greater or less extent affected by what happens in the world economy as a whole.

Similarly, a government's policies about the national language, schooling, and the mass media of communication all affect its people's career prospects and cultural life, while its laws about marriage, inheritance, the care and custody of children, and such matters affect their family life. In certain respects, then, each country may come to have its own *society*. But the boundaries of country and society do not in general coincide. Many countries, especially in the Third World, are in a sense highly artificial, arbitrary creations whose boundaries might as well have been drawn along other lines on the map, and include societies with widely diverse languages and cultures, for example within Nigeria the Yoruba, Ibo, Hausa, and others. At the same time, some societies extend across the boundaries of more than one country, for example, the Samia, parted by an arbitrary boundary between Uganda and Kenya, or the overseas Chinese whose society extends into Hong Kong, Malaysia, Singapore, Thailand, Indonesia, and other countries.

Industrialization and development

Industrial countries have hitherto made lavish use of energy (though they may now be learning to use it a little less lavishly). Ever since the steam engine was invented, heat engines burning fossil fuels have put more power at the elbow of the inhabitants of the industrial countries than was previously available to them from their own muscles and those of other animals, and a limited use of wind and water power. In the 1990s there was a wide difference between the energy consumption of rich and poor countries: some thirtyfold, according to World Bank estimates for 1991.[4]

If energy represents the critical difference in terms of physics, then in terms of economics the concomitant difference is capital. Heat engines and the machines they drive represent capital investment on a vastly greater scale than the simple tools of a non-industrial economy. Those who control them tend to be highly rewarded (alike in public or private ownership), and as industrial capital comes to outweigh land as the principal source of wealth and power, so income disparities are enhanced. At the same time the use of machinery increases the productivity of labour; indeed, the very nature of work is transformed by the application of science, as it comes to be done by machines controlled and directed by human operators rather than being directly performed by their own muscles. So wages are potentially high, and in so far as trade union organization is permitted it can ensure that actual wages correspond to the productivity of labour. Indeed, in countries with a small capital-intensive industrial sector, workers in industry can represent a relatively highly paid and privileged minority, sometimes called an 'aristocracy of labour' (though that is a controversial term).

In the past history of the latter-day rich countries, industrialization entailed a process of capital formation, initially by forced saving and 'going short' out of low levels of income, later by saving and investing out of higher incomes to use power-driven machines to make more machines. In this process there was a shift of the labour force out of 'primary' production (agriculture and other 'extractive' occupations like fishing and mining) into 'secondary' industry including manufacturing. This has been followed in the later stages by a further shift, out of industry as it became more capital-intensive, into inescapably labour-intensive activities, 'tertiary' and 'quaternary', as diverse as retailing, education, social welfare services, and leisure. Industrialization has been only one aspect of development, albeit an important, even pace-setting part. The present-day affluent countries have indeed been through the rise *and fall* of industry, and services now dominate their economies, generating 58 per cent of their combined GNP in 1991, according to the World Bank[5] – which, significantly, dropped the term 'industrial' from its classification of countries in 1989 and substituted 'high-income'.

According to this view, the process of change which came to be known as industrial development or the industrial revolution started at different dates and proceeded at different rates. By common consent Britain was the first industrial country, followed by other western European countries, then Russia and Japan. The United States was a late starter, still a mainly agrarian nation of farm and small town until as late as 1900, but its industrial development was then very rapid and it quickly overtook the rest. In many other countries industrialization started late, or proceeded slowly, or both. The underlying assumption was that development was to be identified with industrialization, and measured by the growth of average income or GNP per head.

From this point of view the 'Third World' consisted of the late indus-trializing, the as yet little-industrialized countries, whose development could be expected to recapitulate that of those where the process had started earlier. Countries of this kind were first called 'underdeveloped' in a report to the United Nations in 1951. The word had not then acquired all its present associations, and as the report itself said, 'an adequate synonym would be "poor countries"'.[6] Later, when 'underdeveloped' came to be thought of as derogatory, they were called 'developing' – an instance of what Myrdal called diplomacy by terminology,[7] for while in some there was indeed rapid growth of GNP per head, in others that was a negligible or even a negative quantity.

Classical perspectives

It goes without saying that nineteenth-century sociological thought, like much nineteenth-century thought generally, was evolutionary. Thus Comte regarded it as one of the aims of sociology 'to discover through what fixed series of successive transformations the human race, starting from a state not superior to that of the societies of the great apes, gradually led to the point at which civilized Europe finds itself today' – that was in 1822. Social development was a product of intellectual development, which albeit somewhat unevenly had proceeded in three stages, culminating in positive (or as we would now say scientific) thought associated with industrial, peaceful social organization.[8]

Somewhat similarly, Herbert Spencer classified societies by the complexity of their organization, and into 'industrial' and 'militant' types. He did not mean by 'industrial' quite what we understand by the term today, and classed some simple and technologically primitive societies as industrial because they concentrated on peaceful production rather than war. Nevertheless he made it clear, by implication if not explicitly, that he regarded industrial societies as superior and more advanced from the evolutionary point of view, for he wrote of 'reversions' and 'partial reversions to the militant type of structure' in advanced contemporary societies including his own. Anything involving coercion or compulsion was 'militant', while 'industrial' societies were based on the voluntary co-operation of free individuals.[9]

Following Spencer, Maine concluded from his study of ancient law that 'the movement of the progressive societies has hitherto been a movement from Status to Contract';[10] and together with the British economists from Adam Smith onwards they laid the foundations for Durkheim's analysis of the division of labour, with its distinction between mechanical and organic solidarity. Mechanical solidarity characterized a society in which there was little division of labour and people were like-minded because they performed similar tasks, and the structure of such a society consisted of homologous segments like clans. Durkheim probably erred in under-estimating the extent of individual differences in such societies, and overestimating the predominance of penal customary law in them.

Organic solidarity was that of the complex society with a high degree of division of labour. Here the social structure consisted of interdependent associations, like industrial enterprises exchanging goods and services with one another. Occupational and other groups would tend to develop their own different sub-cultures, and such a society could no longer rely on common values as a source of solidarity. Durkheim differed from the British school in recognizing that self-interest mediated through free contract does not assure solidarity, since interest makes me today your friend, tomorrow your enemy. He accordingly rejected Spencer's extreme individualism, and looked rather to the rise of new sources of solidarity like professional ethics to maintain long-term non-contractual relations among individuals and groups; while ritual was another way in which groups engendered and maintained their solidarity and cohesion.[11]

Although Marx and Engels differed sharply from the liberal tradition of Comte, Spencer, and the British economists; based their approach on historical materialism; and saw class conflict as a main explanation of social change, they too like their contemporaries put their ideas into a grand perspective of the stages of development of human societies. Originally property took the form of tribal ownership and the social order was an extension of the family. Then the slavery that had always been latent in the family became the dominant institution of society, so that citizens and slaves were the two classes of the city-states of ancient Greece and Rome. The third stage of development was feudal, with peasant serfs instead of slaves as the subject class of producers. And it was obvious enough that what they characterized as the bourgeois capitalist society of their own time had emerged from feudal society when the labourer ceased to be a slave, serf or bondsman and became a free seller of labour power. To bring about that state of affairs, the industrial capitalists had to displace the feudal lords; and Marx wrote that 'The hand-mill gives you society with the feudal lord; the steam-mill, society with the industrial capitalist.'

When Marx became the correspondent of the *New York Daily Tribune* on Indian affairs, and became accordingly more aware of the civilizations of India and China, he saw Oriental society, based on the Asiatic mode of production, as a kind of alternative or by-pass to the Occidental stages of the city-states and feudalism. It was typified by a centrally controlled canalization and other public works, its urban trading class was weakly developed, and it was too centralized to be feudal, while in its social order the unifying function of the tribe was usurped by the despot and his ideological reflex the deity. Marx accordingly wrote in a summary way of the 'Asiatic, ancient, feudal, and modern bourgeois modes of production' as 'progressive epochs in the economic formation of society'.[12]

Among his many contributions to sociological theory, Max Weber, like Marx, grappled with the question of the rise of capitalism, but he rejected

Marx's historical materialism and the economic determinism which it entailed. While capitalism could be seen as a set of institutional arrangements including rational book-keeping, formally free labour, the separation of the household from the workplace, the separation of corporate business property from personal property (by means of limited liability), and the concept of citizenship, such a view saw only the bare bones. The whole structure had to be brought to life, and what inspired it and gave it direction Weber called the spirit of capitalism. This he identified with the Protestant ethic, whose rise he traced in the seventeenth century in the Calvinist sects and the Puritans in western Europe and America. The sense of a calling to be in the world but not of it, to lead a godly, righteous and sober life without withdrawing into a monastery, and to resist all the temptations of the world, provided the motivation for the distinctively Puritan virtues of thrift, honesty, sobriety, diligence in business and sheer hard work. With such virtues it was indeed hard not to succeed, yet if it were wrong to expend resources in personal consumption and frivolous display, what else to do with the profits but re-invest them in the business? The 'elective affinity' between the Protestant ethic and the spirit of capitalism indicated that, so far from religion being a mere superstructure, affording ideological justification for the harsh necessities of the material economic base, the converse might be the case, and religion as an independent factor could play a part in initiating social and economic change.[13]

Tönnies contrasted the 'natural, organic' relations of the family, village, and small town (*Gemeinschaft*) with the 'artificial, isolated' condition of urban industrial society (*Gesellschaft*) in which the original and natural relations among human beings are excluded and all strive for their own advantage in a spirit of competition. Western Europe had passed from a union of *Gemeinschaft* whose prototype was the family, through an association of *Gemeinschaft* with corporations and fellowships of the arts and crafts and 'relations between master and servant, or better between master and disciple', to an association of *Gesellschaft* with the rise of the joint stock company and limited liability. A fourth stage was possibly represented by movements like consumers' co-operation and British guild socialism, a revival of *Gemeinschaft* in forms adapted to the prevailing *Gesellschaft* which might become the focus for 'the resuscitation of family life and other forms of *Gemeinschaft*'. No doubt his nostalgic analysis idealizes the harmony and integration of small-scale rural communities and overrates their advantage; but the notion of *Gesellschaft*, like Durkheim's organic solidarity, expresses the complex interdependence of modern industrial society while deploring its consequent impersonality.[14]

In his work on social development, Hobhouse tried to avoid value-judgements, sought to elaborate 'criteria of advance of a non-ethical character', and identified them as growth in scale, efficiency, mutuality, and freedom. His concept of 'efficiency' resembled Spencer's differentiation of the social structure, with co-ordination of the activities of different parts. Advance in one respect might not necessarily be accompanied by advance in others; thus a growth in the scale of social organization had often been achieved by means of repression and constraint, so that for instance the Greek city-states were smaller in scale than 'some of the great Empires of the middle culture', but enjoyed more freedom. Nevertheless, on the whole the four aspects of social development were so inter-related that there had been advance in all of them together in the history of humanity. Hobhouse's criteria of freedom and mutuality may well have expressed his position as a liberal social philosopher and not been quite as 'non-ethical' as he intended. His criteria of scale and efficiency, however, clearly converge on Durkheim's view of the division of labour.[15]

Among social anthropologists, however, Malinowski rejected evolutionary theories because they encouraged field-workers to look for 'living fossils', primitive customs carried over from earlier stages of social development (as in the work of L. H. Morgan), rather than regarding the institutions of non-western societies as having their function in meeting people's needs in those societies.[16]

The work of Talcott Parsons, the leading figure of US sociology in the 1950s and 1960s, was in large part a synthesis and elaboration of the nineteenth-century European classics, together with some other elements of western social thought, including especially Malinowskian functionalism in social anthropology.[17]

In his early work, Parsons clarified and elaborated Tönnies' distinction between *Gemeinschaft* and *Gesellschaft* into five major 'dilemmas of orientation' which he termed the pattern variables. Four of these had a bearing on the sociology of development, including the first, affectivity versus affective neutrality. The latter was shown when an actor postponed or renounced immediate gratification, as in decisions to save and invest rather than spend on current consumption. We may detect overtones of Weber's Protestant ethic here. Affective neutrality also characterized social relations in modern societies, which tended to be contractual, impersonal, and calculating; the continuing need for affective gratification in these societies was largely concentrated on family life, the one island of security left in which a high level of diffuse affectivity prevailed. As for the other three, Parsons gave a succinct example: 'The American occupational system is universalistic and achievement-oriented and specific.'[18] In other words, compared with other societies, in the USA people tended to be hired for what they could do rather than for who they were, careers were open to talents, and people were paid for carrying out specified tasks, rather than entering into more diffuse relationships. Where people recruited workers or admitted pupils on the basis of kinship, we in western countries called it nepotism and regarded it as incompatible with the ways of modern society.

In a later work, Parsons combined evolutionary and comparative perspectives in analyzing changes in the structures of societies 'ranging all the way from extremely small-scale primitive societies to the new supernational societies of the United States and the Soviet Union'. That evolution entailed differentiation, including for instance the separation of workplaces from households. That did not mean that the older units had 'lost function'; on the contrary, as already noted, just because the household was no longer an important unit of economic production it might well perform its other functions better. However, new roles had to be created in which authority was not derived from kinship; and there was a problem about establishing a new pattern of values appropriate to the new type of society. These new values might encounter severe resistance from groups adhering to older values which were no longer appropriate, a resistance he identified as 'fundamentalism':[19] I return to this subject in chapter 10.

It may be helpful at this point to tabulate the terms in which some sociologists of the classical tradition (including Parsons) have characterized the basic processes of change.

Spencer	from simple	to complex
	from military	to industrial
Maine	from status	to contract
Durkheim	from homologous segments	to interdependent associations
	from mechanical solidarity	to organic solidarity
Tönnies	from *Gemeinschaft* (natural, organic community)	to *Gesellschaft* (artificial, isolated association)
Hobhouse	growth in scale efficiency (complexity, differentiation), mutuality, and freedom	
Parsons (1951)	from affectivity	to affective neutrality
	from particularism	to universalism
	from ascription	to achievement
	from diffuseness	to specificity
Parsons (1966)	adaptive upgrading, differentiation of sub-systems	

Two general remarks may be made at this point about those older theories. First, evolutionary ideas have been called in question, not least among societies or peoples explicitly or implicitly classed as backward or primitive. Nonetheless, it is still very difficult not to think in terms of stages of development, especially about population trends, as in the next chapter; and this is the core of truth in works such as Rostow's *The Stages of Economic Growth*.[20]

Secondly, while some of the founding fathers, notably Spencer, saw a continuity between natural and social science, others, notably Durkheim, insisted that social facts were *sui generis*, in a class of their own, not to be explained in terms of other sciences such as biology and psychology. In Britain, sociology was born in a life-and-death struggle against the eugenics movement, which followed Spencer in seeing progress as the survival of the fittest and biological heredity as the primary factor in social welfare, and favoured encouraging the birth of the fit and discouraging the birth or survival of the unfit. For the leading eugenist Karl Pearson, heredity accounted for nine-tenths of a man's ability, and selection of parentage was the sole effective process known to science by which a race can continuously progress. Countering this, for Hobhouse the calling of sociology was to show that 'the biological conditions of human development are not such as to present any insuperable barrier to progress', and that 'we may expect to find progress, if anywhere, rather in social than in racial modification'.[21] Sociologists in Britain ever since have been consistently wary of anything that smacked of genetic determinism or biological explanations of human behaviour.[22] Likewise in later generations, sociologists generally have rejected socio-biology.[23]

Among anthropologists, Malinowski's functionalism was explicitly biological: the function of a people's culture, their system of institutions, was their flesh-and-blood survival. When Parsons took over Malinowski's concept of functionalism, however, despite some acknowledgement of 'viscerogenic needs', the main emphasis was on the survival of a social system, a much more abstract concept; while his 'pattern maintenance' was clearly a quite different notion from the flesh-and-blood survival of a human population. Indeed, it could sometimes be argued that a people's flesh-and-blood survival would be better assured, and their needs more adequately met, if their social system were not maintained but changed.

In latter-day development studies, in continuity with those earlier controversies, sociologists' aversion to natural science has been evident in suspicion towards technological solutions such as the Green Revolution for 'Third World' problems. Similarly there has been an emphasis on human agency in famines, down-playing droughts, floods, desertification, etc., and highlighting class factors ('famine was always class famine')[24] or the alleged disruption of traditional patterns under colonial rule or capitalist penetration, to the point that 'the very idea of a natural hazard is called in question'.[25]

I now turn to a preliminary outline of the main schools of thought in development studies, to which I give more detailed consideration in chapter 6.

Modernization

When development studies emerged in the 1950s it was a widely held view among economists, political scientists, and sociologists that if some countries were rich and others poor, that must be because the former were advanced and the latter backward; that the former had passed through the stages of development associated with industrialization ahead of the latter. The problem of the development of the poor countries, and the raising of the living standards of their inhabitants, was seen as the problem of how they could catch up – by their own efforts, or with outside help, or both. If they had not done so, or if they responded sluggishly to the efforts of their own government and outside development agencies, there must be obstacles to development. Identifying those obstacles, and helping to remove them, was seen as a contribution which social scientists might usefully make to the process. Thus in Latin America, an inequitable distribution of land was seen as an obstacle to development. Peasants without land rights had little incentive to improve their methods and their holding, while the very rich landlords showed little inclination to invest in industrial development. The whole system was seen as feudal, a view based with some justification on the history of a continent which fell under the domination of Spain and Portugal at a time when the feudal system prevailed there as it did all over Europe. The social structures of Latin American countries, with their landowning military elites, were seen as archaic survivals from a pre-modern era, inappropriate for the needs of the twentieth century. Similarly, in India the caste system with its notion of hereditary occupations – or more exactly a 'lack of unrestricted choice of occupation' – was seen as one obstacle to development. Another was the complex of avoidance and observances of orthodox Hinduism, exemplified by the ban on cow-slaughter, which seriously restricts selective breeding for meat and milk and the rise of a modern animal husbandry that might provide much-needed protein for the Indian masses. And in many places an obstacle to development was found in religions which diverted resources into an unproductive monasticism, or encouraged a fatalistic resignation to the divine will, unlike the Protestant ethic that had played its part in the economic development of Europe and North America; and social scientists looked for latter-day functional equivalents of the Protestant ethic, sometimes with success.

In this style of thought, industrialization was identified with development, and both with modernization. The last was a key word especially among scholars and social scientists working in this field of study in the United States. 'Traditional' and 'modern' were contrasted antonyms, while 'modernization' was the passage or transition from one to the other. It was both political and personal. The modernization of a society and its institutions occurred when people were liberated from archaic restrictions and became free to move – particularly from country to town – to engage in trade, and to enter wage employment; while the modernization of individuals occurred as they became mentally free, through education, literacy, and exposure to the mass media of communication, to imagine things otherwise than as they are, and to make informed choices. That indeed was the nub; United States scholars wrote of modernity in terms recalling those in which Thomas Jefferson had spoken of freedom, as 'the possibility of choice and the exercise of choice'. The crowning achievement of the modern society was the informed participation of its citizens in public life through a democratic electoral political system affording them genuine choices of leaders and policies.

Not all social scientists in the mainstream tradition, however, identified themselves wholeheartedly with the modernization school. Many social anthropologists, accustomed as they were to suspending their own value-judgements and those of the cultures from which they came, and to discipline themselves to work within the cultural traditions they were studying, were unable to accept the prior judgement of the institutions of other cultures that was implied by the phrase 'obstacles to development'. Thus the Indian caste system found an eloquent defender in Louis Dumont.[26] Any implication of irrationality in the conduct of people of other cultures was alien to the whole tradition of social anthropology, which from the time of Malinowski had always alerted its practitioners to elucidate the rationality of seemingly bizarre practices and customs among the people they were studying. Social anthropologists have consistently appeared as the defending champions of those whom they studied, their beliefs and attitudes as well as their material interests.

Among the development economists, too, the so-called 'neo-institutional' school, mostly of Europeans, differed from their United States colleagues. Where the latter no doubt were thinking primarily about Latin American countries which had been independent for a century or more, Europeans were more likely to be interested in countries of Asia and Africa which had lately emerged from colonial rule, and laid greater stress accordingly on their ex-colonial character than on the allegedly 'feudal' nature of their institutions – an allegation that would not always have been easy to sustain. Seers and Streeten stressed the inapplicability of western economic analysis to the prevailing conditions in many Third World countries, with their different institutions and attitudes. Myrdal, too, consistently emphasized the influence of attitudes, institutions, and policies on the course of economic development. Questioning the view that development in one part of an economy necessarily spreads to other sectors, and noting the tendency for it to occur in enclaves with limited spread effects, he went further in pointing to 'backwash effects' by which development in one sector might draw in resources from others and impoverish them in the process. Redistributive policies might do much to counter backwash effects within a country, and level up economic development in different parts of its economy. Internationally they were more intractable.

Underdevelopment and dependence

Explanations of the poverty of poor countries in terms of their alleged backwardness did not go down well in those countries themselves. The very word seemed disparaging and gave offence, in the same way as the word 'primitive' came to be resented by people of the societies and cultures to which it had been applied, and was dropped accordingly from the language of social anthropology. And when the lack of economic development in poor countries was attributed to a lack of Protestant-ethic-type personal qualities such as thrift, industry, and enterprise, those explanations too seemed 'person-blamed'; a case of blaming the victim. For Third World countries were widely regarded as the victims of the past wrongs of colonial rule and the present inequities of the international economic system, not least among the social scientists and other intellectuals graduating from their burgeoning universities and entering the world of scholarship and the service of international organizations.

The intellectual movement associated with the terms underdevelopment and dependence (or 'dependency') began in the 1950s among Latin American economists reacting against the apparent failure of policies based on mainstream development economics to stimulate growth and begin to raise the living standards of the mass of the people. Later, in the 1960s, it became more widely known in the English-speaking world, largely through the writings of A. G. Frank. Gaining many converts, it became part of a general counterblast against mainstream social science.

In that counterblast, Parsons' view that development entails shifts in the pattern variables from ascription to achievement, from particularism to universalism, and the rest, was explicitly rebutted by reference to the particularism and ascription that prevailed in the highly efficient, and also strongly paternalistic, industrial organizations which had brought about the development of Japan. Analysis in terms of stages of development was attacked as concentrating on endogenous factors within each country and neglecting exogenous factors in the world system. It was particularly strongly denied that Latin American societies had ever been feudal; on the contrary, it was asserted that they had been capitalist from the time of the Spanish and Portuguese conquests. The notion of a pre-modern 'traditional' society was attacked as 'denying a history' to the underdeveloped countries, as it seemed to imply that they had persisted unchanged since time immemorial before the impact of industrialism. Equally strongly rejected was the idea of a 'dual economy', with a 'traditional' sector where people earned a living from the land by subsistence agriculture with 'Biblical' methods, and a 'modern' urban industrial sector where money transactions prevailed. The very notion of a traditional society and culture was thus dismissed, and pre-existing differences of language and ethnic identity were played down. On the contrary, it was asserted, there is only one world economy, and consequently one world system of social relations, and it is capitalist, penetrating every nook and cranny from the great industrial and financial centres outwards through national capitals, provincial towns, and small trading centres to the last remote rural hinterland. And if control extended from centre to periphery, profits were accumulated and surplus value appropriated from periphery to centre. The verb 'to underdevelop' was given a transitive meaning; poor countries were poor, not because they were *un*developed or backward, but because they had been and still were being actively *under*developed by rich countries. Political independence, indeed, was something of an illusion in a world in which the main relationships continued to be capitalist and imperialist. It served only to hide the real dependence of the poor countries on the rich, the penetration of their economies by western influences through the multi-national corporations, and the extent to which their ruling elites owed their power to support from western countries, especially the United States.

With its underlying economic determinism, the language and the concepts of this school of thought are recognizably largely Marxist: capitalism, imperialism, the appropriation and expropriation of surplus value in the process of the accumulation of capital, and so on. For this reason, it has often been called 'neo-Marxist'. However, the extent to which it is 'really' Marxist is debatable, and depends in turn upon highly debatable questions about which version of Marxist socialism is to be regarded as authentic. In some of the writings of the school, there are criticisms of Marx as being, like his bourgeois counterparts, a western European evolutionist whose vision of the importance and revolutionary potential of the industrial proletariat is not directly applicable to the Third

World of today. And there are diverse strands and controversies within the school itself.

During the 1970s, it sometimes seemed as if there were just two mutually incompatible ways of looking at the processes of social and economic change in the Third World: that of orthodox mainstream social science, or as its opponents called it 'bourgeois development theory'; and the alternative view stressing dependence and the active underdevelopment of the poor by the rich countries. It would be wrong to call it a debate, for there was little or no dialogue; the two schools of thought talked past each other.[27] Now that appears too simple. To a large extent the 'neo-institutional' school of European development theorists could, as we have seen, be exonerated from the neo-Marxists' strictures. They were aware that backwash effects can impoverish the periphery while development proceeds at the centre; they attached much importance to the colonial history of the present-day Third World countries; and they gave much weight to the international economic system.

The 'Third World'

Although I have retained the term 'Third World' in much of the discussion that follows, it must now be regarded as an outdated concept.

Its origins may be traced back to 1947, when a group of Labour members of the UK Parliament published a pamphlet, *Keep Left*, arguing (among other things) 'for a "Third Force" in world affairs, escaping the polarisation of Soviet communism and American capitalism'. As narrated by the historian Stephen Howe, at about the same time the British socialist Fenner Brockway presented a paper to a conference held at Puteaux, Paris, to set up a Congress of Peoples against Imperialism, in which he put forward 'the object of establishing a Third Force which would unite the peoples of Europe, Asia and Africa for national freedom, democratic socialism, and peace'. Although this was supported by democratic socialists from Asia and Africa, it was opposed by the African nationalists, and, reluctantly, the European socialists agreed to drop the proposal and concentrate on anticolonial aims.[28]

However, the idea did not go away; and in the 1950s it gained currency among French socialists looking for a 'third way' or 'third force' in the politics of their own country more congenial than a conservative nationalism on the one hand or a rigidly dogmatic communism on the other. On a wider scale, too, a third force seemed urgently needed in a world dominated and threatened by the increasingly tense 'cold war' between West and East. Their hopes were raised by diplomatic moves, led by the governments of Egypt, India, and Yugoslavia, and by a conference at Bandung in Indonesia in 1955 of twenty-nine African and Asian states, many of which had recently gained their independence from colonial rule. The phrase then coined by Alfred Sauvy, 'le tiers monde', interestingly embodies not the modern word 'troisième' but the archaic 'tiers', rich in historical associations with 'le tiers état', the third estate of the realm, the common people who rose in 1789 and overthrew the privileged first and second estates of the Ancien Régime, the nobility and the clergy respectively.[29] At that time, then, 'the third world' came to mean those countries which, however diverse, had three things in common: they were poor, they were ex-colonies, and they were non-aligned. Perhaps accordingly they could be thought of as the commonalty of the earth, who might if they united possess the same potential as the Third Estate showed in the French Revolution to transform the existing order.[30]

The term itself, and more important the view of the world it signified, were introduced (or re-introduced) to the English-speaking public largely by Peter Worsley in his book of that title, published in 1964,[31] and Irving Louis Horowitz's *Three Worlds of Development* in 1966.[32] It has since passed into the language of everyday discourse, to be used almost unthinkingly as a variant for 'poor' or 'less-developed' countries. But even before the end of the 'cold war' the term had lost any precise meaning, as some of the so-called developing countries had actually developed while others had stayed poor, and there were increasing disparities among 'Third World' countries. Already it was becoming more realistic to think in terms of 'north' and 'south', rich and poor, more and less developed countries; and moreover not in terms of a tripartite division, but of a continuous scale, based on some criterion measure such as GNP per head or, better, the United Nations' Human Development Index. With the détente between 'East' and 'West' there was no longer an effective 'Second World', and the demolition of the Berlin Wall in 1989 marked also the end of the 'Third World'.

2

Technology, society, and population

The natural history of the human population of the earth from the emergence of *Homo sapiens* to the present day (fig. 1)

There have been two great technological revolutions in human history.* Each was accompanied by a population explosion.[1]

Ten or twelve thousand years ago, *Homo sapiens* was a relatively rare species found living in small bands by hunting and food-gathering. Some human groups do so to this day, or did so till recently, including the Australian aborigines; a few small groups in Africa, such as those popularly called 'Bushmen', and the Hadza of Tanzania; the Andaman islanders; and some Amazon forest peoples.[2] From studies which have been done of the population density of people living in this way, it may be surmised that there can have been no more than 10 million humans on earth before the development of agriculture, and the actual population was perhaps 1 to 5 million.

Between about 9000 and 5500 BC, there occurred the first great technological revolution in human history. It involved a complex of inventions rather than one single crucial discovery. The domestication of a number of plant species, especially the grain seeds, greatly increased the carrying capacity of the land, or at least of land in some parts of the earth, and also made possible the storage of food, and both necessitated and permitted the growth of a settled population. This in turn stimulated the building of houses, an advance on the temporary shelters of food-gathering wanderers. The domestication of a number of animal species had equally complex and fundamental effects on human social

* 'Human' here refers to *Homo sapiens*. If we count other species of the genus *Homo*, all now extinct, and extend our time-scale to the past million years, we could distinguish an even earlier technological revolution corresponding to the making of the first stone hand-axes and similar tools, accompanied by population growth from perhaps around 100,000 or 150,000 individuals to perhaps 1 million.

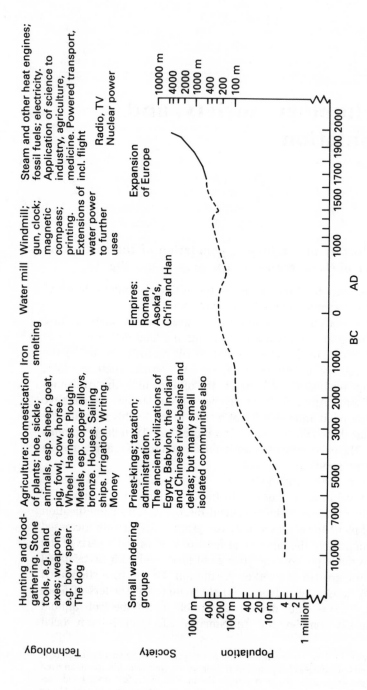

Fig. 1

Note to Fig. 1. Both time and population are plotted on logarithmic scales. Time is plotted on a logarithmic scale of years before AD 3000. This enables the long slow trends of the remote past to be somewhat 'foreshortened' while the rapid increase of the past 300 years can be seen without undue distortion. In the same way, plotting population on a logarithmic scale enables the diagram to show changes in the relative increase rate. The first population explosion from 5 million to 100 million is thus kept in the same perspective as the second from 500 million to some 5,350 million in 1991.

organization; these included sheep, goats, pigs, poultry, cattle, and horses. By adding the muscle power of other animals to that of humans, they made possible the rise of techniques such as ploughing; they added a dependable food supply of meat and milk, together with other animal products such as leather; and they afforded the means of transport and trade between the new fixed settlements of human beings. Along with agriculture, therefore, went the rise of the first towns, and correspondingly that of specialized crafts and manufactures in exchange for the food that was now available in a storable form. Other technological achievements of this period included the rise and elaboration of metallurgy and the making of tools and weapons of bronze and iron; the wheel, with its vast potential for both trade and war; and the wooden sailing ship, which added a limited use of another source of energy to human and animal muscle. And these technological developments were accompanied by remarkable economic, political, and intellectual developments, including the rise of money and systems of accounting; the rise of political authorities – mostly, it would seem, of the 'oriental despotism' type – wider than the kinship or neighbourhood principle; the invention of writing; mathematics, and its application to astronomical observation, surveying, and accounting; and the reckoning of time.

Although the first technological revolution seems from our standpoint like a leisurely affair compared with that of recent history, it was nevertheless a dramatically rapid change compared with the slow processes of evolution by natural selection, which had prevailed before the rise of culture. And like our own technological revolution it was accompanied by a population explosion. By the time of which we have worthwhile estimates, the largest human communities of people subject to a common political authority numbered scores of millions. The Han empire of China, Asoka's empire in India, and Roman rule around the Mediterranean basin comprised populations of around 50–100 million each, and the world's population at the beginning of the Christian era has been estimated at between 200 and 300 million.

Although the technologies of transport and war made empires possible, they did not sustain a system of communications and social interaction which ever approached the scale of the whole earth. Even the empires remained comparatively isolated from one another, while in areas which they did not conquer there continued to be smaller human groups, developing in relative isolation both distinctive cultures – different languages, technologies, kinship systems, systems of political authority, etc. – and also distinctive physical characteristics through the process known as genetic drift. So humankind came to be divided in two ways – by culture and by race.

After that great burst of innovative energy there followed seven thousand years of relative technological stagnation. This stagnation was not quite unrelieved, and we can distinguish two periods within it when significant advances occurred. One accompanied the development of iron smelting, apparently in about 1400 BC, and its spread, together with some inventions of minor importance such as the crane and the pulley at an early stage of Graeco-Roman civilization. The other occurred during a period around AD 1000–1300, with the invention of the windmill (possibly independently in Persia in the seventh century and in Europe about 1100), the gun, the mechanical clock, the magnetic compass and other aids to navigation, printing, and the further development of some older inventions including improved harness, making possible a wider use of animal power, and the application of water power to wider uses. The first great expansion of European influence across the world, indeed, began centuries before the industrial revolution and was based on the technology of guns and sails. Though the evidence is fragmentary, it seems not impossible that these periods of minor technological advance were also periods of population growth. In between such periods, and even to some extent during them, however, population grew very slowly, if at all, and from time to time experienced sharp setbacks from famine, pestilence, or war. From the 200–300 million which most authorities regard as a reasonable estimate for the world's population at the time of Christ, it possibly fell to not much more than half that number around the seventh century AD, rose again until about the thirteenth century, and was then severely reduced by the pandemic of bubonic plague later named the Black Death.[3]

For long periods of history, and still in some places today, human communities experienced high and fluctuating birth- and death-rates in an irregular succession of good and bad times. Good times occurred when the climate and weather were favourable, and crops were good; when there were no epidemics of killing disease over and above normal mortality; and when political conditions were stable and not unduly oppressive. Bad times were those of famine, pestilence, and war: droughts or floods leading to crop failure; outbreaks of disease among crop plants, domestic animals, or the human population themselves; or human-made disasters such as war with its consequent ravages of looting and pillage, the destruction of houses and stocks of food, the spreading of diseases by armies on the move, and the movement of people fleeing from the fighting or from political oppression.

Whether locally or on a wider scale, in bad times starvation or disease resulted disproportionately in the deaths of those most vulnerable: the old and the very young. As times improved, the survivors would now include a higher proportion of active adults than before, with fewer dependants. They might experience a rise in their standards of living, and inherit rights to land and other assets earlier than they would otherwise have expected. Marriages postponed during the bad years would now take place, while existing marriages would experience renewed fertility. The birth-rate would rise, and a recovery or increase in numbers would take place until the next calamity.

Thus the birth-rate and the death-rate, reflecting the patterns of fertility and mortality, were not independent of each other, and tended to move in opposite directions: fertility was low when mortality was high, and vice versa. This effect is to be seen in the figures for India before 1920 (fig. 4 below) and England before 1750 (fig. 5). Similarly de Waal, writing of the famine in Darfur, Sudan, in 1984–5, stated that lower fertility in famines had been attributed to 'amenorrhoea, anovulation, sexual abstinence, and separation of spouses', and that there was likely to be a 'rebound' with a high birth-rate for a short period after the famine.[4]

In many societies, a response to generally high levels of mortality, particularly of children, was high fertility, having many children in the hope that some would survive to look after their parents in old age. However, unchecked fertility and pro-natalist attitudes did not prevail everywhere, and in some exceptional societies fertility was checked in one way or another. This was particularly true of western European societies, where many women married late or not at all.[5] Among non-western societies, a striking case was the tiny Pacific island of Tikopia, where in 1929 the anthropologist Raymond Firth found an express awareness, especially among the elders and chiefs, that there could easily be too many people for the resources available. Population checks included late marriage, with coitus interruptus in pre-marital relationships; abortion, rarely; and in the last resort infanticide.[6] An example on a larger scale was Japan under the Tokugawa shogunate, as mentioned in the case-study below.

From 1650 onwards, however, despite setbacks especially in Africa, increasingly reliable estimates of world population as a whole indicate continuous growth. If it scarcely doubled in the first 1,650 years of the Christian era, from 200–300 million to 545 million, it nearly doubled again in about 160 years and passed the 1,000 million mark in about AD 1810–20. It then doubled in a century, reaching 2,000 million in about AD 1920–30. And it doubled again in sixty years to almost 4,500 million in AD 1981, and was estimated at 5,351 million in 1991.[7]

The demographic transition (fig. 2)

The idea of demographic transition arose in the 1920s when it was clear beyond doubt that in western countries both mortality and fertility had fallen and were still falling, and there was no indication what the eventual outcome might be. Many indeed feared that the birth-rate would fall below the death-rate in those countries and that their population would decline, though those fears were largely dispelled by the 'baby boom' that followed the Second World War. At that time, in the United States the demographer Frank W. Notestein, following the earlier work of Warren S. Thompson, put the demographic transition into the wider context of general modernization.[8] At the same time in Britain the demographer and eugenist C. P. Blacker set out a useful schematic analysis of demographic transition in five stages. According to his analysis, high and fluctuating birth- and death-rates were characteristic of a first, 'high stationary' stage. With a rise in the standard of living and the spread of modern scientific medicine, especially in the field of public health, populations pass into the 'early expanding' stage. In this second stage, the death-rate falls, but fertility remains high or even rises, and population increases at an accelerating rate. After a longer or shorter time, however, many countries have experienced a fall in the birth-rate consequent upon the adoption of a small-family system. There has accordingly been a turning point, marking the beginning of the third stage which Blacker termed the 'late expanding' stage, when although population continues to increase the rate of increase slows up. When births and deaths are again in balance, but now at low levels, we have the fourth or 'low stationary' stage; while the possibility exists that the birth-rate may go below the death-rate, so that we have a theoretical fifth or 'declining' stage.[9]

At the end of this chapter I give case-studies of three individual countries, namely India, England and Wales, and Japan, with the object of showing the different ways in which population trends have occurred and may be related to economic and other changes. Roughly speaking, using these three societies as examples, England and Wales may be said to have entered stage 2 in 1750; stage 3 began in 1877, a date which can be 'pin-pointed' by the Bradlaugh–Besant trial; while by about 1935 or 1940 stage 3 had come to an end, though whether the trends after 1940 deserve the term 'low stationary' is more doubtful. Japan entered stage 2 some time after 1868, and stage 3 came in with the dramatic drop in the birth-rate of 1947–57. India fairly clearly entered stage 2 after the great influenza catastrophe of 1919; whether stage 3 has been reached yet is doubtful.

However, useful as Blacker's analysis is, it will become clear that it does not exactly fit the population history of any of the three countries; still less, it must be emphasized, is it an inevitable sequence to be followed by all. When we come to translate 'high' and 'low' into actual figures, things become more difficult again. Although birth- and death-rates in western

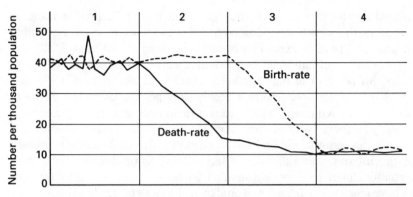

Fig. 2. The demographic transition. (After C. P. Blacker, *Eugenics, Galton and After.*)

Europe before the demographic transition were much higher than they are now, it seems that they were never as high as they were in the recent past in other parts of the world.

Thus whereas in India before 1920 (fig. 4) birth- and death-rates fluctuated between 40 and 50 per thousand, in England (fig. 5) the death-rate fluctuated around 30 and went above 40 only in the last severe mortality crisis of 1729, and birth-rates exceeded 40 only for a few years between 1800 and 1825. Studies of the demographic history of other European countries including Ireland and Norway suggest that, as in England, fertility was limited by late marriage and birth spacing, so that families were not large, especially among the poor;[10] and I refer below (p. 30) to France, where the birth-rate and death-rate fell together, so that Blacker's stages 2 and 3 ran concurrently and there was no period of rapid growth. It has been argued, especially by W. J. Goode, that the demographic and family patterns of western Europe facilitated the rise of modern industrial society there, and I return to this theme in chapter 8.

World population and the 'Third World' since 1950

One of the first acts of the United Nations Organization soon after its inception in 1944–5 was to set up a permanent Population Commission, which encouraged member states to carry out censuses and collect data on fertility and mortality in their territories, and which has since 1948 tabulated and published the resulting data in its *Demographic Yearbook*, giving us for the first time a comprehensive annual survey of population trends throughout the world. That makes 1950 a suitable starting-date for this discussion.

Since that date, death-rates have tumbled, so that whereas a high annual death-rate used to be thought of as one of 40 per thousand or more, by the 1990s anything over 15 was relatively high. According to the UN Development Programme, between 1960 and 1987 the expectation of life at birth in developing countries rose from 48 to 62 years, 80 per cent of the 'Northern' average; while between 1950 and 1988 infant mortality fell from nearly 200 per thousand live births to about 80, a reduction which took the industrial countries nearly a century.[11] There is no mystery about how this has been achieved; it is mainly the result of public health and preventive medicine, an instance of the international diffusion of technology. Some diseases have been virtually eliminated, notably smallpox, whose strains are still cultivated in laboratories only in order to enable vaccines to be produced if another outbreak should ever occur. Others have been controlled, notably malaria. A remarkable early instance of this occurred in 1945–53, when the death-rate in Ceylon (Sri Lanka) was halved, falling from 22 to 11 per thousand in eight years, almost entirely as the direct and indirect result of eradicating malaria.[12]

Rapid recent population growth in many countries has been accentuated by the very rapidity of the fall in death-rates. This has to do with the age- and sex-distributions of populations at different stages. Where birth- and death-rates are high, many children are born, but as each age-group passes through life their numbers are much reduced, and few survive into old age. Such conditions still prevailed in India in 1951, and fig. 3 brings out the contrast between the resulting age- and sex-structure and that of a population with low birth- and death-rates, England and Wales in 1971.

Since 1950 a rapid improvement in mortality conditions has occurred in many poor countries whose populations still exhibit the 'youthful' age-structure with which they emerged from the earlier stage. These improved conditions naturally have their first and most dramatic effect on the mortality of children and young adults; combating the diseases of old age is a slower process, and it is the young who benefit more from measures such as the control of malaria and the improvement of midwifery. The main improvement in mortality conditions, accordingly, is felt just in those age-groups which are most numerous; in arithmetical terms, the most reduced mortality rates are multiplied by the biggest age-groups in the reckoning of overall mortality and the summing which produces the death-rate for the population as a whole, the so-called 'crude' death-rate.

As a simple calculation will show, a stable population in which every baby born lives to the age of exactly 100 years will have a death-rate of 10 per thousand. Needless to say, no country has ever approached such favourable mortality conditions as that, and countries like Sweden, with

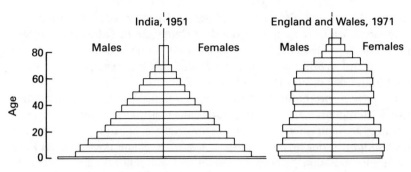

Fig. 3. Age and sex distributions

highly developed public health services backed by adequate resources, have a hard time keeping their death-rates below 12 per thousand in populations which include a due proportion of old people. But in many poor countries today, where the age-structure of the population is a 'youthful' one as a result of past high mortality and present increase, a comparatively modest improvement in mortality conditions enables the crude death-rate to be brought well below 10. It was thought well-nigh incredible when in 1966 the crude death-rate in Japan was reduced to less than 7 per thousand despite mortality conditions which, age for age, were still not quite as favourable as those in western European countries with death-rates of 11 or 12. By the 1990s Japan's performance had been matched by most lower-middle-income countries, according to the World Bank's classification, and by some low-income countries, notably Sri Lanka and China, where infant mortality rates too were far lower than might have been expected from their GNP per capita.[13] Such low crude death-rates could indeed be regarded as 'artificially' low, and likely to rise again in decades to come as the age-structure of the population matures, that is, as the big age-groups now young in those populations survive into old age and fill out the numbers of older people. By 1991, indeed, this seemed to be happening in Japan.

Meanwhile, though, these extremely low death-rates have constituted an important factor in rapid population growth in the world as a whole, commonly called the population explosion. Fertility, the other main factor, is a much more problematic concept, as will appear below.

By 1990, indeed, death-rates in countries classed as 'developed' and 'less-developed' had undergone a remarkable convergence on levels around 10 per thousand (though there is the grim possibility that this figure may rise as the HIV/AIDS epidemic spreads). But there was still a broad contrast in fertility. While birth-rates in developed countries averaged 14 per thousand, in less-developed countries the average was

30, or 34 excluding China's 21. Moreover, there were marked regional differences: 30 in Asia, again excluding China; 28 in Latin America; but 44 in Africa.[14] Clearly if there was a world population explosion it was in the 'Third World'; and since 1950 this has been seen as one of the great issues facing humankind as a whole.

In the past, pro-natalist attitudes have often prevailed. As mentioned above, in many societies such attitudes at the grass-roots were a rational response to high mortality. In addition, some beleaguered minorities have sought to out-breed dominant majorities. Some governments have favoured population growth for reasons of national aggrandizement, to arrest a feared decline in their nation's power and influence in the world, even for military manpower or 'cannon-fodder'. Congruent with such attitudes have been the traditional injunctions of many of the world's religions: 'Be fruitful, and multiply, and replenish the earth, and subdue it.'

Such views became less and less tenable after 1950. In a world of rapidly falling death-rates and population increase, what had been a rational response to high mortality now seemed against all reason, especially to those professionally concerned, such as demographers, economists, ecologists, and conservationists. At the first United Nations population conference in 1954 the prevailing atmosphere was of Malthusian concern about unchecked population growth in relation to limited resources. Only two organized groups stood out: the Soviet Union and the Roman Catholic church. For the former, over-population was equated with unemployment, a disease of capitalism, abolished by socialist planning. The latter were adamant in their rejection of 'artificial' methods of birth control, and implacable in their hostility to abortion in all circumstances. Such indeed has continued to be the case, for despite continuing debate within the church successive popes have reiterated traditional Catholic doctrines on these matters.[15]

In 1969 the Pearson commission (see chapter 13) identified 'the staggering growth of population' as a major cause of the disparity between rich and poor countries. It increased the need for public expenditure on health, education, housing, and water supply; and for aid. Child health and family size were inversely related. Rapidly growing numbers of children increased the burden of dependence and delayed educational improvement. Severe urban problems arose, and inequality was increased by factors such as rising land values and rents.

These problems had been recognized, however, and more than 70 per cent of the population of the developing world lived in countries whose governments had adopted family planning policies. Many parents wanted large families for good and valid economic reasons, not because they were ignorant or improvident; and in such cases access to family planning information and facilities would not make much difference. Nevertheless, 'many of the children born today are unwanted'. The incidence of illegal abortions, and of maternal deaths from them, was high enough to be a serious problem in Latin America and elsewhere, and indicated 'a silent demand for family planning'.[16]

The Pearson commission drew attention, too, to the 'major breakthrough in family planning techniques' that had recently occurred. As they implied, family limitation is much more a matter of motive than of means, and people who seriously want to avoid having children will generally find a way. Indeed, it may be suggested that the new techniques, especially oral contraceptives ('the pill') and intra-uterine devices (IUDs, 'the coil', 'the loop'), had a significance beyond that of merely widening the range of methods available. They were developed with the Third World in mind, even though they have come into widespread use in western countries; and they represent methods by which women could control their own fertility, with important implications for the status of women and the relations between the sexes. However, since 1980 a new factor has arisen: HIV/AIDS prevention strongly indicates condom use.

As the Pearson commission noted, the governments of many 'Third World' countries had adopted policies either explicitly aimed at reducing population growth or having that effect. The lead was taken by India in 1951, as detailed in the case-study below. In China a pro-natalist position was originally taken up in 1949, but that attitude was modified during the 1950s and 1960s. In 1971 the official policy became one of curbing population growth by later marriage, longer spacing, and fewer children, two in towns and three in rural areas. However, even that policy was soon regarded as inadequate, and in 1979 the famous one-child family campaign was launched.[17] By 1990 most 'Third World' states, including the big ones, had adopted policies favouring family planning and slower population growth, and it was estimated that 82 per cent of the population of the 'developing countries' lived in such states. At the same time, support for family planning programmes has been forthcoming from the World Bank and from UN agencies including the United Nations Fund for Population Activities, though these have not always been unequivocally endorsed by United States governments on the ground that they might involve condoning abortion.[18]

In recent times, then, there has been little support for pro-natalist attitudes and policies, and widespread acceptance of the need to check runaway population growth if there is to be any hope of raising living standards in poor countries. Given that acceptance of a broadly Malthusian position, though, there has been much controversy about what governments should do and how they should do it.

At the starting-point of recent and current debates is the 'fertility control' argument that if the rate of economic growth is (say) 5 per cent annually while population increases at (say) 3 per cent, then most of the effort, initiative, and investment that go into economic development are being eaten up by the extra mouths. From this viewpoint, fertility control is seen as a necessary condition of any genuine improvement in living standards, and governments are justified in devoting considerable resources to reducing the birth-rate. Thus Lord Blackett in 1969 calculated that it would pay the government of a typical poor country to spend up to $150 to prevent one birth from taking place,[19] while other authorities have estimated that 'the addition to income per head in a poor country caused by spending £100 on birth prevention is, at very least, fifteen times the addition to income from the best alternative use of £100'.[20]

The 'fertility control' approach, then, proceeds from the top downwards; it implies an active effort on the part of a government to persuade its people to have fewer children. Imbued with such ideas, a government will, perhaps, typically inaugurate a programme and entrust it to a new or existing government department under a responsible minister. An organization will be set up which will recruit staff. Targets will be allotted for the performance of field officers in persuading men to undergo vasectomies or women to be fitted with IUDs. Positive sanctions or incentives will be held out for the fulfilment or over-fulfilment of targets, while negative sanctions such as promotion withheld will be applied to those who fall short. Such pressures on the organization's field staff may be transmitted downwards to the people in the way of bribes on the one hand, threats or coercion on the other. And if that begins to read like an unpleasant caricature, it is in fact not wildly different from what happened in India in 1976, as will be seen in the case-study below.

In reaction against that, with its unpalatable ethical and political implications, some have rejected the proposition that checking fertility is a necessary precondition of economic development, and have tended to assert the contrary. They argue that until people are better off, share greater knowledge and resources of literacy and understanding, can look forward realistically to security in old age without a large family to support them, and above all can expect most of their children to survive, they will have no reason to limit the number of their offspring. Family limitation is seen from this point of view as a result, not a cause: a by-product of economic development. It arises 'spontaneously', it proceeds from below upwards, and it is to be both explained and engendered by socio-economic factors, particularly a rise in incomes; industrialization, and the growth of towns; literacy; schooling, especially of girls; and perhaps most important of all, the reduction of infant mortality. Hence the slogan 'The best contraceptive is development', taken up with enthusiasm at the United Nations world population conference at Bucharest in 1974, when to the dismay of many professional demographers and other social scientists the population issue was debated in frankly political terms.[21]

That position, however, has been controverted in its turn by those who consider that the reaction against the 'fertility control' approach went too far. It is a mistake to regard socio-economic development and family limitation as if they were mutually exclusive alternatives between which a choice has to be made. Governments can pursue both, and each can help the other. It is not necessary to wait till a certain threshold of development has been reached, for family limitation programmes can have some effect at any level of socio-economic development. Nor, in such programmes, need there be pressure 'from the top downwards' to arouse adverse reaction. The key phrase should rather be 'family planning', and this implies encouraging couples to make responsible decisions about parenthood, and ensuring that they have the information and the means necessary to do so. It is partly a matter of the availability alike of both the knowledge and the appliances; partly education in the widest sense, the encouragement of rational discussion in a free and open atmosphere of this as indeed of all issues; and partly of measures enabling women to decide important matters on terms of equality with men. It has been well said that great social changes begin when the previously unthinkable becomes thinkable. The change of mind is what counts, and there is much that governments can do to create a climate of opinion in which that can occur.

This in turn is linked with another issue, about means rather than ends, between the 'clinical' and the 'commercial' approaches. Many of the Third World governments which have adopted family planning programmes have done so through their ministries of health, which have either set up special clinics for the purpose, staffed by doctors and nurses, or charged existing clinics with this extra task. It is argued that this is not only a great waste of the time and energy of such highly trained professional people, which should rather be devoted to relieving suffering and combating disease; it is also a mistake to put about the idea that family planning requires all the solemnity of a visit to the clinic, held perhaps infrequently and at some distance from home. According to this view, governments should concentrate more on making contraceptives available, possibly at subsidized prices, through everyday trade networks like the village store and the itinerant trader, rather as they are in western countries. On the other hand, it can be argued that the only really safe, reliable contraceptive suitable for purely commercial distribution is the condom, which puts fertility unequivocally under male control. All the methods applicable by women require at least some professional help or supervision, whether it is a prescription for 'the pill', implantation of an IUD, or fitting a diaphragm, if they are to be either safe or reliable; while the same is even more obviously true of the surgical sterilization of either women or men. But perhaps this like other issues in the debate is best viewed in terms of 'both and' rather than 'either or'.

Europe's fertility decline reassessed

Considerations of this kind have led to a renewed interest in the history of fertility decline in Europe. Thus in the case of England, those who argue that 'development is the best contraceptive' and that socio-economic factors explain fertility decline can point to the long time-lag of a century or more of population growth, between 1760 when the industrial revolution is conventionally regarded as having taken off, and first intimations of falling fertility after 1877, before rising standards of living led to family limitation. On the other hand, at that time infant mortality was still high, even among the middle classes, who could not realistically have expected that all their children would survive, as the theory would require, before adopting the small-family system.[22]

And if England is one case, France is quite another, where – as Carr-Saunders pointed out long ago – the birth-rate followed the death-rate downwards from the early nineteenth century, with no time-lag and no dramatic downturn like that signalled by the Bradlaugh–Besant trial in England. Confirmation that the French are indeed a special case, with a good claim to be regarded in this respect as the first modern nation, has come from studies which have traced family limitation among the French-speaking *haute bourgeoisie* of Geneva as early as the seventeenth century, long before it was adopted elsewhere in Europe.

Apart from France, where married fertility began to decline appreciably as early as 1800, in most European countries the down-turn occurred no earlier than 1880 and no later than 1920. When the data are analysed in more detail by provinces (or the corresponding administrative units) the concentration of the dates in the decades around 1900 is even more apparent. According to van de Walle and Knodel, 'Europe's fertility decline began under remarkably diverse socio-economic and demographic conditions.' Thus England was largely industrialized (with only 15 per cent of employed men in agriculture) and urbanized (rural population down to 28 per cent) when fertility started falling; whereas Hungary was an overwhelmingly agrarian economy when fertility began to decline there, as it did about the same time. So too was France when its much earlier transition began around 1800, and Bulgaria at the onset of its decline over a century later. 'Literacy was also at very different levels when fertility began to fall – low in France, Hungary, and Bulgaria, for example, and high in England and Wales.' Socio-economic explanations therefore appear inadequate and the rapid spread of family limitation around 1900 in Europe is to be seen rather as an instance of the diffusion of ideas, the explanation for which may more appropriately be sought in the cultural realm.[23]

World fertility trends *c.* 1980

By the late 1970s demographers were beginning to think that the long- and anxiously-awaited turning-point had been reached and that world fertility had begun to fall. As already noted, many 'Third World' governments had adopted policies favouring family limitation. It was reported that contraceptive use was becoming widespread, albeit patchily, and that fertility decline had occurred in most countries, especially in Asia and Latin America, though not in Africa.

That impression was confirmed by the World Fertility Survey of 1974–82. Appropriately enough for so momentous a subject, this was described as 'the biggest social survey ever conducted'. During the 1960s, according to Scott and Chidambaram, 'the population problem' had loomed large in the United States' foreign aid policies, while the United Nations too set up its Fund for Population Activities in 1967. Both had money to spend on population questions, and both perceived a pressing need for better data on fertility. The attitudes of 'Third World' governments to an international population initiative varied widely; some welcomed the idea, while others suspected that the United States' interest was politically inspired or even racist. At the same time they were unwilling to turn away money that could be used to strengthen their own national statistical departments, and a scientifically neutral survey proved to be an acceptable compromise, enabling them to resist pressure to adopt family-planning programmes while gaining better data for their own purposes on what was acknowledged to be an important subject. The United States would not allow the survey to be conducted by the UN or any of its agencies, and in the event the International Statistical Institute was invited to carry it out. The eminent statistician Sir Maurice Kendall was appointed director, the headquarters office was in London, and the UK made the third biggest contribution of funds.[24]

One of the most difficult problems was to devise a core questionnaire, which participating countries were expected to follow closely to enable standard data to be collected and valid comparisons made, but which had to be adapted to different national circumstances and, above all, languages: a difficult balance to strike. Fieldwork began in 1974 in 42 'developing' and 20 'developed' countries, and was carried out through national statistical offices. Sample sizes ranged from roughly 2,000 to 10,000 women, and nearly all the interviewers were women. In all over 330,000 women were interviewed in countries with a total population of over 1,700 million. Analysis took about 20 months on average, up to four years in some countries, and country studies were published as they became available, so that the main trends were emerging before the project was complete.[25]

According to John Cleland, the survey had been well timed. The late 1960s and the 1970s had proved to be a turning-point, and 'by 1980 it was apparent that a massive transition was occurring; fertility was in decline throughout Central and South America and much of Asia, with some major exceptions such as Bangladesh and Pakistan'. On the other hand, however, 'unchanging high fertility' in most of sub-Saharan Africa had been established beyond reasonable doubt.[26]

To cite some of the more detailed findings from the WFS official report: as in Europe in the past, in countries experiencing fertility decline, such as Colombia, Malaysia, and Turkey, births tended to be clustered in a narrow age-range, normally 20–29, whereas in high-fertility countries such as most African and Arab countries the age-range was wider. Women with more schooling tended to have fewer children, especially in countries where a substantial fertility decline had occurred. Contraceptive awareness varied widely, and in some African countries few women had ever heard of modern methods; also Nepal, but see below. Contraceptive use likewise ranged from 1 per cent in Mauritania and Yemen to 64 per cent in Costa Rica, about the 'developed'-country average. The survey attempted to elucidate the various purposes for which women use contraceptives, whether 'postponing', 'spacing', or 'stopping'. Spacing had important effects on child mortality; children born within 2 years of a preceding birth were much less likely to survive to the age of five. A family planning programme could therefore directly contribute to a decline in infant and child mortality. Moreover, women who had used contraception for spacing were presumably more likely to use it when they wanted to stop. Likewise the survey collected the first large body of comparable data on breast-feeding, with its important implications for health and welfare, spacing, and total fertility.

Finally, the survey went into the number of children a mother wanted as compared with the number she actually had: desired family size in relation to total fertility. Associated with this was the concept of 'unmet need' (rather like the Pearson report's 'silent demand for family planning'). Clearly there was an unmet need when a woman did not wish to become pregnant but was not using a modern, efficient method of contraception, or was actually pregnant. By this test there were very high levels of unmet need in many 'developing' countries. If the desired family size was less than the actual total fertility rate, and if women did no more than managing to avoid unwanted pregnancies, there was the prospect of a substantial fertility decline, though in many countries to levels that still implied rapid population growth.[27] For example, in Costa Rica desired family sizes were no lower than in many other Latin American countries, but the total fertility rate was one of the lowest in the region. Clearly this reflected, not lower preferences, but better implementation of preferences. Even so, Costa Rican fertility would have been substantially lower still if all unwanted births had been avoided.[28]

Some criticism of the World Fertility Survey centred on the survey method itself, with its shallow rapport between subject and interviewer, its tendency to present questions in the form of categories none of which quite fits the subject's attitudes or experience, subjects' tendency to give polite, socially approved, 'correct' answers, etc. Thus the Australian demographer John C. Caldwell thought that asking a woman whether she wanted another child or not was 'deficient if not ludicrous' in leaving out complex power relations with her husband, in-laws, and others. He favoured more intensive studies on a smaller, local scale, going into greater depth about such matters. It was of course a limitation of the WFS that it was exclusively a survey of women, and data on husbands' attitudes was collected in only two countries, Egypt and Thailand.

According to Caldwell's own theory, fertility decline turned essentially on the distribution of resources within families. In societies based on familial production, net resources tangible and intangible flowed 'upwards' from young to old, and also 'sideways' from females to males. The old were venerated and pampered, while children worked and contributed to the family's production from an early age. High fertility made sense in these circumstances, and Caldwell stressed his underlying assumption that all societies are economically rational. (The opposite assumption, that fertility behaviour in the 'Third World' arises largely from ignorance, and needs to be changed through education and persuasion, had given rise to much trouble at World Population Conferences.) The all-important transition took place when the resource flow was reversed, and resources flowed 'downwards' from old to young. This happened when wage-earning predominated over familial production, and particularly when all or almost all children went to school. More resources were then devoted to the care of children, so that to some extent the same forces made for low fertility and low mortality, particularly infant and child mortality. Clearly the study of intrafamilial resource flows is extremely sensitive and difficult, and requires methods more like those of social anthropology than demography. I take up Caldwell's work in more detail in chapter 8.[29]

Another critic of the WFS was Robert Chambers, an authority on rural development, who quoted a report from Nepal, where after the national survey there had been a much smaller-scale sample study succeeded in turn by a follow-up and cross-check. At each stage the proportion of women stating that they had heard of various contraceptive methods rose dramatically. Those who said they knew about condoms, for example, went up from 5 per cent in the national survey to 45 per cent in the small-scale inquiry and 95 per cent in the follow-up. Low responses in the national survey, which had pointed to lack of awareness as a major problem, were attributable rather to an unintelligible questionnaire using a highly literary form of the Nepali language, the sensitivity of the whole subject of contraception, and the social setting in which interviews were carried out. Once the subject had been broached in the first survey, however, it seemed that women felt freer to discuss it in the subsequent interviews.[30] On the other hand, in Costa Rica 83 per cent of women gave the same response in a second interview as they had in the main survey 18 months before to questions about preferred family size.[31]

Most fundamentally, Scott and Chidambaram criticized the WFS's basic survey instrument, the core questionnaire. Even after modification by committees and researchers all over the world, its implicit assumptions were 'that potential mothers regard the bearing of children as a voluntary and controllable act (controlled, indeed, by themselves alone)'; that they have 'clearly formed and coherent attitudes regarding the number of children they want, and that their behaviour will rationally reflect such attitudes'. The inapplicability of such assumptions in the 'Third World' was shown by the consistent finding that many women in nearly all countries said they wanted no more children but were doing nothing about it, even when contraceptives were readily available: behaviour which some might regard as inexplicably inconsistent.[32]

Despite such criticisms, however, since the World Fertility Survey it has become generally accepted that, with a few exceptions especially in Africa and the Middle East, fertility in the world as a whole has fallen and will continue to fall. Sadly it has to be said that if anything the inexorable onset of the HIV/AIDS epidemic will accentuate this trend.

HIV/AIDS

Unknown before 1981, the Human Immunodeficiency Virus (HIV) and the Acquired Immune Deficiency Syndrome (AIDS) first came to medical attention, and spread rapidly, in the USA among male homosexuals ('gays') and intravenous drug users. The manner of its appearance among marginal groups gave rise to some misapprehensions about its true nature, and led to the disease itself and its sufferers being stigmatized. Secondly, it appeared early and has spread almost entirely by heterosexual intercourse in inter-tropical Africa, affecting men and women in more or less equal numbers. This is the area with by far the highest prevalence rates, most of all in Uganda and adjoining countries. Thirdly, in many countries of Asia and north Africa the virus was introduced later, around the mid-1980s, and is not yet so prevalent, though it is said to be spreading fast especially in India and Thailand.

According to United Nations estimates, in the early 1990s about 15 million people worldwide were HIV-infected, more than 12.5 million of them in developing countries including 9 million in Africa.[33] Second only to its paramount importance as a world public health issue, therefore, it has become a development issue.

So far, by about 1990 the overall demographic effects had been slight. AIDS-related deaths had made little or no impact on overall death-rates nor had they checked population growth, though according to the World Bank HIV/AIDS was already starting to reverse long-term declines in child mortality. Estimates of the future course of the pandemic are highly speculative and depend on many unknown factors. Early estimates suggesting population decline in the worst-affected African countries have been revised by more recent forecasts of only modest reductions in these countries' recently rapid rates of growth.[34]

The selective effects on particular groups are more serious, however. AIDS-related deaths occur disproportionately among adults of prime child-rearing and working age, leaving fewer adults to shoulder the burden of dependence and provide for the very young and the very old. Even more selectively, it appears that among those more at risk are the educated elites; HIV prevalence rates are higher in towns than in most rural areas, and this is related to the 'urban bias', the concentration in towns of people with longer schooling and higher qualifications and skills. The care and treatment of AIDS sufferers represents a claim on poor countries' exiguous health services which may be difficult to meet without crowding out the needs of other patients with treatable conditions and a hope of recovery. With or without medical help, the care of AIDS sufferers imposes heavy burdens of exhaustion and distress on carers such as kin or neighbours.

Prevention has everywhere involved highly charged personal, moral, and political issues. It has entailed open and non-judgemental discussion of subjects such as male homosexuality, intravenous drug abuse, and prostitution, without discouraging people at risk of infection from seeking advice and changing their ways (using condoms, clean needles, refraining from anal sex, etc.). Sex education in schools is a perennially sensitive and highly controversial subject, and the more so when health hazards make it necessary to give explicit instruction on such matters to young children. A heavy emphasis on condom use is unpalatable to some, especially moralists who regard it as encouraging promiscuity.

Underlying such attitudes is the stigma attached to the disease. Many people regard AIDS sufferers as morally unclean, at best the victims of their own misdeeds. Mistaken beliefs that it is dangerous to approach or touch AIDS sufferers have led to their being denied help, ostracized, assaulted, even driven out of their homes by people fearful for their own or their families' safety.

Studies by Barnett and Blaikie in Uganda vividly illustrate many of these general considerations. Thus the selective havoc of AIDS-related mortality was apparent in two heavily affected villages where young adults of prime child-rearing age (men 30–34, women 25–29) had been almost wiped out.[35]

A consequential problem was the large number of children whose parents had died. Some stayed on in the parental home, partly in order to maintain their right to the land, including one who as a 12-year-old had taken responsibility for her five siblings aged 2 to 9, growing simple food-crops and cooking for them, and even managing to keep them in school. Others were helped by kin and neighbours. Many were taken in and looked after by grandparents, a solution that might seem to accord with outdated stereotypes of 'the extended family' in a 'traditional society'; but there were problems. Many elderly poor people who had lost their own adult offspring had to look to their grandchildren to care for them in their old age, and meanwhile could not afford to send the grandchildren to school but had to keep them at home, earning money making handicrafts such as woven mats, baskets and the like. In Caldwell's terms, resources in such families flowed upwards from young to old, and some children were found to be neglected, malnourished, and in poor health.

Some of the problems of prevention were symbolized by three Uganda slogans. The government's AIDS Control Programme said 'Love carefully', but the Roman Catholic Church said 'Love faithfully', and a third slogan was 'Zero grazing', 'grazing' being a Uganda euphemism for having sex with many partners, or 'sleeping around'.

Uganda teenagers, asked to write school essays on the subject, were clearly well informed about the medical cause and nature of the disease, and well aware of the selective damage it was inflicting on Uganda's economy and society. Most of all they blamed the irresponsible behaviour of the educated elite, and they showed scant sympathy for the sufferers.[36]

And for many in Uganda AIDS was not the most immediate problem. In a country devastated by civil wars, disorganized by political turmoils, impoverished by financial mismanagement, with a largely black-market economy, and in which armed robbery was rife, people had more pressing concerns. The possibility of dying of AIDS in five to seven years represented a longer time-horizon than these immediate hazards.[37]

However, in contrast to such attitudes, remarkable initiatives had been taken in Uganda to help sufferers and carers. Notable among these was a manual on AIDS care produced by two doctors at the national teaching hospital, recommending simple diagnostic and treatment methods along with a few inexpensive drugs affording much relief for sufferers. Another was The Aids Support Organization, TASO, a voluntary self-help and support group for sufferers and their carers. Beginning in 1987, by the early 1990s TASO was reaching more than 30,000 people a year, and its activities included 'counselling, condom education and distribution, home care, income-generating activities, feeding programmes, and payment of orphans' school fees'.[38, 39]

Case-study 1: India (fig. 4)

India has a particular interest for the study of population trends in poor countries on two counts. First, it represents a leading case of a country in which adequately reliable estimates exist of the birth- and death-rates in conditions of high and fluctuating fertility and mortality. These are afforded by the analysis carried out by Kingsley Davis of the census data gathered under British rule between 1881 and 1947. They refer to the old undivided India, including the parts which are now Pakistan and Bangladesh, but only to those provinces which were under direct rule, and excluding the princely states. Figure 4 shows the high fluctuating birth- and death-rates around 40–50 per thousand before 1920, and in particular the appalling catastrophe of the 1919 influenza epidemic, which almost literally decimated the population of the sub-continent. After 1920, with a falling death-rate and a birth-rate which remained above 40, this population may clearly be regarded as having entered Blacker's stage 2; but right up to the time of independence in 1947 no one could be sure that famine and catastrophe might not return. The British administration's main concern accordingly was to prevent such calamities by means which Davis describes in detail – the development of irrigation, transport for famine relief if it should be necessary, and health measures.[1]

It was not until after the separate independence of India and Pakistan that a problem was recognized of rapid population growth, and as described by Myrdal the new government of India in successive Five-Year Plans became the first government in the world to adopt a policy positively favourable to family limitation.[2] This is India's second chief interest accordingly. At first the government was feeling its way, but when the expected opposition from religious authorities was not

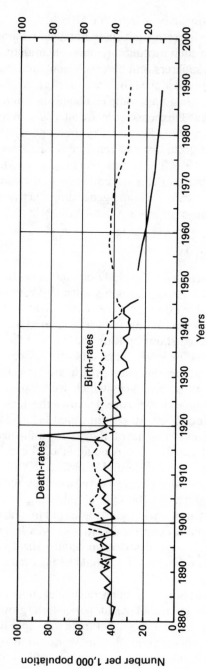

Fig. 4. Estimated birth-and death-rates, India. The two parts of the graph are not strictly comparable because of boundary and other changes.

(Sources: 1881–1946, office of Population Research, Princeton University: reprinted by permission of Princeton University Press from Kingsley Davis, *The Population of India and Pakistan* (copyright 1951 by Princeton University Press). After 1950, UN *Demographic Year-books*.)

encountered it embarked upon a programme characterized by a clinical approach and concentrating upon male sterilization by vasectomy as its chosen method. But only limited success was achieved, and by the late 1960s the birth-rate was estimated by the UN Population Division to be still over 40. Ironically, it was Dr Karan Singh, who as minister of health was responsible for the family planning programme, to whom the slogan 'The best contraceptive is development' is attributed – the slogan which, as has been mentioned, was taken up with enthusiasm at the world population conference in 1974; for only two years later he appeared to swing over to the opposite position, when he was reported as saying in effect that it was no use waiting for education and economic development to bring about a fall in fertility; a direct assault was needed.[3]

The effect of that 'direct assault' was political disaster. By April 1976 there were widespread complaints that junior officials had shown an excess of zeal in carrying out the sterilization programme and had gone far beyond government policy in order to meet their monthly targets. Some groups felt they had been unfairly picked on, such as teachers in Uttar Pradesh who were told to be sterilized or lose a month's pay. Even though the extent of the abuses may have been exaggerated, rumours of coercion and harassment were rife. There were riots and a major political storm; and the ensuing general election in 1977, held after a postponement in an atmosphere of crisis, resulted in the fall of Mrs Indira Gandhi's government. After such turbulent controversies, both the Janata Party who succeeded to power in 1977 and Mrs Gandhi when she was re-elected in 1980 adopted a more cautious approach, but the family planning policy was continued with a generally rising trend in sterilization, and other contraceptive measures.[4] By 1989, the birth-rate had fallen to 30.5, the death-rate to 10.2.

Case-study 2: England and Wales (fig. 5)

Our knowledge of the earlier population history of England is based on the painstaking work of local historians, co-ordinated by the Cambridge demographers E. A. Wrigley and R. S. Schofield, on the Anglican parish registers of 404 parishes recording 'every wedding, christening, and burying' from 1538, when the clergy were first obliged to keep such registers, to 1871. Calculating birth- and death-rates from registration data requires also knowledge of population size, which was lacking before the first census in 1801 and its successors at ten-year intervals since. Wrigley and Schofield overcame this difficulty by the ingenious statistical device of 'aggregative back projection', starting from a date when the population size and composition was known, and working backwards, adding deaths and subtracting births to give the size and composition in

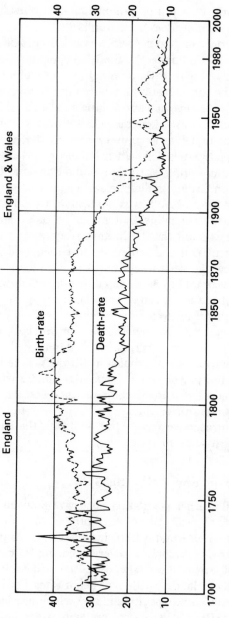

Fig. 5. Birth- and death-rates, England and Wales. Civilian deaths only 1915–20 and 3 Sept. 1939 to 1946.
(Sources: for England 1700–1871, E. A. Wrigley and R. S. Schofield, *The Population History of England 1541–1871*. For England and Wales, 1871–, Registrar-General's Annual Reports and succeeding official sources.)

preceding years. For this their base-line was the 1871 census, though civil registration data were also available from 1837.[1]

Figure 5 shows Wrigley and Schofield's estimates for England from 1700 to 1870, and from 1871 onwards the Registrar-General's published figures for England and Wales.

As will be seen, England before 1750 well exemplifies Blacker's stage 1 with widely fluctuating fertility and mortality, the birth-rate depressed during mortality crises and 'bouncing back' after them. Between 1651 and 1691 the population fell slightly, then rose again slightly to 1751 and more rapidly thereafter. During the seventeenth and early eighteenth centuries marriage ages were high, averaging 27 to 28 for men and around 26 for women, and whether deliberately or not fertility was restricted as a consequence. There were wide local variations, and in one parish, that of Colyton in Devon (which attracted much attention early in these studies for its unusually complete register), men actually married women older than themselves, many nearing 30 and more than halfway through their childbearing period, while births were widely spaced. That proved to be an exceptional case, but more generally a sizeable minority of men, and even more of women, never married, as many as 25 per cent at times during the early and mid-seventeenth century. (I have already cited Hajnal for the view that this pattern was long characteristic of western Europe.)

From 1750 onwards the death-rate fell, possibly as a result of medical improvements; while marriage ages fell and the birth-rate rose, possibly in relation to new employment opportunities in widening markets as the industrial revolution gathered pace.

The fall in the death-rate was arrested by the 'health of towns problem' in the early Victorian era, and it hesitated around 21 to 24 from about 1820 to 1880 until the sanitary reforms which were the achievement of that unsung hero of English history Edwin Chadwick.[2] That long hesitation was a special feature of the experience of this country, part no doubt of the penalty of being the first industrial country, and not repeated elsewhere.

The circumstances in which the birth-rate began to fall in the late 1870s are now fairly well understood.[3] Following Malthus' work, published in 1798, there had been some advocacy of family limitation, especially by the early radical Francis Place, but it had fallen on deaf ears.[4] By 1870, however, the rising middle class were experiencing a number of checks to their standard of living – falling prices which disproportionately reduced profits and investment,[5] and an absolute shortage of domestic servants – along with other changes that made children a source of new expense, such as the introduction of examinations for the civil service, Army, Navy and other professions, the concurrent rise of the so-called Public Schools (actually private and very expensive), and some minor changes like the custom of taking holidays by the sea. At the time when the middle classes were motivated to limit their families, the trial of Charles Bradlaugh and Annie Besant in 1876–7 on charges of obscenity arising from a book on birth control, and the wide publicity it received in the press, gave them a knowledge of the means. The use of contraceptives, beginning among the well-to-do, spread down the social scale and by the 1950s was widespread throughout the population.[6] The death-rate meanwhile had levelled at around 12 per thousand. Since the Second World War there have been two 'baby booms'. The first culminated in 1947 when the birth-rate was 20.5 per thousand, the second in 1964 when it was 18.6. In between it fell to 15 in 1955, and in the late 1970s it fell below 12 per thousand, about the same as the death-rate. Population growth has accordingly been slow and irregular at rates between one per cent and, recently, zero.

Blacker's four stages then, may be seen as having occurred in this country as follows: the first before 1750; the second from 1750 to 1877; the third from 1877 to 1940; and the fourth since the Second World War. The other main feature of the experience of this country lies in the extreme slowness of the changes, which took over two centuries here in contrast to the way they have been telescoped in some later-developing countries into scarcely more than two or three decades.

Case-study 3: Japan (fig. 6)

For over two hundred years, from the gradual expulsion of foreigners in 1615–28 to the incursion of Commodore Perry in 1852, Japan was completely secluded from the rest of the world by the deliberate policy of the ruling Tokugawa shogunate. Censuses were taken at frequent intervals during this period, and though these enumerated only the commoners and excluded the nobles, samurai, and rich merchants, they show a variation of no more than 10 per cent. The checks which kept population so remarkably stable included natural disasters like volcanic eruptions, but also deliberate measures – infanticide among commoners, and abortion among the nobility and gentry – to preserve a limited inheritance on land which was visibly limited.

After 1852, and especially after the Meiji Restoration of 1868, the new ruling class decided that rapid industrial development was essential if the country was not to be conquered and subjected to the colonial rule of one or other of the European powers. The immediate effect on population was an increase from its Tokugawa level of 35 million in 1873 to 55 million in 1918. It is not known exactly how this occurred; certainly the death-rate fell, but its fall may not have been immediate, while the birth-rate

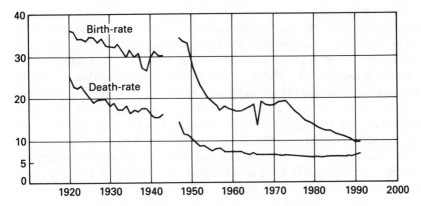

Fig. 6. Birth- and death-rates, Japan
(Sources: 1920–1935, Irene B. Taeuber, *The Population of Japan* (1958). Subsequent data from UN *Demographic Yearbooks*.)

may well have risen with the abandonment of traditional family-limitation practices in response to the rise of new opportunities and the migration to the new industrial towns.

Modern vital statistics were instituted in 1920, from which date we have a clearer picture of trends. Figure 6 shows that the fall in the death-rate from 25 in 1920 to 11 in 1950, comparable to that which took 130 years in England and Wales (*c.* 1810 to 1940), was achieved in Japan in 30. Meanwhile, the birth-rate remained high at first, though with a suggestive slight drop in the late thirties. Population growth was fairly rapid accordingly at around 15 per thousand or 1.5 per cent, from 55 million in 1918 to 73 million in 1940.

At this time it began to be recognized that population growth was a problem, and a government commission in 1927–30 recommended that planned parenthood should be encouraged and there should be a reasonable diffusion of birth control. The government rejected this report; in the then climate of opinion, the obvious answers to population growth lay rather in agricultural improvement at home and imperial expansion abroad. However, some influential people continued to believe in the desirability of birth control, and the government did not interfere with the sale of contraceptives and the spread of information.

But the decisive events took place in 1948 with the passing, amid great political confusion, of the Eugenic Protection Law, which came into force in 1949 and in effect legalized abortion. The effect was dramatic. By the early 1950s well over a million abortions were performed annually in Japan, something like one to every two live births; and the birth-rate fell with unparalleled rapidity from 34 in 1947 to 17 in 1957.[1]

The great wave of abortions at that time has been followed by a quieter spread of the knowledge and use of contraceptive methods, and as in other industrial countries the birth-rate has fluctuated at levels well below 20 per thousand. Meanwhile, the death-rate has fallen to the extremely low level of 6–7, for reasons analysed above; so that population growth has continued at around 1 per cent – a rate of increase, however, that does not appear to be beyond the capacity of a country whose industrial growth rate has reached 10 per cent in recent years. Moreover, as already indicated, the death-rate must rise in decades to come as the older age-groups fill out, and unless Japanese attitudes to family size change once more it is likely that the population will stabilize over about the next thirty years.

Suggestions for further reading

Carlo M. Cipolla, *The Economic History of World Population* revised edn (Harmondsworth, Penguin, 1978)

Colin McEvedy and Richard Jones, *Atlas of World Population History* (Harmondsworth, Penguin, 1978)

Georges Tapinos and Phyllis Piotrow, *Six Billion People* (New York, McGraw Hill, 1978)

World Fertility Survey: Major Findings and Implications (London, World Fertility Survey, 1984)

John Cleland and John Hobcraft (eds.), *Reproductive Change in Developing Countries* (Oxford, Oxford University Press, 1985)

Tony Barnett and Piers Blaikie, *AIDS in Africa: Its Present and Future Impact* (London, Belhaven, 1992)

Population Bulletin, quarterly (Washington, D.C., Population Reference Bureau)

3

The colonial episode and the race question

Most of today's poor countries underwent at some time the experience of colonial rule. There were many variations of that experience, and it ended in some places before it had begun in others. Thus after the conquests that began around 1500 in the age of Columbus, the former Spanish colonies in South America became independent republics in the wars of 1810–26, while Portugal peacefully ceded Brazil's independence in 1822. British supremacy in India, established in fact by about 1805, was formally declared in 1858, and came to an end in 1947, while a number of other south Asian countries also became independent about that time. In Africa, although a few small coastal enclaves were established as early as the fifteenth century, in most of the interior the colonial experience was even later and even shorter. Partition among the European powers took place after 1880, and in many areas colonial administration was not effectively established until after 1900. Then, within a lifetime, there was a rush to independence around 1960, the so-called 'year of Africa'.

Meanwhile, Russian expansion overland from the seventeenth century onwards brought the whole of north-eastern Asia under their control by the late eighteenth century. Russian colonization was then extended to Alaska and to enclaves on the north American Pacific coast as far south as California, till the United States purchased Alaska in 1867. Meanwhile, too, although the European states did not completely subjugate China, they asserted their power there during the nineteenth century when their nationals enjoyed extra-territorial rights and immunity from Chinese law, and territorial concessions created enclaves of foreign rule on Chinese soil. The Japanese, having narrowly escaped a similar fate, took the initiative by annexing Taiwan (Formosa) in 1895, and after defeating the imperial Russian forces went on to occupy Korea and Manchuria in 1905. Less successfully they attempted to extend their empire to

Mongolia and China in the 1920s and 1930s; more briefly still they overran all of south-east Asia and the western Pacific in the early 1940s, before their defeat in the Second World War brought their overseas expansion abruptly to an end in 1945.

Colonization was not a uniform process. There were wide differences among the pre-existing cultures of the peoples subjected to colonial rule, and equally wide variations in the nature and timing of the colonial experience. These differences have had much to do with lasting diversity among the countries and major regions of the 'Third World'. Thus the development economist Morris D. Morris distinguished three types of 'developing countries'. The first was characterized by a long involvement in foreign trade and town life, as in Latin America, and also countries such as South Africa, Lebanon, and possibly Turkey. The second included countries with long-sustained urban traditions, extraction of surpluses from densely settled village systems, and small but important literate elites, as in most of south and south-east Asia and north Africa. The third category included 'tribally-organized' societies such as those in Africa south of the Sahara, also Afghanistan and some Arab countries. These started at very low levels of GNP, far lower than western countries before industrialization; and, I would add, in African societies a limited technology compared with either western or Asian civilizations.[1]

Leaving aside the empires of ancient and medieval times – Roman, Ch'in, Asoka's, Byzantine, Ottoman, Mongol – I concentrate in what follows on the overseas expansion of Europe, though it may be that some aspects of the colonial experience can be more widely generalized. For example, the position of Koreans in Japan in the aftermath of empire seems not unlike that of people from the Caribbean and the Indian sub-continent in latter-day Britain.

Over large areas of the globe, the expansion of Europe resulted in people of 'white' appearance and European descent dominating 'native' or 'coloured' populations. The sheer fact of conquest gave rise to myths about superior and inferior races which were readily believed by the white conquerors. In some countries, political independence from the original colonial power was attained by 'white' communities who continued to dominate populations of non-European descent. In that way a colonial situation became internalized in such places as South Africa and the southern states of the USA, while the independence of Brazil and some other South American countries may be seen in a similar light. Elsewhere, too, attitudes of racial superiority have persisted although the circumstances that made them plausible have long since passed away. Equally persistent have been the bitterness and resentment of the formerly subject peoples once regarded as backward or primitive. Even though the age of empire has come to an end, an awareness of the colonial past and demands for 'decolonization' continue to be important in the modern world.

The meaning of the word colony has changed. Originally 'a settlement in a new country', in its dictionary sense the term was applied, for example, to British settler communities in countries such as Canada, Australia, and New Zealand. After the First World War those colonies gained greater autonomy and for a time were officially styled Dominions; while Colonies were countries such as Nigeria, Jamaica, and Kenya, where small numbers of Europeans dominated large non-European populations, and which could literally have been called dominions. The more recent usage of the word colony has persisted in common speech too, and I have adopted it here.

A thumbnail sketch of colonial history, *c.* 1500 to 1960

1 Sixteenth to early nineteenth centuries

The age of European expansion falls into two major periods. The first was that of 'guns and sails', when in only a few decades after 1500 Europeans gained an absolute predominance over the oceans that enabled them to conquer the Americas, wholly occupy many islands round the world, and establish small enclaves on the coasts of the African and Asian continents. For nearly three centuries, however, their dominion did not extend far inland. No serious attempts were made to extend territorial conquest inside Asia, while Africa, with its lethal diseases, long resisted Europeans and as late as 1876 only 10 per cent of the continent was under white occupation. The Americas were different, sparsely populated by technologically primitive peoples who readily succumbed to European infectious diseases; even there, however, until the eighteenth century the areas under effective European control, as distinct from nominal sovereignty, were mostly close to the sea.[2]

The search for gold was a prime object of many European overseas ventures, while some settlements were established also to trade in tropical products such as spices and handicrafts such as silk, and others like St Helena to act as supply and repair depots for the sailing ships that carried on the trade. South African history, indeed, began unpretentiously with a Dutch settlement at the Cape to establish 'a cabbage patch on the way to India'.[3] Settlements in temperate zones, such as the original thirteen colonies in New England, lived off the land by means of family farming. In some tropical colonies, however, large-scale plantation agriculture became the main economic base.

Some places where Europeans established themselves were uninhabited before (for example, Mauritius, the Falkland Islands); in others, the native population became extinct, or was extinguished (for example, the Caribbean islands, Patagonia, Tierra del Fuego, Tasmania). In some such places the present-day population is wholly of European descent, the society is a transplanted version of a European society, and the colonial situation in the later sense of the word does not exist; Tasmania and the Falkland Islands are cases in point. Elsewhere, Europeans brought in labourers from an African or Asiatic mainland. In Mauritius, for example, French settlers brought in indentured labourers from India, while later immigrations added 'Creoles' (of mixed descent including African ancestry) as clerks and skilled workers, and Chinese shopkeepers, to make up the latter-day plural society.[4] Similarly, Indian labourers were brought under indenture agreements to the plantations of Guiana and the West Indies. But by far the biggest population movements of this period resulted from the trade in African slaves.

That trade began in the mid-sixteenth century with the shipment to Brazil of slaves from the Portuguese West African possessions of Guinea, São Tomé and Angola. People of other European nationalities soon joined in, including French and British, while the first twenty black slaves in North America were sold from a Dutch warship to Virginia settlers in 1619. It expanded in the mid-seventeenth century when the Portuguese administration in Brazil, under Jesuit missionary pressure, stopped the enslavement of native Indians there; while the growth of French and British plantations in the West Indies provided a market for British slave traders.

The trade reached its peak in the eighteenth century, when slaves were taken from Mozambique as well as from the west coast of Africa. It is estimated that between 1500 and 1810 some 10 million African slaves were shipped across the Atlantic. The biggest number of these went to Brazil, followed by Spanish America, the British Caribbean, and French colonies in America.[5] In those areas mortality from tropical diseases was heavy, and the slave population was continually topped up with fresh imports from Africa, mostly of men. In the United States by contrast, the tendency was for the population to increase, and for most of the period few slaves were imported. By 1825, though the USA had imported fewer than any other part of the New World, it had the biggest population of black slaves, nearly all of whom had been born into slavery there.[6]

The overall demographic impact on the population of Africa is not clear. Some authorities have considered that it declined or showed no increase during the period of the slave trade, and have made allowances accordingly in their estimates of world population by continents.[7] However, according to McEvedy and Jones, only at the slave trade's peak in the late eighteenth century, when some 75,000 slaves a year were being shipped across the Atlantic, can it had done more than slow down the rate of increase in sub-Saharan Africa as a whole.[8] But the selective effects may have been greater; if those enslaved and transported were predominantly young adult men, the burden of dependence would fall more heavily on those left behind, possibly leading to a general impoverishment and increased mortality. Moreover the effects were not felt equally over the whole continent; West Africa was by far the most heavily affected region.

Slavery was a traditional institution in many African societies, and those involved in the trade included African chiefs who made war on their neighbours, captured slaves, and sold them for guns to make further wars. On the east coast of Africa, Arabs too were involved both as captors and as traders. Europeans traded in slaves rather than captured them, and in the case of British merchants a further complication was Lord Justice Mansfield's judgement in 1771 which effectively meant that slaves could not be brought to England or they would at once become free. The shipowners of Liverpool, Bristol, and London accordingly worked the 'black triangle' – out with trade goods (cloth etc.) to West Africa; across with slaves to the West Indies, the notorious 'middle passage'; and home with plantation goods.[9]

By the end of the eighteenth century, slavery had become a major issue in British politics. The anti-slavery movement whose parliamentary spokesman was William Wilberforce drew support from the humanitarian convictions of men such as Samuel Johnson, Horace Walpole, and above all Thomas Clarkson. It was also supported by the political opponents of the upstart West Indian plantation magnates whose monopolies had been discredited by the rising school of liberal economists. Free trade, private enterprise, individual liberty and the abolition of slavery cohered in a new set of social, political, and economic principles, and the anti-slavery movement achieved its two prime objects with the prohibition of the slave trade in 1807 and the liberation of all slaves in the British empire in 1833.[10]

Following Britain's lead, the United States outlawed the foreign slave trade in 1808, though slavery remained a domestic institution until after the civil war in the 1860s. Elsewhere too the British government took the initiative in suppressing slavery, subject as it was to the converging pressures of humanitarian reformers on the one hand, and, on the other, British plantation owners who, having been forced to give up slave labour themselves, did not see why their competitors should still have that advantage. Thus it was in a treaty with Britain that Brazil agreed in 1831 to outlaw the slave trade, though it was not effectively stopped for another 20 years, and it was not until 1881 that slavery was abolished in Brazil itself. Meanwhile the Royal Navy maintained anti-slave patrols around the coasts of Africa from 1807 to 1869, intercepting consignments of slaves and putting them ashore at settlements like Freetown in

Sierra Leone.[11] A British consul was posted to Zanzibar in 1841, partly to look after the interests of Britain's Indian subjects there, and partly to help curb the Arab slave traders. And British public opinion hero-worshipped David Livingstone not least for his lifelong dedication to suppressing the slave trade, while the conclusion some drew from his life and death was that it would never be stopped until much of Africa was brought under British rule.[12]

This first period of European expansion, then, ended in the early nineteenth century with the independence of the white-dominated societies of the Americas, and the suppression of the slave trade.

2 Mid-nineteenth century to 1960

During this period, substantial areas of the major continents, away from the sea, were brought under European control. Lands in the temperate zones of North America, Australia, New Zealand, and southern Africa were opened up to white settler farmers, while the Russian empire extended eastwards across northern Asia. These developments were made possible by technological innovations, particularly the railway, the steamship both at sea and in inland waters, and later the internal combustion engine; and some crucial medical discoveries, especially quinine, which enabled Europeans to survive despite the diseases of Africa and Asia.

Thus, for example, the extension of British rule in India was a lengthy process and it was not until 1860 that most of the country was under either direct administration or indirect rule through the princes. Burma was annexed in two bites in 1852 and 1886. A British trading base was established at Singapore in 1819, but it was several decades before Malaya came under effective administration. Meanwhile in the mid-nineteenth century the French and Dutch too were consolidating their 'spheres' in Indo-China and Indonesia respectively.[13] As for Africa, even the basic geography was still unknown and being explored in the 1860s and 1870s, the 'scramble for Africa' took place after 1870, the spheres of influence of the major European powers were not settled till the late 1880s, and actual administration in some of the remoter areas was not a reality till after the First World War.[14]

Between the two world wars, as already noted, some parts of the European empires were already becoming more independent in fact, and there were the beginnings of resistance to European rule especially in India. The Cripps mission of 1943 made Indian independence certain as soon as the war was over; once India was independent there was no holding the rest of the Asian empires, while 'freedom' movements in African colonies could hardly be denied their independence in their turn; and so, by what seemed like an irresistible logic of events, soon after 1960 (and with certain exceptions of which more below) colonial rule was a thing of the past. It remains to emphasize how short was this second period of European expansion and colonial rule. In some places it all happened in a single lifetime; thus Harry Thuku, honoured at the independence ceremonies in Kenya in 1963, remembered the days before the white man came.[15]

The nature of colonial society

The salient feature of colonial society was foreign control. In European colonies this was particularly true of economic life, Christian missions, and government.

Economic institutions

Not all colonies were acquired in the direct prospect or hope of economic gain. On the contrary, many in Europe saw them as 'millstones round our necks'; for example, a reluctant Liberal cabinet in Britain was with difficulty persuaded to annex Uganda, partly to forestall German control of the source of the Nile, and partly by a church campaign to protect the missions and their converts there.[16] But clearly it was important to make a colony pay its way, and all colonial regimes were concerned to promote economic activity that could serve as a tax base.

In a few places this could be done by encouraging indigenous enterprise, as for example in Uganda where cotton and later coffee as export cash crops were introduced by the combined efforts of the British administration, the Anglican mission, and the local African chiefs. Such cases were exceptional, however, and reliance on native sources of supply was more usually regarded as unsatisfactory; the goods were not always available in sufficient quantity, and the quality was variable, so there was always a tendency for foreign enterprises to secure sources of supply such as mines or plantations under their own control. Thus wild rubber tapped from forest trees gave place to the standardized product of rubber plantations.

In some places, the soil and climate and the sparseness of the native population made for family farming by white settlers rather than plantation agriculture; thus the United States were long divided between the north, where the family farm predominated, and the plantation economy of the south. Similarly, farming prevailed in Australia and New Zealand, where the native populations were small and greatly outnumbered at an early stage by the settlers. There a colonial situation arose to a limited extent, as large stock farms in Australia rely on the services of stockmen of aboriginal or mixed descent, while in New Zealand there were wars over land rights between Maoris and Pakehas (whites) in the nineteenth century and some tension persists today. More pertinent perhaps to the 'Third World' is the settlement by farmers of European descent that occurred in countries such as South Africa, Zimbabwe, Algeria, and Kenya. Though their technical and economic achievements were in many cases very great, such white minority communities posed intractable political problems with their ruggedly possessive attitudes towards the land and the country they occupied.[17] Under colonial rule they were often at loggerheads with the administrative officials sent out to govern them, whom they characteristically regarded as fatally 'soft on the natives'. It was partly over this issue, indeed, that American colonists rebelled against British, Spanish, and Portuguese rule in the eighteenth and early nineteenth centuries. Similarly, though British governors in Australia enjoined settlers to 'live in amity and kindness with' the aborigines, they had the greatest difficulty in restraining them from punitive expeditions that degenerated into cruel and indiscriminate shooting.[18] White settler communities tended to identify themselves strongly with the mother country and loudly protest their loyalty; hence 'Algérie française!' and the long-conditioned insistence of the Rhodesian settlers on their British identity. When the home government has seemed determined to betray their own kith and kin by handing the country over to the majority of its people, however, there has been an abrupt swing into disillusionment and a determination to maintain a 'civilized' state of affairs in a unilateral declaration of independence with white minority rule.

Where the predominant form of agricultural enterprise was the plantation, however, different situations were created. European managers came and went on leave and retirement, and did not put down roots like settler farmers. As Myrdal pointed out, plantations represented extensions in tropical colonies of companies incorporated in the metropolitan countries. Their alien control and management led to dividends and a large part of salaries being remitted abroad or used to purchase foreign goods rather than to stimulate demand on the local market. Not only did the higher salaries go to alien managers, but also skilled workers, foremen, and even some unskilled workers were brought in from other countries. In south Asia the gulf between the European upper caste and the masses of unskilled workers was widened by the employment of middlemen, many of whom were 'Oriental aliens', and by the system of managing agencies. Though managers might sometimes be uneasy about the way these intermediaries were treating the workers, they were too dependent on them to be able to do much about it.

In Myrdal's judgement, plantations as a form of industrialized agriculture played an indispensable part in economic development, raising average income levels (though not everyone shared in the increase) and stimulating investment in the infra-structure of buildings, roads, ports, and railways. Even though these, like the associated commercial and financial institutions, were geared to the foreign-dominated export sector, they could become part of the local economy and be used for wider purposes. And on the whole the independent governments of south Asia left them alone. Threats to nationalize them, as in Sri Lanka, or actual nationalization, as in Indonesia, were on the whole disastrous; the threats scared off new capital, while the actuality led to inefficiency and corruption.[19]

Large international corporations still control plantations in many poor countries, where they exemplify the 'big firm, small country' syndrome to which I refer in chapter 4. Though from an economic point of view they represent a somewhat unassimilable legacy of the colonial period, socially and politically they have posed fewer problems than farming by European settlers. Even more than the latter, however, plantations and mines alike depended on a plentiful supply of cheap labour. In the early period of colonial history this was largely provided by slaves. After the abolition of slavery, recourse was had to other methods of recruitment.

In many societies there were traditional obligations to work for public purposes for a few days or weeks a year. Thus in many Asian societies people were required to turn out when needed to repair and maintain irrigation canals, dams, and embankments. In some African societies people had to mend the chief's fence and till his fields, yielding food for councillors and litigants at his court, and a famine reserve. Sometimes these customary obligations could be usefully modernized, like *bulungi bwansi* (literally 'good works underfoot') in the kingdom of Buganda, by which people were required to maintain minor roads and village tracks. In effect it was a tax payable in labour rather than money. Under colonial rule, however, there were instances where forced labour was raised, not for public purposes, but for private employers, and not for a few days or weeks but for long periods.[20] Thus according to Myrdal the indigenous systems of forced labour which colonial regimes inherited in south Asian countries were adapted to induce large-scale movements of labour. Such practices could be challenged and made the subject of campaigns in the home country. For example, in the early days of British rule in Kenya similar activities on the part of the administration there were publicized and discredited by missionaries led by J. H. Oldham, and the government was forced in 1921 to abandon the formal compulsion of Africans to work on the settlers' farms.[21] Moreover, forced labour of this kind was officially proscribed by international agreement in 1926.

Another method of labour recruitment, with some elements of 'voluntariness' about it, was by means of contracts or indentures. These often involved men working in places far distant from their homes and with restrictions, sometimes severe, on their freedom of movement. As Myrdal put it, 'Foreign labourers, isolated in unfamiliar surroundings, were more docile, more easily organized for effective work, and more permanently attached.' In south Asia he gave as examples the Indian and Chinese labourers respectively in the rubber plantations and tin mines of Malaya, Indian workers in Burma and Sri Lanka, and the Chinese brought into Java both as coolies on the tobacco plantations and as intermediaries between the government and the indigenous people.

Yet another form of pressure upon men to enter employment was that of imposing money taxes in circumstances when there was little option but to earn the money by working for settlers, mines, or plantations, at whatever wages were offered – and clearly such circumstances put native workers at a disadvantage and made for low wages. To cite Myrdal again, it was private employers who consistently complained of labour shortage and urged colonial governments to do something about it. The difficulties of attracting local people into wage employment were indeed serious, but 'the matter was never considered on any assumption other than an extremely low level of wages'. Governments themselves do not seem to have had the same problem: 'some very large undertakings, such as the construction of railways and public works in India after 1860, seldom suffered seriously from labour shortage, though wages rose conspicuously as the demand for labour increased'.[22]

It will have become clear how strongly the economic institutions established under colonial rule were oriented to the export of primary products for a world market. The point is made most vividly by a map which shows how the railways built in African colonies linked the mines, the plantations, and the white-settled farming areas to the sea; they did not link one African country to another.[23] Though an infrastructure was certainly built up, it may not have been the precise infrastructure that the present independent governments would have preferred. As will be seen in chapter 4, many poor small countries remain very dependent on primary exports, and this perhaps has been the most persistent economic consequence of their colonial past.

Missions

Christian missions were integrally involved in European overseas expansion in ways that went far beyond the preaching of the gospel. They founded branches of the churches that had sent them, which were long dominated by European clergy until these were replaced by men locally born and ordained. They concerned themselves with healing bodies as well as with saving souls, so that in association with mission stations there grew up dispensaries and hospitals, soon followed by schools for training nurses and other medical personnel. Schools were needed too for the general spread of literacy, well-nigh indispensable as that was for membership of the church, while higher and more specialized education was required for the training of native clergy and catechists. Schools needed books and other equipment, so that the missions' activities extended into commerce and industry as they initiated and controlled printing works, bookshops, and workshops where materials such as school furniture were manufactured. Furthermore, in some areas it came to be felt that people's material standard of living had to be raised if they were to be able to care as Christians should for their children and other dependants in a house with minimum sanitary and hygienic arrangements, such as soap and mosquito nets. Some missions accordingly developed an 'industrial' side, training men as skilled craftsmen, and introducing cash crops to enable people to earn money for bibles, clothes, and school fees. For example, in Uganda the Church Missionary Society's industrial missionary, Mr Borup, in partnership with government officials, was largely responsible for introducing cotton as a cash crop. Moreover, it was the CMS who set up the organization for collecting, processing, and exporting the crop with capital raised in Britain largely from wealthy Christian philanthropists who for many years got very little in the way of dividends.[24]

In Africa a large mission station was like a whole town, with its hospital, schools, seminary, workshops, bookstore, and houses of foreign missionaries and native adherents, all centred on a large church or cathedral. Some like medieval European cities even had walls round them, for some missions were established before colonial government and the whole station might have to be defended against attack.

Mission stations thus afforded a refuge for those who needed protection. For example, freed slaves found safety in stations like that at Freretown near Mombasa, while during the female circumcision crisis of the 1920s (see below) the Protestant missions similarly extended protection to girls who refused clitoridectomy, and were themselves attacked in consequence. Such circumstances further heightened their character as settled communities with an economic base, different from the surrounding areas and acting as change agents in relation to the life of those areas.

Throughout colonial history, the missions championed the rights of the natives against exploitation by European enterprises or unjust treatment by government officials. For example, Jesuits in Brazil resisted the enslavement of the native Indians, establishing stations at strategic river confluences to stop slave traders penetrating up-stream, to intercept convoys coming down-river, and to settle the freed captives on land where they could live and be evangelized.[25] Similarly, I have already mentioned the missions' successful campaign against forced labour in Kenya.

Missionaries, however, did not always make themselves popular with the native people of colonial territories. Despite their concern for the latter's welfare, they were necessarily deeply committed to changing many aspects of the indigenous cultures. The local deities were condemned as false gods, to be abjured by the convert along with customs and practices which from a Christian point of view were immoral. Some of those practices may now seem to us comparatively harmless, and missionaries were not always able to distinguish between the essential core of Christian teaching and western European cultural preconceptions; it was only half in jest that some were said to have brought Christianity, chemistry, and cricket in a single package. Forms of dress and dancing, for example, which by today's standards seem inoffensive enough, were stigmatized as indecent by Victorian missionaries. Not all the traditional practices they condemned were so innocent, however. In Kenya there was a storm over clitoridectomy, traditional among the Kikuyu in initiating young women. The missionaries objected not only to the dangerously unhygienic way that was done, for the same objection to male circumcision could be met by having it carried out by trained staff in a hospital or dispensary, as was in fact done in Christianized versions of similar rites elsewhere in Africa. 'Female circumcision' was different, as it had lasting harmful results. Missionaries accordingly urged their converts not to allow their daughters to undergo initiation, and (as already mentioned) sheltered those who refused it. From a Kikuyu point of view, however, that seemed a totally unwarranted interference in an integral part of their traditional life. In the conflict that ensued, government officers who not long before had been under missionary pressure to stop forced labour now found themselves leading forces of police to protect the lives and property of their missionary critics who, as it appeared, had made themselves quite gratuitously unpopular by their tactless handling of the matter.[26]

And there was resentment of the long-continued occupancy of positions of authority in the churches by Europeans. Different churches had different approaches to this problem. Roman Catholic missions soon established schools from which a few young men with the necessary intelligence and vocation might pass into seminary training and eventually be ordained. It was a slow process, and many dropped out, though those who did were a source of educated manpower as teachers and in the government service. Once ordained, there were no distinctions between local and expatriate priests; their celibacy helped, as they lived without wives and children in the same clergy houses, and when there were enough local priests a whole diocese eventually passed from missionary hands into those of a local secular clergy. Some Protestant missions, too, took higher education and the training of clergy seriously. Among Anglicans, however, there was a distinction between the mission, financed from donations in England, and the 'Native Anglican Church' (as it was often called) which was locally supported. Frugal though the living standards of Anglican missionaries were, native Anglican clergymen and their families were even poorer materially, and this caused a certain amount of feeling within the church. At the same time, some other Protestant denominations tended to be slower to ordain local men, thus giving an appearance of trying to keep control of church affairs in white hands.[27]

Resentment of foreign domination extended accordingly to Christian missions and missionaries, dedicated though they were to the good of the people among whom they worked. It had much to do with movements to set up independent churches, as detailed in chapter 10.

Government

The government of colonies was characteristically regarded as administration rather than politics. Power in a colony was wielded by officials of the metropolitan country who were responsible to the home government rather than to any local body. Local legislatures were, it is true, set up to distinguish when the Governor or Viceroy was giving an order from when he was making a law. Typically they consisted of a majority of senior government officials and a minority, usually appointed rather than elected, of 'unofficials', influential local whites whom the government wished to placate and conciliate by involving them in the process of law-making. In some British colonies white settlers complained that such arrangements amounted to taxation without representation and denied them their basic democratic rights. That argument was used to sustain a claim for making government responsive, if not altogether responsible, to a very undemocratic electorate, namely the local white minority. Under strong settler pressure, that claim was conceded in some settler-dominated colonies such as Kenya and Southern Rhodesia (now Zimbabwe). Elsewhere, generally speaking, it was only in the later stages of colonial rule that non-whites were nominated to membership of legislative councils, and only on the eve of independence that they were elected by popular vote. Meanwhile, administering a colony was viewed as an art comparable to administering a government department at home – making sensible rules and seeing that they were obeyed, collecting revenues and using them efficiently for approved purposes to the satisfaction of a government auditor, and generally attending to the business of government in an orderly manner.

The pre-existing societies differed widely in the extent to which their institutions could form the basis of modern administration under colonial rule. Thus at one extreme Indian civilization included indigenous scripts and literatures; money, banking, and credit institutions; and a tradition of political organization extending back to the empire of Asoka. At the other, the social and political organization of some East African tribes was not recognized as 'government' at all by the early European explorers, there was no indigenous writing, and a rudimentary currency had only recently been introduced by Arab slave traders. Modern administration clearly had to start from the beginning in such places, and there are records of the well-nigh comic confusion that occurred when taxes in kind were introduced before money was familiar and widespread. African political systems themselves, however, differed widely, and in places such as the emirates of northern Nigeria and the interlacustrine Bantu kingdoms of Uganda there were despotic monarchies with appointed chiefs and organized courts recognizable as 'government' by Victorian Englishmen. A policy of indirect rule was appropriate in such areas and (whether or not under that name) was adopted by the British also in others including the sultanate of Zanzibar and the kingdom of Tonga, and above all the princely states in India, and likewise by the Dutch in Indonesia. Indirect rule had great advantages. People were governed in the way to which they had been accustomed. The legitimacy of traditional authorities was recognized and confirmed, backed in the last resort by the metropolitan power. Control was exercised over what those authorities did with their powers, and they could be required to use them to introduce health measures, schools, cash crops, and the like for the general benefit and advancement of the people; the introduction of cotton in Uganda, noted above, was a case in point. At the same time the lower levels of administration were staffed cheaply with local subordinate officials rather than expensively with expatriates; thus it used to be said in jest in colonial Africa that the only member of the administration not entitled to go on leave to Britain was the chief. For such a person, though, there were difficult dilemmas. The more modern his style and the measures he introduced, the more discontent and opposition he was likely to arouse. But if he failed to make the changes required of him, or represented too vigorously the views of his people, he was subject to pressure from above by officials who in the last resort could dismiss him and send him into exile.[28]

In colonies where there was a native population, some account had generally to be taken of the indigenous system of law. On the one hand, the colonial administration existed precisely in order to ensure that Europeans' lives and property came under the same kind of protection as they might at home, and that contracts to which they were party could be relied on, if necessary, for enforcement in the setting of a congenial legal system. On the other hand, however, where the local people had their own institutions for dealing with offences and settling civil disputes, there might be little need to interfere, and much to be said for leaving well alone. So native law and custom might be recognized, though generally only so far as it did not conflict with 'natural justice' or some such concept, meaning the fundamental preconceptions of the colonial power's law. It applied only to minor criminal cases in which the accused was a native, and civil cases in which both parties were native. Generally, too, there was a right of appeal to the colonial power's courts. Furthermore, in the plural societies that grew up under colonial rule (see below), immigrant communities other than those of the colonial power might have their own customary laws, especially about marriage and inheritance, and these were not always well accommodated into the laws of the colony.

The effect was generally to sharpen distinctions between different communities or categories of people, and to give legal sanction to them. Where two systems of law existed enforced by two sets of courts, the question of who was subject to which had to be legally defined. For example, in East Africa under British rule the prime distinction was that between 'Africans' or 'natives' on the one hand, and 'non-natives' on the other. An African or native was defined as 'a person who is a member of, or one of whose parents is or was a member of an indigenous African tribe or community'. Persons whose legal status was so defined were subject to the jurisdiction of officially appointed or recognized chiefs, and had to obey their lawful orders in matters like health control, soil conservation, and the brewing of local beer. Non-natives were not subject to the jurisdiction of African chiefs, but they did pay more tax. Within that category, distinctions between Europeans and Asians were made as a matter of administration rather than law.[29] Elsewhere in Africa, in French and Belgian colonies a distinction was drawn between '*indigènes*', who were subject to customary law, and others, who were subject to metropolitan law. The latter were of course primarily the Europeans, but they included also those Africans whose superior education and occupation put them into the category variously known as *assimilé*, *immatriculé*, or *évolué*.[30] Thus where the British adopted a set of categories based on birth and amounting to a race distinction, the French and Belgian administrations enabled a small elite to move out of the category of 'natives' and gain the same rights and responsibilities as Europeans.

All colonial governments, then, exercised law-and-order functions, collected taxes, and set up the framework of modern administration, though in doing so they often drew invidious distinctions between categories of people, particularly Europeans and natives. In partnership with Christian missions, and to an extent that differed in different places, they introduced modern social services such as health and education. Possibly the greatest achievement of some administrations was famine control, as already noted in India (chapter 2), and in Africa according to John Iliffe.[31] Most also laid the foundations for economic development by public investment in the infra-structure of harbours, railways, roads, and public buildings; indeed, that aspect of the colonial legacy is visible today even in such minor details as police uniforms and the rule of the road.

Another legacy of empire in most former colonies is that of a language of wider communication. Although Japanese does not seem to have taken deep root in Taiwan, Korea, or other parts of the former Japanese empire, at the other extreme Spanish was firmly implanted in most of Latin America during centuries of colonial rule and is now the universal language of the region, while Portuguese is the language of wider communication not only in Brazil but also in Mozambique, Angola, and the other former Portuguese colonies of Africa. In Africa and Asia, whatever the variety of the local vernaculars, at least some people in a colony learned to speak and write English or French, or some other language with a wider currency in the world. Thus an elite were left with the key to a wider world of knowledge, culture, and political and commercial opportunities. As a result, the educated elites of former British colonies enjoy close and easy communications with the whole of the English-speaking world, including the United States, while those of former Belgian and French colonies gravitate more naturally to the French-speaking world. Most of Africa is accordingly divided at present between Anglophone and Francophone countries, whose leaders communicate more easily among themselves and with outsiders than they do with each other – a cultural equivalent of those railways that run straight to the sea and not to neighbouring African countries. I return to the question of language in chapter 9.

Under colonial rule, nearly everywhere a start was made on education, or more strictly schooling. (It can of course be maintained that no society lacks a system of education, for all prepare and socialize children somehow for their adult roles; not all, however, traditionally did so through specialized institutions like the school.) Colonial governments generally ensured from the first that there were schools for Europeans' children, while schools for the natives were mostly pioneered by missions and later maintained and extended in partnership between the two. Widely different policies were pursued in different colonies. In some there was an emphasis on primary schooling; for example, in the former Belgian Congo (Zaire) it was assumed that while some Africans needed to be trained in basic industrial skills as craftsmen, railway workers, and the like, higher posts would be filled by Europeans for the foreseeable future. When in the 1950s that assumption was clearly open to question, the rapid establishment of higher education, including three universities, had all the appearances of a death-bed conversion, and the institutions concerned had had very little effect on the situation when independence eventually broke upon the country. In some other colonies, in contrast, governments early assumed a responsibility for native education including higher education; among British African colonies, Uganda and the Gold Coast were notable in this respect. In yet others such as Kenya, the rise of African education took place in a difficult atmosphere of opposition from white settlers, though it went ahead there rapidly nonetheless.[32]

Colonial governments therefore faced the issue still central to educational policy in poor countries, that of the balance between primary schooling for the greatest number on the one hand and higher education for a fortunate few on the other. Under colonial rule, emphasizing primary schooling could look suspiciously like holding back native advancement. It was associated with settler pressure in colonies such as Kenya and Rhodesia, and campaigned against by missionaries and nationalist political leaders; while colonial governments less subject to settler pressure, like Uganda, did more to encourage the emergence of an indigenous elite. Ironically, the latter policy has more recently been stigmatized as elitist for engendering disparities of income and privilege, while the former has been endorsed as egalitarian, cost-effective, and more conducive to economic development. I discuss the issue further in chapter 9.

Western medicine too was introduced into colonies by Europeans, for whom indeed it was a necessary condition of their very survival. Thus according to John Iliffe the first hospitals in Africa were set up by the Portuguese and Dutch in their coastal enclaves primarily to treat their own sick sailors and soldiers.[33] As empires extended into the interior, it was in similar circumstances that colonial government medical officers worked in the early days; their first responsibility was the health and survival of the European officials, then that of others; European 'unofficials', natives employed by the colonial government as policemen, clerks, and the like, and lastly the native population at large. Where public health was concerned, the first requirement was to create townships, cantonments, and government stations as islands of health control – pure water, sanitation, refuse disposal, malaria eradication – where Europeans could live and work efficiently. Arrangements for treating the sick followed a similar pattern, with government hospitals for Europeans separate from those for the native population. At the same time, western medicine was also introduced by the missions, for whom, as already noted, healing bodies and saving souls were inseparable. As with schooling, therefore, medical services and hospitals had dual origins in government and missionary activities.

The European community

Although as seen by the native or subject people the white conquerors may have seemed a united force, there were diversities and conflicts of interest among different groups of Europeans. Settlers clashed with government officials over land questions and the conditions of native labour, while missionaries championed native rights against both. All tried to outmanoeuvre one another, not only in the colony itself, but also in the metropolitan country, where missionaries could enlist support from their parent churches while commercial interests too could bring pressure to bear in the home capitals. Generally speaking, however, the native population knew little of these conflicts, as many Europeans much of the time assented in effect to a conspiracy of silence out of a sense that, however deep the disagreements, white prestige and even perhaps their very survival depended on maintaining a united front.

Moreover, in British colonies the appearance of white solidarity was accentuated by one special and peculiar institution known as the Club. Writing of Uganda in the 1950s, Sofer and Ross described how in a small European community this was the focus of European activities, providing the only recreational facilities for many miles. Membership was open to both sexes, and members met there after work for drinks, conversation, and games, as well as for organized activities such as amateur dramatics. In the smallest stations, non-membership involved isolating oneself almost completely from the European community. In the larger centres other facilities were available, but it was considered the 'right' thing to be a club member. The club's exclusiveness was heightened by the fact that not even all Europeans were regarded as suitable for membership, as those whose work bordered on the manual or whose English was not good were assigned to the 'non-clubbable' category.[34] The club was accordingly the meeting place for those who exercised authority at the local level – the District Commissioner and his senior assistants, specialist officers of the government service (medical, education, agriculture, veterinary, police, works, etc.), the bank manager, senior managers of the oil companies, and the like. Here, in a setting and an atmosphere that reinforced their sense of national and racial identity, the top people and their families mingled informally in circumstances giving every plausibility to the suspicion that they could from time to time settle important affairs behind closed doors – closed, as we have seen, even to some Europeans, and certainly closed to all natives.

Populations of mixed descent

In many colonial societies, sex relations between people of different 'race' – which meant primarily between Europeans and others – were subject to an ambiguous disapproval. Ambiguous, because it might well be a sign of manly prowess for a white man to have a black mistress, while sex relations the other way about between a black man and a white woman were much more heavily penalized as symbolizing the black man getting above his place. Such attitudes extended the usual dual morality of sex relations into the race-relations situation. A man must gain experience, but equally he must protect his sister's honour; so there are two sorts of women, the virtuous who are good for marriage, and the other sort, who are socially inferior. In a race-conscious society white men clearly tend to class black women in the latter category.[35]

Colonial societies differed widely, however, in the extent to which such unions might be regarded as legal marriages whose children were legitimate. That affected both the number of people of mixed descent and their status, with important consequences for the latter-day social structures of former colonies. Two contrasting examples will illustrate the point.

In Brazil, despite some evidence of prejudice and discrimination in the past, hard-and-fast colour bars were avoided and racial categories kept flexible and open. From the earliest times of Portuguese settlement, inter-marriage and the founding of legitimate families of *mamelucos* were encouraged by both church and state, since they increased the Catholic population and added to the number of loyal subjects of the Crown.[36] Those attitudes set patterns that long persisted, according to studies carried out in the 1940s and 1950s mostly by North American scholars. Thus Wagley quoted a study by Hutchinson of a rural community among whom only a small minority including the local planter-aristocracy could trace a purely European descent. A second class of bureaucrats, professionals, and technicians included the rest of the pure whites and some of mixed ancestry. There was a third stratum of fishermen, craftsmen, and wage workers, and a fourth of casual workers without a regular income. These two lower groups included a few *brancos de terra* (of ancestry mainly white but known to be mixed) with mulattoes and a majority classed as Negroes.[37]

Paler skins and European appearance predominated at the higher levels of income, power, and prestige. There was, however, a widespread acceptance of 'whitening' or 'purifying the blood' through mixed marriages, resulting in a complex, fluid class structure in which race was only one factor and wealth, occupation, and schooling also counted. Brazilians said that 'a rich Negro is a white man and a poor white is a

Negro', and had a rich vocabulary of racial terms – *branco, branco de terra, indio, negro, mulatto, mameluco, preto, cabra, cabo verde, caboclo, escudo, pardo, sarara* – reflecting a fluid situation characterized by ambiguity and vagueness. As for discrimination, Bastide put it epigrammatically: 'A Negro is not refused a post because he is a Negro – he is told that unfortunately it has just been filled; he is not refused promotion – he fails to pass the medical examination.' The interracial etiquette of avoiding reference to people's colour was at variance with the actualities of prejudice and discrimination. Nonetheless, both the practical difficulties of rigidly classifying so mixed a population, and the official view of Brazil as a colour-blind society, had prevented social colour bars or overt legal discrimination from arising.[38]

From similar origins South African society evolved along completely different lines. The early Dutch settlers at the Cape brought in slaves from Madagascar, Mozambique, and the East Indies, and assimilated the indigenous Hottentot population into serfdom. Unions between the settlers and the women of these slave communities were sometimes recognized as marriages, especially if the women had been baptized; as time went on, however, they came to be regarded as concubinages, and the woman's children however begotten were slaves, until the abolition of slavery in all British dominions in 1834. Later in South African history the attitudes of white people towards unions with non-whites became more and more unfavourable. Entrenched as an integral part of South African white culture, those attitudes were embodied in laws denying the status of marriage to any union between a white and a non-white person (Prohibition of Mixed Marriages Act, 1949), and making sex relations between such persons an offence (Immorality Act, 1927, amended 1950 and 1957). Since mixed unions became so difficult, it seems likely that most of the so-called Coloured population of South Africa are the descendants of the early unions referred to above. Most speak Afrikaans as their home language, and keep up their original culture, especially the Malays who remain Muslims though otherwise their culture is Afrikaans and western. To a large extent, then, the Coloured people may be regarded as a self-contained and mainly endogamous group. In contrast to the complex and fluid system of racial categories in Brazil, therefore, in South Africa there were just four: White, Coloured, Bantu, and Asian. The process of 'whitening' as it was called in Brazil had its equivalent in 'passing' in South Africa; the Population Registration Act of 1950 had the express aim of eliminating it, and an administrative framework was set up in which each person's race was a legally defined status, from which it was very difficult to get reclassified.[39] Doubtless all this will be changed following the election that brought the African National Congress to power in 1994.

Plural societies

Finally, in many places colonial expansion created a type of society that, following J. S. Furnivall, has been termed 'plural'.[40] In such societies people thought of themselves, and were thought of by others, as belonging to different 'communities' associated with different occupations and social statuses, marked off by racial appearance, and distinguished by cultural features such as language and religion.

In a colonial society there were always at least two such communities, white and natives; usually, however, there were more. While the slave trade took populations of African descent to the Americas, migrations of free or indentured labour took many more people to distant parts including East Indians to the Caribbean, Chinese and Indians to many parts of south Asia, and Indians to South Africa. Slave and labour migrations are only part of the story; others besides Europeans migrated on their own initiative in search of trade, such as the Indians who took part in the opening up of East Africa, and the Chinese in Malaya and Mauritius. Migrant communities of this sort became closely associated with particular occupations or other economic interests such as retailing. In many countries, indeed, a person's identity as a member of one or other of these communities might be more important than citizenship of the new state. The governments of newly independent countries have accordingly had an uphill struggle to engender a common culture and sense of identity as part of the task of nation-building.

Though it is necessary to refer only briefly here to this aspect of the colonial heritage, it is one that has been of the utmost importance in shaping the present-day social structures of many poor countries. I return to this subject in chapter 12.

The question of exploitation

It is often alleged that the present-day rich countries owe their affluence to their past and continuing exploitation of the poor. In so far as it concerns the colonial past, the question calls for some consideration here.

Exploitation may be said to occur when a transaction or relationship between two persons or groups makes one better off at the expense of the other. Unlike bargains freely made that benefit both parties, such arrangements are clearly unlikely to be entered into willingly if the disadvantaged party understands the consequences. Generally they involve coercion, or ignorance and gullibility, or both.

It will have become clear from the foregoing that there was much exploitation in colonial history, particularly in the early period. Slaves were victims of the grossest exploitation of all, forced as they were to work for no more than the barest subsistence to enable them to live and breed more slaves. Forced labour too was exploitation. Other labour recruitment practices like the contracts and indentures mentioned above had a semblance of voluntariness about them, yet it may reasonably be surmised that workers' ignorance and gullibility were often exploited when they ventured into the unknown on long-term contracts to far-distant places where their freedom of movement was restricted. Such practices were by no means universal, however, and by the end of the colonial period employment in foreign enterprises often paid far better than alternative occupations, particularly traditional subsistence agriculture; a state of affairs that has continued, as seen in the next chapter.

Exploitation could also be said to occur when people were deprived of access to land or other resources on which they relied for their subsistence, and were left with little choice but to work on plantations, mines, or settlers' farms. However, plantations and farms often made more productive use of land than formerly, and were a source of employment and incomes. Thus in south Asia, according to Myrdal, 'Of the four main types of agriculture, plantations yield by far the highest returns per unit of land, followed by wet paddy, sedentary dry farming, and shifting cultivation'; moreover, the plantations were 'labour-hungry', though many managements shopped around for cheapest labour and the employment did not always benefit the local people.[41] Widely different land policies were adopted by different colonial governments in pursuit of the 'dual mandate' doctrine that required them to balance the rights and interests of the native peoples on the one hand and the most effective use of natural resources on the other.[42] For example, in British East Africa there was the greatest possible contrast between Uganda and Tanganyika, where paternalistic administrations laid prime emphasis on protecting native land rights and made very little land available for plantations and settlers' farms, and Kenya, where wide areas in the so-called Highlands were set aside exclusively for white settlement.[43] Moreover, improved health conditions under colonial rule resulted in population growth, but in Kenya extra land for African subsistence agriculture was not available as it had been pre-empted by its alienation to white settlers. The land issue became bitterly contentious and had much to do with the guerrilla campaign in the 1950s known to Europeans as 'Mau Mau'. Similarly, in Ceylon (Sri Lanka), according to Myrdal, 'the planters laid their hands on uncultivated land in the hilly districts around the villages in the very period when an extension of the land under food crops was becoming urgent as population was increasing'.[44]

Some colonial governments, especially in the early days, forbade or discouraged native competition with European interests, either locally or in the home countries. A much-cited example is that of Indian cotton textiles, undercut in the early nineteenth century by British machine-made goods which entered India duty free, while Indian manufacturers could not retaliate as the export of textile machinery to India was at first prohibited, then subject to a duty which was in turn repealed in 1860.[45] Similarly, restrictions were imposed on coffee-growing by Africans in Kenya from the early days of British rule till about 1950. The Kenya settlers even tried to get similar restrictions imposed in Tanganyika, but the administration there resisted their pressure and encouraged native coffee-growing on Kilimanjaro and elsewhere. Later, the Kenya administration reversed its policy and encouraged Africans to grow coffee there too.[46]

To be sure, profits were made from colonies. As Myrdal pointed out, they accrued to a few, including shareholders in the metropolitan countries and Europeans settled in the colonies; while the costs of empire, in so far as they were not borne by the colonies themselves, fell upon the whole nation, including the working class whose sons died in colonial wars. After the Second World War, national liberation movements in the colonies increased the costs of policing them, and it became increasingly difficult to justify those costs to the home electorates. In Britain's case, according to Myrdal, after the first period of crude exploitation the colonies were probably never very profitable. It was free trade with, and investment in, the areas of European settlement in temperate zones, rather than colonialism in Africa and Asia, that built up Britain's prosperity in the late nineteenth century. So 'the British were cool and rational rather than generous and idealistic in giving up their South Asian colonies . . . The French and Dutch acted differently because they did not see their own interests.'[47]

It seems quite clear, indeed, that industrial countries have prospered more without colonies than with them. Thus of the seven countries with the highest GNP per capita in 1991, five – Switzerland, Sweden, Denmark, Finland, and Norway – had no colonies, while Germany was deprived of them after the First World War, and Japan's spectacular rise as an industrial nation took place with redoubled vigour after it too had been deprived of overseas possessions in 1945. As for the United States, despite phrases like 'American imperialism' they never had much of an empire, and for long were indeed the leading anti-imperialist power, whose representatives frequently chided countries like Britain and France for the sin of having empires.[48] Thus it was under United States pressure that the British government sent the Cripps mission to India in 1943, so ensuring India's independence as soon as the war was won. And when countries such as Britain and France divested themselves of their colonies they too may have benefited in their turn. Freed of their imperial commitments ('east of Suez', in the symbolic phrase) after 1960, and relying on nuclear weapons for defence against a direct attack upon themselves, like other western states they were able to reduce their armed forces and military expenditure to unprecedentedly low levels and devote correspondingly more of their resources to their public health and welfare services.[49]

In Britain's case, mention may also be made of the Colonial Development and Welfare scheme. Initiated in 1929 and extended in 1940 and 1945 despite the war, this took effect mainly in the 1950s when substantial grants were made from the British treasury to colonial territories for purposes such as rural development and the establishment of university colleges, and was a forerunner of what we now term aid.[50]

We may therefore conclude that although exploitation did occur at some times and in some places, in general colonial rule became less exploitative as it went on, and was a source of benefits as well as costs. Despite some exploitation, the economic returns from colonial empires were disappointing, and the countries that had them were better off when for one reason or another they gave them up.

It has been argued that even in purely economic terms exploitation is not incompatible with mutual benefit.[51] Even though both parties gain from an exchange, one party may consider that they are not getting their fair share of the benefits. In social and psychological terms this may be termed 'quasi-exploitation'. Domestic service, for example, is not necessarily exploitative if people are not forced to be servants and if their remuneration in cash and kind is as good as in other occupations open to them, even though the result is that rich people appear to be making themselves comfortable at the expense of poor. As mentioned in chapter 4, domestic service reflects wide disparities of income, and is still widespread in poor countries. During the age of colonial expansion, western European societies were highly inegalitarian, and well-to-do people employed servants. In the colonies they employed black servants, so adding a racial distinction to an economic disparity. Later, when income disparities diminished in the metropolitan countries and domestic service declined there, in the colonies white people could still employ black servants. Thus, writing of Uganda in the 1950s, Sofer and Ross singled this out as the main reason why European immigrants decided to stay, or to return.[52]

And if material, economic exploitation is classed as 'instrumental', following de Vos we may further distinguish 'expressive' exploitation when, as he put it, 'socially dominant members of a society make indirect use of others for a psychological advantage'. This occurs in caste societies when socially exploited pariahs as part of their occupation perform tasks regarded as innately polluting. The dominant group depend on these out-castes, want them to continue, and cannot practise violence against them, so separate themselves off as 'sacred' from the 'unclean' out-castes who accordingly become necessary for the maintenance of a secure definition of their superior social status.[53] Some personalities may thrive in a society in which they have someone to despise and patronize, even though they may be doing nothing but good to the despised and patronized; and this may have applied in colonial societies to the more paternalistic kind of missionary, administrator, teacher, or technical officer.

The view from below

I have emphasized throughout that colonial regimes were widely diverse. Some were economically exploitative and politically repressive, alienated much land to white settlers, used forced labour for mines, plantations, or settlers' farms, and neglected native education, health, and economic development. Others by contrast were mild and beneficent, imbued with a 'development and welfare' mentality, alienated little land, encouraged native education and welcomed the emergence of an indigenous elite. Thus among African colonies we may contrast Kenya and Algeria on the one hand with Uganda, Tanganyika, and Senegal on the other. All, however, were characterized by invidious distinctions. To adapt Jean-Paul Sartre's epigram, not so very long ago the earth had 2,000 million inhabitants: 500 million people, and 1,500 million natives.[54] Colonial society embodied white superiority in every aspect of modern life: their technological mastery, their control of economic, political, and religious organizations, legal distinctions between Europeans and others, and even the arrangements for health care which seemed to show that some people's lives were considered more valuable than others. In such circumstances, benevolent paternalism seemed to diminish human dignity scarcely less than outright exploitation.

For example, Maguire recounted how in Sukumaland in central Tanganyika a development scheme which, it can hardly be doubted, would if implemented have materially raised people's living standards, came to grief through being imposed from above. Plans were at an advanced stage before local people were informed, let alone consulted, and the scheme was linked with ambitious but unpopular proposals for representative local government on multi-racial lines. Widespread non-co-operation with government orders for livestock improvement and the like drew from the administration the fatal response that 'sometimes people have to be coerced for their own good', and mass demonstrations degenerated into riots that were brutally repressed.[55]

Whether harsh or mild, exploitative or beneficent, then, colonial regimes were almost always resented by those upon whom they were imposed, and especially the more intelligent, educated, and urbanized people among them. What was resented was first and foremost foreign rule, then the exploitation, real or imagined, associated with it. Thirdly there was a reaction against some Europeans' disdain of indigenous cultures, and fourthly a resentment of colour bars and the personal humiliations that went with them. Those sentiments found expression in a literature of protest which has had a continuing influence in shaping intellectual and political movements in the Third World, as men who later became political leaders set out their manifestos, often in auto-biographical form.[56]

This literature ranged in style from the dignified, urbane and moderate tone of Jawaharlal Nehru[57] to the passionate polemics of Frantz Fanon.[58] It embodied two responses to the white-dominated world. One was to assert that 'men of colour' were fully equal to whites, and could perform similar tasks and rise to similar challenges. The other was more backward-looking. An early example was the preface to Jomo Kenyatta's *Facing Mount Kenya*, an ethnological text imbued with a political message to 'all the dispossessed youth of Africa: for perpetuation of communion with ancestral spirits through the fight for African Freedom . . . '[59] It was hard to reconcile the two responses, for the more competent the formerly subject peoples showed themselves at coping with the modern world, the more it was by acquiring and exercising scientific knowledge and administrative skills not particularly characteristic of the indigenous cultures of those who, in the poignant words of Aimé Césaire's poem, had 'never invented anything'.[60] That posed deep dilemmas for cultural and literary movements like that of *négritude* or 'the African personality', about which Wole Soyinka remarked that 'A tiger does not go around proclaiming its tigritude – it just pounces.'[61]

Decolonization

The call for decolonization, loudly voiced in recent times, linked two demands. One was that the expansion of Europe should be reversed by its contraction, and required the former colonial powers to relinquish their overseas possessions. The other was for the end of foreign rule, or in other words the self-determination of peoples. Nearly everywhere the two coincided, the former colonies' inhabitants were glad to see the backs of the white conquerors, and the liberation (or abandonment) of colonies was almost completed by the early 1960s. The remaining colonies include the bitterly disputed Falkland Islands, and a number of relatively non-controversial islands of strategic and scientific importance with few if any permanently settled inhabitants, such as Ascension, South Georgia, Kerguelen, and the Crozet Islands. By far the biggest population still under colonial rule at the time of writing are the people of Hong Kong, due to return to Chinese rule on the expiry of a British lease in 1997.

But though that may well mark the end of the colonial era, we still live in a world dominated by the rich countries; and protest against that domination and disparity can be powerfully expressed in terms evoking echoes of the colonial past.

Thus as Julius Nyerere recalled in 1990, there were times when the imperial nations, especially those of western Europe, were proud of their colonial empires, and saw no reason to hide their domination over others. Their total political, and hence economic and social, domination depended in the last resort on military power, seldom deployed but always known to be there.

All that had changed since 1945, with the setting up of the United Nations and the recognition of a universal right to national independence, while military occupation by one country of another against its people's wishes was internationally condemned. 'This means that colonialism in the traditional and political sense is now almost a thing of the past', while 'gun-boat diplomacy' had been largely replaced by 'covert action' and even that had its limitations. So a new strategy had been adopted, based on the use of economic strength to achieve technological and cultural domination. 'Aid' was currently flowing from South to North through adverse terms of trade, indebtedness, and payments for information. It was 'Economic Colonialism' that was now attacking the independent nations of the 'Third World'.[62]

Suggestions for further reading

Alfred Crosby, *Ecological Imperialism* (New York, Cambridge University Press, 1986).
Barbara Ingham and Colin Simmons (eds.), *Development Studies and Colonial Policy* (London, Frank Cass, 1987)
Philip Mason, *Patterns of Dominance* (London, Oxford University Press, 1970)
Carlo M. Cipolla, *European Culture and Overseas Expansion* (Harmondsworth, Penguin, 1970)

4

Economic conditions

Measuring disparity and development

The GNP measure

The most obvious way of starting to investigate the differences between rich and poor countries, or individuals, is to compare their incomes. As I explain below, there are certain pitfalls in this approach to the differences between rich and poor countries, but up to a point it is a good and useful one.

There are three possible measures of a country's collective income, and of these the one most commonly used is the gross national product or GNP. The *gross domestic product* or GDP is the value of all goods and services produced in the country, usually valued 'at factor cost', that is, adjusting for indirect taxes and subsidies. *Gross national product* is the gross domestic product at factor cost, plus any balance of income received from abroad. *National income* is gross national product net of depreciation. It represents the resources available for current use after setting aside sufficient to maintain the nation's stock of capital equipment, and is the best measure accordingly; however, it is more difficult to calculate, since it is hard to arrive at estimates, or even a satisfactory definition, of depreciation; and it is not available for as many countries as is GNP.[1]

Most countries have statistical departments which calculate and publish an annual estimate of the GNP in the national currency. This can be converted into a standard currency (by convention US dollars) at an appropriate rate (usually the official rate of exchange). The average for the population, or GNP per capita, enables us to see at a first rough approximation what the average income is in each country and how it compares with others. Since 1978 these estimates, along with other data, have been compiled by the World Bank from figures supplied by national statistical offices together with other sources, and published in the Bank's annual *World Development Report*.

They show, first, how wide a difference there is between the richest and poorest countries. In 1992 among the 40 'low-income economies', excluding China and India, the average GNP per capita was 370 US dollars; among the 23 'high-income economies' it was US $22,160, sixty times as much.

The disparities between the world's richest and poorest people are almost certainly wider still. Data are lacking on internal disparities within many countries, especially poor countries; however, estimates by the United Nations Development Programme (UNDP) for 1988 suggested that the incomes of the richest 20 per cent of the world's people exceeded those of the poorest 20 per cent by a factor of at least 140 to 1.

Secondly, the data confirm that differences in GNP per capita do broadly correspond to differences in real resources and living standards. For example, in poor countries in 1990 there was one physician for every 11,190 people, in high-income countries one for every 420. The average infant mortality in poor countries was 91 per thousand live births, thirteen times the rich-country average. However, among countries at similar average income levels there prove to be wide differences in real indicators such as infant mortality. Judged by such criteria, some have done better than would be expected from their GNP per capita, others less well.[2]

Thirdly, account must be taken of trends over time. Economic development as measured by growth in GNP per capita has taken place in some countries, while in others it has been nil or negative, so that positions in the league table are constantly changing. Between 1980 and 1992, indeed, negative growth rates were reported from 18 of the 42 low-income countries, though not from India, where reported growth was substantial, or China, where it was spectacular.

The limitations of the GNP measure

Since the 1960s it has been recognized that the GNP measure has considerable limitations.

Most basic is the unreliability of the official figures. There is a general problem, especially in the smaller low-income countries, about the quality of the data reaching the national statistical office, while the office itself may be short of skilled staff and other resources. A particular problem arises over agricultural statistics; in countries where substantial quantities of farm produce are consumed by the farmers' households with no money changing hands, estimates have to be made of the areas under crops, the expected yield, and the prospective money value of the goods if they were sold in local markets; and when these estimates are made by overworked and under-supervised field staff, it will be appreciated that they may be subject to considerable error. A related point is that some government statistical offices, for whom producing a GNP figure may be a matter of national and professional pride, may concentrate on economic statistics to the detriment of data urgently needed for health and welfare purposes, particularly on short-term trends in infant mortality and nutrition.[3]

Secondly, estimates of GNP per capita are average figures. In themselves, and in the absence of other data, they conceal income disparities within countries. Inter-personal income distribution is a complex subject with many aspects, including disparities between rich and poor households; between men and women, old and young, even within the same household; between towns and rural areas; among different classes and different ethnic groups; among regions within countries. This is particularly important when growth in GNP per capita is taken as a measure of development. In a country with wide disparities between rich and poor, a positive growth rate may merely mean that the rich are getting richer. Other data are needed to ascertain how widely the benefits of economic growth are being spread. To be sure, data are available for some countries on the distribution of income among households, while indirect evidence of how widely resources are being spread is afforded by real indicators such as the infant mortality rate and school enrolments.

Thirdly, there is the rate-of-exchange problem. For the purposes of comparing average incomes in different countries, figures computed initially in each country's national currency have been converted to a common standard, conventionally the US dollar. However, official exchange rates, as used by banks and in the world currency markets, are unsatisfactory for this purpose. They change suddenly when a national currency is devalued (or more rarely re-valued upwards); they can be artificially manipulated by governments and central banks; they are related to current and expected future interest rates and rates of exchange, expectations which are often self-justifying. The need was for a set of exchange rates based on purchasing power parities (PPP), representing for each country how much of its currency would be needed to buy a defined standard combination of goods and services. The formidable task of compiling such a table has been the subject of a continuing International Comparison Project (ICP), initiated by the United Nations in 1969. This has produced a set of 'conversion factors' analogous to rates of exchange, known as the Purchasing Power of Currencies (PPC), and defined as 'the number of units of a country's currency required to buy the same amounts of goods and services in the domestic market as one dollar would buy in the United States'.[4]

These calculations have confirmed what had long been believed, that official market rates of exchange grossly undervalue the currencies of many poor countries, resulting in an underestimate of their real income per capita. In 1990, according to UNDP statistics, there was a threefold underestimate for India (GNP/capita US \$360; real GDP/capita PPP \$1,072); fourfold for Nigeria (290 : 1,215); fivefold for Sri Lanka (470 : 2,405). This does something to mitigate the extreme disparities in income cited at the start of this chapter. In PPP\$ terms the average real income of the 'least developed' countries was \$740; among the 'industrial' countries it was \$14,440, some twenty times as much.[5]

Dissatisfaction with per capita GNP as a measure of economic progress (or lack of it) extended beyond purely statistical considerations to substantive questions of development policy. The nub of the matter was well expressed by Morris D. Morris, who pointed out that only eight of the fastest-growing developing countries might raise their GNP to the rich OECD countries' average in less than a hundred years, and only sixteen in a thousand years (presumably at current rates of growth). In other words, on purely arithmetical grounds, and quite apart from the environmental concerns discussed in chapter 5, it seemed highly unlikely that poor countries could 'catch up' in any foreseeable future. However, Morris continued, there did seem to be possible strategies for providing 'many of the basic elements of a decent existence before incomes have risen very much'. This raises a fundamental question: is a frugal but 'decent existence' the best that can be hoped for in poor countries, meeting basic needs without rich-country resources and choices? Clearly this question is central for aid and development, and relates particularly to the 'basic needs' approach discussed in chapter 13.

Human welfare and development: the search for a new index

In the 1970s the perceived need for an alternative to the purely monetary GNP led to a quest for a measurement system minimizing if not entirely eliminating money and consisting wholly or mainly of real indicators of the quality of life. Reviewing in 1979 many previous efforts including those by the UN, UNRISD (UN Research Institute for Social Development), OECD, World Bank, and other organizations and individuals, Morris criticized them all as excessively complex. For example, Jan Drewnowski of UNRISD had proposed a 'level of living index' including nutrition, clothing, shelter, health (access to medical care, prevention, longevity), schooling, leisure, security (of the person, of ways

of life), the social environment (including restrictions on or freedom of
social and political activity), and the physical environment (ranging from
the depressing ugliness of shanty towns to the inspiring townscape of
model cities).[6] Not only was this obviously complex, but it also involved
aesthetic and political value-judgements. Morris further criticized some
composite indicators for an underlying assumption, no doubt stemming
from Rostow, that there is 'some desirable or optimal pattern' of development; and for their explicit concern with economic development rather
than welfare.

For his own Physical Quality of Life Index (PQLI), Morris set out to
ensure that it should be 'unethnocentric', and should not assume that
there is only one pattern of development. It should measure results, not
inputs (for example, not expenditure on education, not numbers of
schools and teachers, but literacy); and it should reflect the social
distribution of those results. The three objective and ascertainable
measures that met all his criteria were: infant mortality, expectation of
life (at age one, to avoid double-counting infant deaths), and adult
literacy. These indicators were scaled from 0 to 100, and averaged, to
give a single index figure for each country. The literacy index was,
simply, the literacy rate, the percentage of adults able to read and write.
The infant mortality index was arrived at by placing each country on a
100-point scale from 'worst' to 'best', the highest ever recorded since
1950 (229 in Gabon) to the lowest (8 in Sweden, or say 7 to represent
the lowest realistically attainable); and similarly with the expectation of
life at age one.

Morris' findings were as we have since come to expect, and as I have
indicated above. There was a general correlation between GNP per capita
and his PQLI among countries classified into broad income groups, from
an average PQLI of 40 in low-income countries to 92 in high-income.
But '"money is not everything"'; within each group of countries the
correlations were not strong. In the early 1970s some high-income
countries, particularly oil-rich Arab states, had relatively low PQLIs. On
the other hand, some low- and lower-middle-income countries had
relatively high PQLIs, including Sri Lanka and Costa Rica.[7]

In its first annual report in 1990 the UN Development Programme
(UNDP) adopted a Human Development Index (HDI), rather like Morris'
PQLI but including a money component. It combined the expectation of
life, this time at birth; the adult literacy rate; and a measure of real GDP
per capita, derived from the purchasing-power-adjusted GDP estimates of
the International Price Comparison project. The mathematics were
complex, but in essence the HDI was intended to measure where each
country stood between the shortest and longest expectation of life
(41.8 years in Afghanistan and 78.4 in Japan); the lowest adult literacy

(12.3 per cent in Somalia) and 100 per cent; and how far short its real GDP per capita fell below the average official poverty line, PP-adjusted, in nine industrial countries, representing 'the North's minimum purchasing power', income above which was disregarded.

In later annual reports a modified version was introduced. Expectation of life at birth was still the single unadjusted demographic measure. The educational attainment indicator, however, combined the adult literacy rate (weighted two-thirds) with mean years of schooling (weighted one-third). The money measure was derived by even more complex calculations from the real GDP per capita in purchasing-power-adjusted dollars (PPP$), this time taking into account income above the poverty line, though on a sharply tapering scale, to enable finer distinctions to be made among the industrial countries.[8]

In its 1990 report, the UNDP recognized that it made a difference whether human development took place in a democratic or an authoritarian framework, and they hoped that a quantitative measure of such aspects of freedom as free elections, multi-party political systems, an uncensored press, the rule of law, free speech, and personal security could be devised and incorporated in the HDI.[9]

The UNDP's tabulation of HDI against GNP has amply confirmed Morris', finding that there is no automatic link between income and human development. According to the 1993 report, countries whose HDI outranked their GNP were, in order: Sri Lanka, China, Chile, Costa Rica, Tanzania, and Colombia; while the converse was true of others including Algeria, Gabon, Saudi Arabia, South Africa, and the United Arab Emirates. Changes in HDI over time were considered to be as significant as its level in marking a country's progress; however, the question arises whether the use of the HDI as a time series may not be invalidated by statistical changes in the components of the index and their weighting.

The HDI was also able to take account of disparities within countries as well as comparisons among them. Thus a gender-disparity-adjusted HDI could be calculated, showing that, while 'no country treats its women as well as it treats its men', adjusting for gender disparity raised some countries in the HDI league (Scandinavia, France, New Zealand) and lowered others (Canada, Switzerland, Japan). Likewise, where the data were available, adjustment could be made for income distribution among households, raising South Korea's HDI score, lowering those of Malaysia, Turkey, Mexico, Panama, Jamaica, and, most of all, Brazil. Regional and rural–urban differences could be analyzed, revealing for example wide disparities in India between Kerala and Punjab on the one hand and Bihar and Uttar Pradesh on the other. And ethnic disparities could be analysed, notably in the United States.[10]

The economic characteristics of poor countries

Sectors

There are many ways in which an economy may be thought of as divided into 'sectors' or areas of economic activity. We hear much of the public and private sectors. Another distinction, useful in the past, was between the 'cash', 'monetary', or 'modern' sector and the 'non-monetary', 'household', 'traditional' or 'subsistence' sector. In the language of development economics there are 'leading sectors' with (optimistically) 'spread' or 'trickle-down' effects, or (pessimistically) 'backwash' or 'polarization' effects on the rest of the economy. Studies of town life in the 'Third World' have identified an 'informal' sector of small-scale private enterprise in contrast to the formal state sector and the equally formal sector of large-scale private corporations. And everywhere, large or small, there is a 'black market' sector of illicit activities, tax evasion, company fraud, smuggling, laundering the proceeds of illicit drugs trading, extortion rackets, etc. The concept of sectors may be misleading if it leads us to think of them as more self-contained than they really are; in fact all sectors in an economy are involved with each other, goods and services are traded among them, and people may be active in more than one sector in the course of a day.

To begin with the distinction between 'cash' and 'subsistence' sectors: in the first, goods are produced and services rendered for money, cash transactions prevail, and money values are placed on everything. In the second, goods are produced and services rendered without money payments, though money may be used in gifts. Many transactions take the form of barter, while many goods and services are valued in personal terms such as reciprocity, family sentiment, honour, or neighbourliness.

In the past it was probably the case that men tended to be more involved in the first sector, women in the second; and this may still be true, though to a diminishing extent. Moving in different social milieux affected such things as the languages they spoke. For example, in Uganda in 1968 many men and few women spoke Swahili, the lingua franca in trade and employment (see chapter 9).

Being non-monetary, the second sector largely escapes statistical notice. Most of the goods produced and services rendered without money changing hands may not figure in the official statistics at all, while it is doubtful whether those that do are correctly valued, such as the agricultural estimates mentioned earlier in this chapter. A false distinction has sometimes been made between food crops, assumed to be for a household's own consumption in the subsistence sector, and cash crops. Food crops can be cash crops too; a family may eat some and sell some, especially if they live near a town or have access to some other market.

In all countries much production is carried on by unpaid labour in the household, notably preparing and cooking food and other domestic tasks. In 'Third World' countries in the past it was probably the case that people's needs were met in the non-monetary sector to a greater extent than in industrial countries, and traditionally even more so. It used to be said in the old Africa that to build a house the first thing was to brew beer; kinsfolk and neighbours came to drink the beer, and helped to build the house. Economic development has generally involved more and more such activities becoming the subject of money values and transactions, so that the household sector has shrunk, but there seems little prospect of its disappearing altogether. On the contrary, its importance continues to be overlooked and underestimated, especially in relation to the unpaid work of housewives in the home; it would be a mistake to regard it as vestigial.

In low-income countries the extent to which the non-monetary sector is overlooked and underestimated is even greater, and with it the economic activity of women. It is indeed ironic that the phrase 'economically active' has come to mean involved in paid work in the cash economy, for the original derivation of the word economy itself was from the Greek for household management. And to imply that women who are not in paid employment are not working is both inaccurate and insulting, for in most countries they do most of the housework and look after the old and the very young, while in many poor countries they do much of the cultivating too.

In low-income countries, then, many needs are met (however inadequately) in the traditional subsistence sector without the intervention of money. By contrast, the modern cash economy is represented by such institutions as mines, factories, banks, and commercial offices, pervaded by a thoroughly businesslike outlook and the fullest use of money, credit, and international exchange. At least one commodity or product in each of the poor countries is thoroughly modern in this way – copper in Zambia, the tourist trade in Kenya, or in India such sectors as the iron and steel complex as Jamshedpur, the commercial centre of Calcutta, or the Bombay stock exchange. Often such sectors appear as enclaves or islands of economic and technological modernity in contrast to the life that surrounds them.

Leading sectors, spread and backwash

The very prosperity of such sectors or enclaves tends to heighten the disparity between them and the rest of the economy and society. To some extent such 'growth poles' generate economic growth in nearby sectors. For example, industrial or mining development in one part of an African country may stimulate food-growing as a cash crop in nearby rural areas, and some of the earnings of workers in mine or factory may generate increased incomes among local farmers. Further afield, however, the migration of men to the mines may result in depressed conditions in the rural tribal areas as those left behind – women, old people, children, the sick and handicapped – struggle to maintain themselves and their dependants by traditional methods on the land. As with men, so with capital; even one with quite a modest capital to invest, such as a small shopkeeper, may rate his prospects better in the thriving industrial area than in the impoverished countryside. Such effects cumulate and reinforce one another. So, according to the older development economics, while a 'leading sector' was generating 'spread effects' in neighbouring sectors, those more distant might be experiencing 'backwash' or 'polarization', though more recently it has come to be recognized that spread effects are far outweighed by backwash.

In either case, however, a leading sector may be an industry, such as mining, iron and steel, or textiles. Or it may be thought of in geographical terms as a town and its hinterland, while the areas experiencing backwash are more distant rural areas. Or the leading sector may be a minority – a class, a racial group, or one of the communities in a plural society like the Asians in East Africa or the Chinese in Malaya. Economic development by its very nature seems prone to engender regional, class, and communal disparities. These have serious political and other repercussions, and I revert to this important point in subsequent chapters.

The precariousness of the cash sector

The modern cash sector of the economy of many poor countries, however, has hitherto tended to be narrowly and precariously based on the export of a small number of primary commodities such as coffee, cocoa, sugar, copper, bauxite, or rubber. Not only does the foreign trade of some 'Third World' countries consist largely of a few such exports, but their whole economy is also dependent on foreign trade. Industrial development in some countries has reduced this dependence. For example, by 1991 exports from India were diverse and mainly of manufactured goods, a far cry from the days when tea, cotton, and jute were the export staples; likewise Brazil's export earnings from machinery, vehicles, and other manufactured goods far exceeded those from coffee. But many if not most poor countries still rely heavily on a few primary staples. According to UNDP, that reliance left them very exposed to the fall in commodity prices by nearly a half that took place between 1980 and 1991, most sharply between 1989 and mid-1991. Coffee was, after oil, the developing countries' largest primary export; and in two years coffee export earnings were halved, with devastating effects for wage labourers and small producers. For example, between 1986 and 1989 Uganda's coffee exports rose by a quarter in volume, yet total export revenues fell from $395 million to $273 million. As in other parts of the world, most of that fall was borne by the coffee-farmers.[11]

And if the rewards of cash farming are precarious, so also are those of salaried employment in countries with high rates of inflation (often attributable to war, or extravagant military expenditure, or general financial mismanagement). When inflation erodes the real values of wages and salaries, people may revert to the subsistence, non-cash sector to meet their needs, growing their own food and bartering with neighbours when money prices reach absurd heights. Uganda again affords vivid examples. By the late 1970s, according to one observer, 'the formal economy had for all intents and purposes collapsed'. Another reported that in 1989 Ministry of Health staff had not been paid for three months; and when salaries did come, they were impossibly low. Some health workers acquired land and grew their own food, leading for instance to complaints about one medical assistant that he was always in the swamp working on his rice. 'At one large facility, the staff had worked out a rota for brewing millet beer to sell.' (Traditional subsistence or modern cash sector?) But most entered the illicit economy known as *magendo*, exacting fees or bribes for services that were officially free, or requiring more than the officially fixed charge. Many health workers, still imbued with an ideal of how a free national health service should function, regretted this state of affairs, but could only ask, 'My friend, what shall I eat?'[12]

Nor can it be supposed that life in the subsistence sector offers any kind of safe haven of rustic simplicity, frugal yet secure in a 'traditional' way of life. On the contrary, it too is precarious, at risk from disease (health conditions are worse in the country), natural disasters such as droughts, floods, and earthquakes, and human-made disasters such as war, civil disturbances, political oppression, ethnic hostility, and religious persecution.

Debt

'Third World' countries differ widely in their indebtedness. In 1990 India and Brazil had large debts, but these are big countries with large GNPs, and their debt : GNP ratios were comparatively low at 25 per cent. The debts of some other countries too, such as Guatemala, Botswana, Iran, and South Korea, amounted to less than 40 per cent of their GNP. But the least-developed countries, especially in Africa, were collectively in debt to the extent of a whole year's GNP. These were just the countries most dependent on a few export commodities. Not only was their position precarious for the reasons given above, but they were also trapped in what seemed an intractable paradox, spelt out as long ago as 1933 by the economist Irving Fisher, and quoted by UNDP in its 1992 report: the more such countries try to earn foreign exchange and repay their debts by exporting those staples, the more they force prices down in a glutted market. So 'the more debtors pay, the more they owe'.[13]

Thus in Uganda, according to Sarwar Lateef of the World Bank, in 1987–90 the terms of trade deteriorated by 64 per cent, mainly because of the fall in the price of coffee. Uganda's debt problem arose largely from the Obote II government's heavy borrowings from the IMF on non-concessional terms in the early 1980s. Even after that debt had been reduced by about a quarter under a World Bank scheme, with the fall in the price of coffee nearly four-fifths of the country's foreign exchange earnings were going to meet debt-service obligations, leaving insufficient to pay for petroleum and other essential imports, and presenting the government with a perpetual cash-flow problem.[14]

Uganda was not the only country to experience problems of this kind. During the 1980s, while world commodity prices fell, debt obligations rose partly because rich countries' governments raised interest rates to counteract inflation. Together these trends resulted in a reversal of the net transfer of resources to developing countries. Between 1983 and 1991 the net flow was from 'South' to 'North', from poor to rich, returning to a positive flow after 1991.[15]

Military expenditure

Possibly the United Nations' most telling statistic was that in 1992 world military spending at $815 billion equalled the combined income of almost half (49 per cent) of the world's people. Military spending in the developing countries amounted to $125 billion. Re-allocation of a quarter of this to health, education, and family planning would be enough to achieve the following targets:

12 per cent would provide basic health care, immunization, and safe drinking water, and greatly reduce malnutrition;

4 per cent would halve adult illiteracy, provide universal primary education, and level up the education of girls and women with that of boys and men;

8 per cent would provide all willing couples with a family planning pack, and (it was hoped) stabilize world population by the year 2015.

Over the period 1988–92 the chief arms exporters to developing countries were, in order, the Soviet Union, USA, France, China, and UK; ironically, all permanent members of the Security Council. 1988–92 was, however, a period of rapid change after world military expenditure reached an all-time peak in 1987. Arms exports fell, along with military expenditure generally, largely through drastic cuts in the armed forces of Russia and other successor states of the former Soviet Union. Among the developing countries the ten chief arms importers included India, Saudi Arabia, Iraq, Iran, and Pakistan.

It used to be said that developing countries spent more on their armed forces than on health and education. However, over a longer period from 1960 to 1990–1, military expenditure by developing countries as a whole has fallen: as a percentage of their combined GNP, from 4.2 to 3.5 per cent, about the same as the industrial countries; and in relation to their expenditure on health and education, from 143 per cent (nearly half as much again) to 60 per cent (three-fifths). Of course it can always be argued that poor countries can ill afford expenditures of that order. Moreover, there are wide variations. Countries with notably high levels of military expenditure include Iraq; Saudi Arabia, and some neighbouring states; Myanmar (formerly Burma); Mozambique, Angola, and Ethiopia.[16]

High military expenditure has implications far beyond the economic consideration of resources forgone that might have been used to further human development. Large armed forces can serve as the power-base for military coups, and once in power military leaders favour high military expenditure to reward their faithful supporters and maintain themselves in power. I return to this subject in chapter 12.

'Big firm, small country'

Much of the world's economic activity has been carried on in recent decades by trans-national corporations or TNCs, formerly known as multi-national corporations (MNCs) or enterprises (MNEs). According to the 1988 report of the United Nations Centre on Transnational Corporations, the biggest TNCs had sales greater than the aggregate output of most countries, and the biggest 600 accounted for a fifth to a quarter of the total value added in the world's market economies, much of the world's exports and imports, and the greater part of foreign direct investment (FDI). If their sheer economic might towered above that of all but the richest and most powerful states, it will be appreciated how little influence a small state in a poor country could exert over these giants.[17]

TNCs were highly selective in their investment in developing countries.

According to the Canadian economist G. K. Helleiner, most TNC investment had been in a few newly industrializing countries (NICs) such as Brazil and Taiwan, and oil-producing countries such as Venezuela and Libya.[18] According to the UNCTNC the TNCs found many low-income countries unattractive for investment purposes for various reasons: lack of infrastructure, geographical remoteness making for high transport costs, shortages of trained skilled labour, political instability, serious internal strife, and low or negative economic growth giving little prospect of an expanding market. In such countries, foreign direct investment by TNCs offered no substitute for official development assistance.[19]

However, TNCs' activities are not confined to foreign direct investment; as Helleiner pointed out, since 1970 a hundred per cent foreign ownership has ceased to be their dominant role, and they are involved in many different ways in mediating interaction with the world market, particularly buying and selling goods, and selling services such as technology, management, and marketing.[20] Of particular moment to low-income countries who depend heavily on one or a few primary export staples was the UNCTNC's finding in 1985 that 'Eighty to ninety per cent of the trade in tea, coffee, cocoa, cotton, forest products, tobacco, jute, copper, iron ore, and bauxite is controlled in the case of each commodity by the three to six largest transnationals.'[21]

Some aspects of TNC activities in developing countries were well illustrated by G. L. Beckford's study of plantation agriculture in the Caribbean in the 1960s. For the firms that owned them, their plantations were only part of the whole, and it was the profitability of the whole that mattered more than the efficient use of resources in each plantation. This led to what Beckford termed 'perverse supply responses' to changes such as a price rise; while increasing acreage and output overall, the firm might reduce production in one country, so not allowing that country to benefit from the higher prices. Clearly that would constitute exasperatingly capricious behaviour from the point of view of the government concerned.

Further, a large firm might control much or most of the exports of a particular commodity from an individual state; and the land area covered by its plantations might be so large as to make it virtually the only source of local employment. Rising productivity due to technical improvement might enable relatively high wages to be paid, especially if the workers were able to form and join a trade union, but possibly at the cost of increased unemployment.[22]

Since the time of Beckford's study TNCs' activities have become more complex, and no longer centred on investment. By 1980 the Brandt commission (see chapter 13) pointed out that TNCs need not always bring capital with them; in some cases that could be borrowed locally, and TNCs could be partners in joint ventures.

However, a continuing issue has been that of transfer prices. A considerable proportion of world trade – as much as 30 per cent, according to the Brandt commission – was carried on within these giant firms, or between them and their subsidiaries. It is very much within the firm's discretion how to price these transactions, and it is to the firm's advantage to do so in such a way as to avoid paying taxes in a country with high tax rates and make the firm's profits, quite legitimately, in a country where they attract less tax. The low price for fruit from a TNC's plantation in Beckford's study was one example. Another, cited by UNCTNC, concerned low transfer prices for timber exported by logging companies to their subsidiaries elsewhere in the world, so avoiding paying any corporate income tax at all to the host country's government. Clearly, as the Brandt commission said, while such practices reflected the companies' legitimate business interests, they might conflict with the developmental objectives and national interests of host countries.[23]

Opinions differ about the extent and scale of transfer price manipulation. For obvious reasons there is little reliable evidence, but according to Helleiner some of it bears out developing countries' anxieties, while the attention paid to the question by the tax authorities in industrial countries gives some indication of its importance.[24]

In the world as a whole, TNCs employed at least 65 million people, about 43 million in their home countries and 22 million abroad including an estimated 7 million in less-developed countries. So some 3 per cent of the world's 'economically active' population were contributing 20 to 25 per cent of its value-added. This indicates that the TNCs were predominantly capital-intensive enterprises with high labour productivity and an advanced technology, and indeed the UNCTNC 1988 report suggested that one of their most important contributions to development and modernization was in the field of technology transfer.[25]

That had to be paid for, of course, though according to Ghertman and Allen the governments of less-developed countries tended to demand that transfers of technology should be free of charge. The 'Third World' view was that the research and development (R&D) has already been done and paid for in the rich industrial countries, and a second payment should not be required, while the TNCs responded that royalty payments were necessary to finance future R&D. A related issue, remarked on also by Helleiner, was the nature of the technology to be transferred. It seemed that the governments of less-developed countries tended to regard 'appropriate technology' as obsolete, polluting, and 'a sort of racism', and to insist that the TNCs should apply only the most advanced technology.[26]

Like Beckford, the UNCTNC noted that the high productivity of labour in TNCs enabled them to pay higher wages and salaries than local firms to a few privileged workers. Indeed, the UNCTNC's 1974 report described the high labour standards and earnings of TNC employees as 'a mixed blessing', creating an elite labour group and accentuating disparities in wages.[27]

Of the TNCs' employees in developing countries about 2 million were women, according to the UNCTNC in 1988. Many were employed in the service sector, a few in white-collar occupations such as bank employees, but most as cleaners, waitresses, shop assistants, and the like. A small and dwindling number were still employed in agriculture, alone or with their families, in TNC-owned plantations dating back to colonial times producing crops such as tea and rubber, and in which their position was generally inferior to men. Women wage-labourers were employed too in fruit-picking, -packing and -canning, though these occupations were classed as industrial. In industry generally, women's work was mostly repetitive, labour-intensive, and low-paid. This was especially so in export processing zones (EPZs), where perhaps a million women found work who would otherwise be unemployed. So the EPZs had been of some benefit to the workers, but almost certainly much more to the TNCs; and they had not done much to alleviate unemployment in developing countries.[28]

When a TNC's plants were shut down in line with the firm's global strategy the direct and indirect effects on local employment were great, and even if this did not happen often the precariousness and lack of control by the host country were always there. This sense of powerlessness was an important underlying factor in reactions against TNCs.

In former colonies TNCs recalled foreign domination and control, while as in colonial times the ostentatious living standards of their expatriate personnel aroused resentment. Local intellectual elites might see TNCs as obstacles to desirable social and political developments. TNCs were further criticized over issues such as promoting the sale of baby foods to the detriment of breast-feeding. TNCs engaged in advertising and the mass media came in for particular criticism for the loss of indigenous cultures and regional and national identities, and for promoting a homogeneous, tasteless world culture.

In the past, according to UNCTNC's 1988 report, there had been allegations of undue political influence over host countries' governments. Most of these, however, dated back to the period roughly 1945–75 when 'a substantial degree of hegemony' over the world economy was exercised by TNCs based in the United States. Since the mid-1970s there had been fewer such allegations as the international scene had become more complex, with the rise of Japanese- and European-based TNCs, together with some based in 'Third World' countries, and more detailed regulation of TNCs' activities by host governments in the 1980s.[29]

On being a latecomer

It may be useful at this point to summarize the advantages and disadvantages of being a latecomer on the scene of economic development.

On the one hand, late-developing countries can take advantage of the experience gained, often slowly and at great cost in human life and suffering, in the countries where the technological revolution began. In no field is this more evident than that of public health and preventive medicine. No country need now repeat the 'health of towns problem' of Victorian England. As has been pointed out in chapter 2, reductions in mortality which took a century or more to achieve in western countries have been accomplished in latter-day 'Third World' countries in three or four decades. In industry, too, some latecomers have profitably copied the models and methods devised in the early-industrializing countries. This was a successful strategy in the early stages of Japanese industrial development. More recently it has been from some newly industrializing countries such as Taiwan and Korea that the mass markets of the world have been flooded with goods such as tennis shoes and transistor radios. Another example of imitative development has been that of village industrialization in the Punjab, where local craftsmen began by applying traditional metal-working skills to making spare parts for western products such as sewing machines, diesel engines, pumps, and farm machinery, and went on to produce all the components and assemble them for export as well as for the local market.[30]

And if the technology can be borrowed in a metaphorical sense, so can the capital literally be. That said, it is not sufficiently appreciated that in recent years low-income countries have been financing high rates of investment mostly from their own resources, and a serious deficiency of domestic savings has been a problem mainly confined to the smaller low-income countries.

On the other hand, the technology available to be 'borrowed' from western countries is characteristically capital-intensive, making available highly paid employment for a few, and in some people's opinion 'inappropriate' for the needs of low-income countries: though, as already noted, that view tends not to be taken by the governments of those countries. Moreover the word 'borrowed' is a misnomer here, for technology protected by patents or trade secrets has to be bought and paid for. As for borrowing in the literal sense, I have already pointed out that many low-income countries have become burdened with debts which it seems unlikely they can ever repay, so that their current and future development is already heavily mortgaged, especially their foreign exchange earnings. Meanwhile their need to borrow is increased by balance-of-payments deficits, most acutely in oil-importing countries. Repayments and interest charges due on old debts require yet more new borrowing, and so the problem is compounded.

Furthermore, as noted above, whereas the early-industrializing countries exported their manufactured goods in a world in which they found ready markets and few competitors, later-industrializing countries find export markets closed against them both by tariff barriers and by the commanding positions of already established industrial enterprises. It is for reasons of this kind that the recapitulation thesis needs to be somewhat qualified, and it has to be recognized that later-industrializing countries cannot pass through exactly the same stages of development in a world that has changed. Some would go further and say that it has changed to their disadvantage. The early-industrializing countries, it is said, in their role as imperial powers, set up a world division of labour in which they themselves concentrated on manufactured exports to exchange for raw materials produced in their dependencies. Now those countries have abandoned their empires and sought self-sufficiency in protected markets, relying on their own resources and depending less on the rest of the world; and their former colonies have been left in the lurch, deprived of markets for the export of goods for whose production they have natural advantages.

Labour, employment, and earnings

In considering employment and wages in poor countries it should be constantly borne in mind that two-thirds or more of the labour force work in agriculture, many on small family farms producing mostly for their own consumption. How well they fare depends largely on how much land they can cultivate. Those with too little land to keep a family, and those with no land at all, generally resort to working for others at low wages, starting at starvation level or below. Some of the poorest people in the world, indeed, are the landless poor in South Asia.[31]

Only a small minority work in industry, which generally means moving to towns, where jobs are better paid. Thus for example in Kenya in 1974–5, according to the economist Arthur Hazlewood, the great majority of the labour force were small farmers, and some 80 per cent of the population lived on the land. In 1980 average wage earnings in agriculture were £215 a year, in manufacturing £742, in finance and insurance £1488.[32] But though jobs in industry are better paid they are scarce, and in many cases even becoming scarcer as modern capital-intensive methods supersede jobs formerly done by large numbers of relatively unskilled labourers.

It was with only slight and pardonable exaggeration that in 1970 the development economist Gerald M. Meier coined the phrase 'development without employment'. In the 'less developed countries' taken as a whole, urban employment was growing more slowly than either the urban population or industrial output. Clearly this made for high rates of urban unemployment as people – mostly men – moved into towns in the hope of being among the favoured few to find modern-sector jobs at wages far exceeding anything available in the rural areas.[33] More recently UNDP have identified 'jobless growth' as 'a new and disturbing phenomenon' affecting many parts of the world including industrial countries.[34]

In these circumstances, Sir Arthur Lewis warned of the consequences of 'premature decasualization'. Modern managements tended to dislike casual labour, and preferred to employ regular full-time workers who fed better, worked better, and caused less trouble. Unions too found casual workers difficult to organize. But when some formerly casual workers got full-time jobs while others became altogether unemployed, there was a serious social problem.[35]

In a capital-intensive industry with a few relatively skilled workers, wages play a comparatively small part in total costs and management have little reason to resist wage claims when they are pressed by a well-organized trade union. The governments of poor countries, too, may favour the payment of high wages especially by big foreign enterprises; high wages may be viewed as a kind of 'tax' limiting repatriated profits and making more of the benefits available locally. Similar considerations may apply to generous fringe benefits. Local pressures by both governments and unions for such benefits may in turn predispose enterprises to invest in capital-intensive methods, importing the necessary machinery.

To an increasing extent, selection for the few highly paid jobs in the modern sector has been by means of formal educational qualifications gained through the school system. This puts a premium on schooling and certification, with important consequences alike for disparities of income, discussed later in this chapter, and for schooling itself, to which I turn in chapter 9.

For the rest, however, unemployment is too simple a term. Outside the ranks of the favoured few in modern-sector jobs – the aristocracy of labour, as some writers have described them[36] – people are not on the whole found to be sitting helplessly about doing nothing. On the contrary, many struggle for a livelihood in ill-rewarded labour-intensive activities in what I termed the 'indigenous private sector', now more generally known as 'informal'. The need to recognize this sector introduces a qualification into the dual sector model with which I began, useful though that is as a first approximation. As detailed in chapter 7, the informal sector includes the myriad tiny businesses and self-employed individuals who in poor countries carry on small-scale manufacture by handicraft methods, minor repairs, food processing, and the like, along with the activities of small shopkeepers, street hawkers, water sellers, and casual labourers. Domestic service, too, which has all but disappeared in rich countries, is still a widespread institution in low- and middle-income countries in response to much wider disparities of income which make it possible for substantial numbers of people to employ others for no more than a twentieth or a thirtieth of their own incomes.

According to the World Bank, in many developing countries 'achieving greater equity and promoting social justice have been important goals', most commonly pursued through minimum wage legislation. Protected wages and salaries in the formal sector may be of little avail where there is rapid inflation, as has been seen in Uganda; however, in some countries especially in Latin America government salaries and statutory minimum wages are index-linked. In the Bank's view, minimum wages tended to reduce employment in the formal sector; and as the informal sector comprised 'small family enterprises that usually lie outside the purview of government labour regulations', minimum wage laws tended to increase inequalities between the formal and informal sectors.[37] This issue is not confined to the 'Third World'; minimum wage legislation has become the battle-ground for conflicting policies between Conservative and Labour parties in Britain, between the UK government and the rest of Europe, and between the European Union on the one hand and the IMF and World Bank on the other: truly a battle of the giants.

The conditions analysed above did not prevail everywhere, however, and the economist Rakesh Mohan's study of the Colombian cities of Bogota and Cali in the 1970s is interesting largely because of their exceptional nature. Economic growth had been steady at around 6 per cent (augmented to an unknown extent by the illicit drugs trade); while, thanks to employment-promoting government policies, employment had grown at a similar rate and faster than output. There was no great flood of migrants into towns, little unemployment, and no discernible informal sector. Nor, on the other hand, was there a protected formal sector, and demand and supply in the labour market were more or less in balance. Male production workers were not particularly well paid, and certainly did not constitute an 'aristocracy of labour'. Disparities in incomes were still wide, but had become somewhat less so, and fewer people were in poverty, though persisting disparity was evidenced by the 100,000 'maids', almost 20 per cent of women workers, about one to every five or six households. In contrast to some other countries where social welfare benefits have been appropriated by the well-to-do, in Colombia they were described as 'less unequal than incomes'. There had been universal primary education for some time, and secondary schooling especially for girls was expanding rapidly. Water, sewerage, sanitation, and roads were 'nearing universality'; there was good public transport, and flat-rate fares enabled workers from the urban fringes to take jobs in the city centres.

In those conditions, according to Mohan, higher earnings were most strongly associated with: (1) being male. In most countries worldwide, women's earnings are a half to two-thirds those of men; in Colombia it was nearer a half, but increasing as more young women completed secondary school. (2) years of schooling, with a 'certification bonus' for successful completion at each level. (3) work experience. For most workers that increased with age, but for workers with primary schooling or none, earnings levelled off in early adulthood. Another factor of some significance was living in a 'good' part of town; not only as the consequence of higher earnings, for obviously rich people live in rich neighbourhoods, but also as cause. Possibly a 'good address' indicated good schooling, and perhaps ability and a will to succeed.[38]

But to return to the conditions more usual in 'Third World' economies: I have already emphasized that the different sectors are in fact closely involved with one another, and the boundaries between them are not clear-cut. For example, households of quite modest means can employ domestic servants, and avail themselves in other ways of labour-intensive services available at 'informal sector' prices. From one point of view this may look like exploitation; from another, it represents one way in which some limited 'trickle-down' occurs, and purchasing power is diffused from the favoured few to the poor.

Another way in which this happens is through the money which migrant workers send home, or bring with them when they return. Considerable attention was paid to this in earlier studies of labour migration in Africa.[39] There, modern-sector employment represented for many men an episode, though it might last for anything from two to twenty years, rather than an irreversible move to town life. Meanwhile they had an active interest in maintaining the traditional way of life in their home areas, and their own place in it, with a view to their eventual retirement. While the prime purpose was to help maintain wives and children, migrants also sent money home to oblige relatives by helping them with such things as their debts, fines, bridewealth, and fares to go abroad and seek work in their turn.[40] At that time it was mostly internal migration within a country or territory, or could be so regarded when, for example, Uganda and Kenya were not sovereign republics but adjoining territories under British rule between which people moved freely. Some labour migration crossed international boundaries, however, such as that from Rwanda and Burundi under Belgian mandate into Uganda under British rule (and it was noted how sensitive that was to movements in the rate of exchange between sterling and the Belgian franc).[41] In more recent times the international aspects of labour migration and workers' remittances have come to the fore with the recognition that some 'Third World' countries have come to depend heavily on this source of foreign exchange. Thus in 1992, according to the World Bank's statistics, workers' remittances added (in round figures) 11 per cent to India's earnings from merchandise exports and over 20 per cent to those of Pakistan, Sri Lanka, and Turkey; 45 per cent to those of Bangladesh; 54 per cent to those of Morocco; 76 per cent to those of Mexico; and 86 per cent to those of Jordan; and they exceeded the merchandise exports of Egypt and El Salvador by over 70 per cent.[42]

Corruption

No country is free from corruption, and in the nature of things it is obviously impossible to cite statistics.

Its economic consequences were well analysed by M. J. Sharpston, who distinguished between 'efficient' corruption which occurs when scarce resources command an illicit price which corresponds to their scarcity value, and 'inefficient' when the price is lower. From an economic point of view, efficient corruption has the same effect as a complete absence of corruption in rationing scarce resources for which a government licence or permit is required, though it puts the proceeds of the sale of those licences or permits into private hands rather than the public exchequer. It may happen, though, that corruption is inefficient because people, including officials, are 'naturally obliging and more inclined to give you the stamp you need on your document than not'.

Generally speaking, high tax rates and complex and stringent controls on economic life, combined with 'inefficient' corruption, make for the widespread evasion of laws and regulations. Thus smuggling will be commonly practised if rates of duty are high but customs officers do not ask for large bribes; if the rate of duty is lower, it may be as cheap, or almost as cheap, to pay it. Likewise it may be a nice question whether to pay one's income tax in full or bribe the inspector to reduce the assessment.

One argument favouring or at least condoning corruption is that it can 'oil the wheels', for example in securing the prompt import of a vital spare part without which much production is being lost. Another is that it may encourage investment by affording a means of accumulating capital; for example, corrupt politicians may invest their ill-gotten gains in bus companies or similar enterprises with a local development potential – though they may also invest them in Switzerland or Wall Street. Thirdly, corruption may have some redistributive 'trickle-down' effects, especially by spreading the benefits of office among the official's wider kin. In a study of the educated elite in East Africa it was stated that the demands of kinsfolk for a return on their investment in his education might be a factor leading a government official or teacher to accept bribes.[43]

On the other hand, according to Sharpston, corruption tends to divert scarce human resources, particularly in management, 'into "fixing" rather than producing'. Secondly, corruption tends to lower the standard of the services provided by all parts of the public sector. If officials are overworked but corruptible, so that a small bribe will lead to prompt attention to important papers while others wait, then there will be an incentive to introduce delays in order to attract bribes for circumventing them. Where such practices are widespread there will be a general acceptance of delays and inefficiency and hence costs to the whole economy. Thirdly, it seems likely that redistribution 'downwards' from the well-to-do to their poor relations only partly offsets the tendency for persons in positions of power and influence, already well rewarded with overt and legitimate earnings, to command a covert, illegitimate extra price for their services. In other words, it seems overwhelmingly probable that most bribes are paid by the poor to the rich, and the net effect of corruption is to increase disparities of income and wealth.

At higher levels of decision-making, with a corrupt government money can buy favourable treatment over such matters as taxation, tariffs, government contracts, grants, concessions, and subsidies. Local industrialists may be able to manipulate government policies to suit their interests. Even more, large foreign firms 'may virtually buy up the government and run the country as an unconsolidated subsidiary'[44] – an extreme case, indeed, of the big firm, small country syndrome.

Disparities within poor countries

Many writers have drawn attention to wide disparities of income, wealth, and privilege among the people of poor countries. Thus Peter Berger likened Brazil to 'a Sweden superimposed upon an Indonesia'; while Indian authors have coined such phrases as 'the island republic' and 'Middle India' for the well-to-do minority, only some 2 to 3 per cent of the population of that vast country yet amounting to that of many a western state, with their middle-class attitudes and way of life.[45]

To parody George Orwell, all income distributions are unequal, but some are more unequal than others. The simplest measures indicate the share of all incomes received by different groups: the top 10 or 20 per cent, the lowest 20 or 40 per cent. From the different possible measures I single out the share of the top 10 per cent. The figures below, published in the World Bank's 1994 report, relate to studies mostly carried out in the 1980s, not for all countries, and not all on the same basis.

By the ten-per-cent test, the least unequal income distributions were those of the Scandinavian countries, the Netherlands, Japan, and countries such as Poland and Hungary recently under communist rule. In these countries the top 10 per cent of households received 20 to 22 per cent of all household income.

In the USA the top 10 per cent's share was 25 per cent, and several other western countries returned similar figures. In Britain the top 10 per cent's share rose from 23.3 per cent in 1979 to 27.8 per cent in 1988.

In some of the poorest countries too the top 10 per cent's share of personal income or expenditure was around 25 per cent: 24.6 per cent in China, 27.1 per cent in India, 24.6 per cent in Bangladesh, and 25.2 per cent in Sri Lanka; but 46.5 per cent in Tanzania, despite its socialist intentions and policies.

In most middle-income countries the share of the top 10 per cent was between 30 and 40 per cent; while the country brave or brazen enough to report the most unequal income distribution was Brazil, where the top 10 per cent's share of all personal income was 51.3 per cent.[46]

Such disparities have to be seen in relation to a number of factors. Very few traditional societies lacked any form of social differentiation, and in most parts of the world there were disparities of poverty and, if not wealth, at least a modest degree of comfort, before modern development began. Thus in Africa, according to the Cambridge historian John Iliffe, besides 'conjunctural' poverty when people ordinarily self-sufficient were thrown into want by some crisis such as famine, there were always many people in 'structural' poverty: the physically and mentally disabled, lepers, the very young especially orphans, widows, and the very old, who were not always as well cared for as the myth of the 'extended family' would suggest.[47]

In most pre-industrial economies the principal asset was land, and there were wide differences between the privileged minority of land-owning families and the rest of the population in Asia and even more in Latin America. A partial exception was Africa, much of which was sparsely populated, so that land had little scarcity value, and traditional aristocracies such as the Tutsi of Rwanda and the Hima of Ankole tended to keep their wealth in the form of cattle. In some societies the landed gentry are or were the military class; they exercised political power through patronage and through their control of the organs of government; and they were also the educated class, able, since they could afford to send their sons to good schools and keep them there for longer, to dominate the professions and the administration of government.

In some countries, landowning aristocracies have been overthrown. In others their dominance has been undermined as industrial capital has overtaken land as the leading economic asset in an industrial economy, to be superseded in its turn by investment in services. In yet others, however, economic development has been such as to consolidate or even enhance their privileged position if they were adaptable enough to diversify their assets.

Pre-existing disparities apart, economic development itself has often been a process in which some people become better off while others at best stay as they were, if they are not actually made worse off. Sometimes the leading sector has been an industry, such as textiles or railways; or a region, 'the North', compared with a backward agrarian 'South'. In many cases, however, economic development has been the work of an enterprising minority, socially defined as a religious denomination or an ethnic group; I take up this aspect of development in chapter 10.

I have already pointed out how closely earnings in the formal, modern sector are related to investment in human capital through schooling and qualifications. Educational diplomas and professional qualifications are valuable assets yielding their possessors high returns, and the opportunities to gain them are not equally open to all; I have more to say about this in chapter 9.

At the very top of the occupational scale, a few people are often found to be remunerated as highly as their rich-country counterparts. This can hardly be avoided when they work for the same firms, the transnational corporations, or when like medical practitioners, university professors, or senior government administrators they can 'brain-drain' (supposing they are free to do so) to comparable posts in western countries or to international organizations – where, indeed, eminent people from the 'Third World' are specially welcome. Applying world standards of comparison to the top salaries of top people, however, stretches out the scale of income disparities within poor countries compared with the meagre earnings of subsistence family farmers and landless farm labourers.

Yet another aspect of disparity is that of urban–rural differences. Average earnings are higher in town than in the country; the towns are where the better-paid jobs are, and town-dwellers include most of the people best able to articulate their interests, organize, and exert power (including the 'aristocracy of labour' organized in trade unions). Towns have better public services, such as water, schools, and hospitals, and fewer people living in poverty. Despite television pictures of squalid slums in 'Third World' cities, the overwhelming majority of the world's poor live in the country. So striking are urban–rural differences worldwide that the development economist Michael Lipton has identified 'urban bias' as the chief reason for the failure of economic development to benefit the poorer people in the poorer countries.[48] I return to this subject in chapter 7.

Redistribution with growth

As has been seen in the World Bank's figures for the 1980s, if we range out countries in order by their per capita GNP we find a general tendency for disparities of income to be somewhat less at the ends of the scale and somewhat more in the middle. According to one interpretation, that of the pioneer development economist Simon Kuznets, this is what we should expect. In the poorest countries the poorest people's incomes had to be 'a fairly sizeable proportion' of the meagre average, otherwise they could not survive. In countries with higher average incomes the relative share of the poorest groups could be smaller without their material position having become impossible. Moreover, the experience of the present-day developed countries at earlier stages in their development suggested widening inequality in the early stages because of disruption of traditional pre-industrial ways of life. Narrowing inequality occurred in later stages of development, partly through state welfare benefits, health and education. For example, in the UK the share of the top 5 per cent fell steadily from 48 per cent in 1880 to under 20 per cent in 1957. Kuznets accordingly saw 'a long swing in inequality: widening inequality in the early phases of economic growth; becoming stabilized for a while; then narrowing in later phases'.[49] In other words, a graph relating disparity to development would be shaped like an inverted U.

Further research into this subject was carried out in the early 1970s by Hollis Chenery and others for the World Bank and the Institute of Development Studies at the University of Sussex. According to their findings, the graph relating inequality to current per capita GNP was indeed inverted-U-shaped, but that was not the most striking thing about it. Rather, it was the wide diversity of middle-income countries in this respect, as shown by the wide scatter of points on the graph. This indicated that there was ample scope for different circumstances, most of all different government policies, to affect the outcome in countries at around the same level of average income. In some, economic development had indeed involved some people getting much richer while others were little or no better off, and the relative deprivation of the poor had increased; but in others the reverse had happened, and lower-income groups and households had shared proportionately, or even more, in the gains from economic development. In Chenery's phrase, there could be redistribution with growth: a phrase which summed up an approach to development briefly espoused by some in the world of aid in the 1970s at a time when there *was* growth:[50] see chapter 13.

In Chenery and his colleagues' terms, Brazil could be regarded as a case of growth without redistribution. According to the World Bank economist Peter Knight, during 1960–79 '[m]ost Brazilians shared some of the real economic growth', but the rich gained much more than the poor, and grew richer faster than the poor grew less poor. Development was concentrated on heavy industry, particularly automobiles, producing motor vehicles and other hardware for the 'Sweden' while not doing much for the 'Indonesia' of the rural poor. Associated with it was the pioneering development of 'gasohol', vegetable alcohol as a motor fuel. From some points of view this was a commendably 'green' development, a renewable energy source less polluting than petroleum. However, it was produced from sugar grown on big plantations with heavily subsidized credit, setting up a three-way competition for the best land with export crops and domestic food production, increasing the concentration of landholding, and not doing much for the rural poor. Disparities between rich and poor were reflected in an infant mortality rate markedly higher than that of comparable Latin American countries at similar levels of per capita GNP. To achieve redistribution with growth, Knight urged the need for land reform, as small farms were more productive and employed far more labour; and measures to shift demand towards basic public services and 'wage goods'.[51]

For Chenery and his colleagues, India represented the country of little redistribution and slow growth. Five other countries seemed to have moved appreciably towards lessening disparities, in some cases deliberately, in others as a side-effect of policies with other aims.

Cuba in the 1960s represented drastic redistribution with nil or even negative growth, though growth followed in the 1970s.

In Tanzania and Sri Lanka there was redistribution 'on purpose'. In Tanzania, exceptionally, there was no need for land reform as there was plenty of land in that sparsely-populated country. Infrastructure development was concentrated on rural roads, schools, and clinics, while differentials in public-sector earnings were drastically reduced as salaries were cut while low wages were allowed to rise.

In Sri Lanka landholding, never very unequally distributed, was further redistributed, and small farmers benefited from import substitution policies and from Green Revolution technical improvements. During the 1970s there were ambitious schemes for subsidizing and rationing basic foods; there was very little malnutrition, and the infant mortality rate was the lowest in any low-income country. These schemes were judged too costly, however, and after 1979 they were scaled down, but they still benefited both farmers and the poorer half of the population alike in town and country.

But the exemplars of redistribution with growth were South Korea and Taiwan. In both there had been severe dislocation following the end of Japanese rule in 1945, and in Korea the devastating war of 1950–3. In South Korea, drastic land reform under United States pressure transformed the country from a land of rack-rented tenants, paying 50 to 90 per cent of the value of their crop to absentee landlords, to one of prosperous small farms. Tight control of the economy was exercised by a government the prime aim of whose policies was growth; their consequences for distribution, though not unwelcome, were not foreseen. (The policies included at first industrialization through import substitution, which also benefited farmers; then export expansion in labour-intensive consumer non-durables; high interest rates to encourage saving and discourage capital-intensive investment; and keeping the value of the currency low to encourage exports.) Between 1964 and 1970 unemployment fell; the real incomes of the poorest 20 per cent of the population doubled; agricultural wages doubled, and other wages also rose (an increase in which trade union activity played no part); while the real incomes of the poorer 40 per cent increased at the same rate of 9 per cent annually as that of the economy as a whole.

The even more shining example was Taiwan. Here too there was land reform. The ownership of capital in both agriculture and industry was widely dispersed, and both were very labour-intensive, so that there was little difference between agricultural and industrial incomes. Government policies did not favour upward pulls on industrial wages either by transnational corporations or by trade unions, and in other ways resembled those of South Korea: import substitution followed by export-led growth, high interest rates, and currency devaluation. Development was helped by US aid, and by the migration of people with skills and savings from the mainland. As in South Korea, too, policies aimed at growth also resulted in redistribution on an unprecedented scale. Between 1953 and 1961, while the economy as a whole grew at 7 per cent annually, the incomes of the poorest 40 per cent grew even faster at 23 per cent.

Suggestions for further reading

United Nations Development Programme, *Human Development Reports* (New York, Oxford University Press for UNDP, annual)

World Bank, *World Development Reports* (New York, Oxford University Press for World Bank, annual)

Ruth Leger Sivard, *World Military and Social Expenditures* (Washington, D.C., World Priorities, biennial)

Poverty and Landlessness in Rural Asia (Geneva, International Labour Office, 1977)

John Iliffe, *The African Poor* (Cambridge, Cambridge University Press, 1987)

Robert Chambers, *Rural Development* (London, Longman, 1983)

Margaret Hardiman and James Midgley, *The Social Dimensions of Development* (Chichester, Wiley, 1982)

5

Environmental concerns

But is it possible? It is a much controverted issue whether the economic development of poor countries, and particularly their industrialization, can be carried to a level approaching that of rich countries without the world as a whole running into environmental constraints.

Thus Paul Ehrlich and Anne Ehrlich wrote in 1970 that most of the underdeveloped countries would never, 'under any conceivable circumstances, be "developed" in the sense in which the United States is today. They could quite accurately be called the "never-to-be-developed countries".' The earth was overpopulated already, as the limits of food production by conventional means had very nearly been reached. Indeed, 'world agriculture today is an ecological disaster area'. It was already leading to loss of soil fertility and erosion, and was vulnerable to even minor natural disturbances. As for other resources, the annual production of such materials as iron, copper, and lead would have to be increased six- to eightfold if the world's population used them at United States rates. However, to bring the present world population up to United States standards of equipment – railways, automobiles, electric wiring, structural steel, etc. – would require the extraction and smelting of far greater quantities at far higher rates, ranging from 75 times as much for iron to 250 times as much for tin. Even if that were possible, the energy consumed might endanger the heat balance of the earth, with possibly disastrous effects on climate. The partial industrialization of the earth had already caused intolerable pollution of air and water; 'our environment cannot stand "world industrialization"'. Accordingly Ehrlich and Harriman did not hesitate to describe the industrial nations as 'over-developed' and to call for their 'de-development'. The underdeveloped countries should at the same time be 'semi-developed', that is, their standard of living should be improved, but not to the extent of raising their GNP per head to contemporary United States levels.[1]

Such views were not unanimously endorsed by other scientists, and some were strongly controverted. They were criticized by John Maddox as exaggerated and alarmist, lacking in historical perspective and innocent of economic understanding. Maddox also pointed to the danger that statements by citizens of affluent industrial countries that others could never hope to enjoy a similar affluence, though made in all good faith by scientists of integrity primarily in criticism of trends in their own society, were likely to be misunderstood and misrepresented. They risked alienating people in countries 'not yet rich enough to aspire to the kind of freedom from pollution on which the more prosperous nations have set their sights'. Suspicion that conservationist arguments might be a means to thwart the industrialization of poor countries seems to have contributed to the difficulty in finding a common platform for the international conference on the human environment at Stockholm in 1972.[2]

A spectrum of concern

In recent debates the issues raised by Ehrlich and Ehrlich have been extended into a spectrum of concerns:

First, concern for poor countries, their peoples, and their development prospects. Can there ever be enough copper, aluminium, etc., and energy sources, to raise their living standards to something like western levels? And can it be done without unacceptable pollution of their environment, or their neighbours', or the earth as a whole? Related to these, but lying outside the scope of this book, are concerns in rich countries about each other's activities, for example sulphur dioxide emissions in the UK damaging Scandinavian forests. This whole area of concern was addressed most notably by the Brundtland commission (see chapter 13). It raises again the fundamental question posed in chapter 4: is a frugal but decent 'semi-developed' life the best that can be hoped for in poor countries, meeting basic needs without rich-country resources and choices?

Secondly, there is concern for all human beings about threats such as global warming, leading to the melting of the polar ice-caps, rising sea-levels, and the flooding of cultivated river deltas and coastal cities; and the depletion of the ozone layer admitting more ultra-violet radiation and giving rise to skin cancer.

Thirdly, there is concern for the natural environment as such, for example marine pollution, or the destruction of natural habitats endangering wild species such as the orang-utan in equatorial rain-forests. To some extent this involves also a concern for the interests of human beings; for example, marine pollution is of direct concern for seafarers' health and safety, and a threat to fish stocks and bathing beaches. Likewise, natural habitats such as equatorial rain-forests represent resources of bio-diversity of possible future use to human beings, for example pharmaceuticals from plants as yet unknown, unclassified, and un-analysed. In some representations, indeed, the human interest predominates, in others it is secondary or incidental, introduced apparently as an additional argument for conservation.

Fourthly, at about this point on the spectrum some environmentalists' concern is to protect the natural environment *from*, or *against*, human activity: a position which Brundtland was most careful to avoid.[3] This shades over into a concern for wilderness for its own sake. Some accord the need to preserve substantial areas of wilderness a higher claim than current human well-being, though in the hope that future generations will still be able to 'stand in quiet awe' at natural spectacles such as wildlife on the Serengeti plain.[4] Thus for Laurens van der Post the 'great battle for wilderness' was 'beyond politics, sociology, and nationalistic ideals'.[5]

But preserving designated areas of wilderness often works against local people's interests by restricting or denying access they once had to needed resources. Obviously that creates hostility and provokes actions such as illicit hunting, stigmatized as 'poaching', in national parks, or foraging for firewood in state forest reserves.

To some extent this has been recognized in some of the more moderate conservationist thinking. Thus George Stanley of the US Department of Agriculture Forest Service recognized that conflict is likely to arise over wilderness designation if it results in local economic hardship. Moreover, '[i]f wilderness is provided without a parallel effort to offer a range of amenities and recreational settings for the whole population, it will be difficult to retain the necessary political support for wilderness'.[6] Similarly, David Anderson and Richard Grove in their study of conservation in Africa remarked that the influential World Development Strategy of the World Wildlife Fund and the International Union for the Conservation of Nature (WWF/IUCN) paid lip-service to linking development with conservation and involving local people, but assumed that at root the conservationists' vision of society must prevail: 'Ultimately the behaviour of entire societies towards the biosphere must be transformed.'[7] Or as another conservationist put it, 'Our . . . distinguishing characteristic is that we care. We are tuned in to the needs of future generations more than most people.'[8] The authoritarian potential of such attitudes is obvious, and a parallel has been drawn between the coercive aspects of conservationist programmes and centrally planned socialist states.[9]

Parts of the spectrum of concern are exemplified in studies of droughts and other natural disasters, famines, ecological concerns, and nature conservation, especially in Africa. Western television viewers are assailed from time to time by harrowing pictures of the sufferings of poor people in famine-stricken areas. Often there is an immediate generous response (a leading example was Bob Geldof's Live Aid in 1985) as the contrast between famine in Africa and food surpluses in Europe and America pricks 'the conscience of the rich'. But then there are doubts. Does it really help to send food? Is food what is most needed, considering the logistical problems and unavoidable delay in getting it there? If not food, then what might be of help? Need famines happen at all? Can they be foreseen, and averted by timely action? Are famines evidence of ecological breakdown, over-cultivation, over-stocking, over-population?

Hunger, drought, and famine

Hunger has always been a common experience in many areas of the 'Third World'. Many African peoples regularly went through a hungry season between planting crops early in the rains and harvesting them a few months later, especially if the previous year's crop had fallen short and food stocks were running out before the next harvest. Thus the anthropologist Audrey Richards wrote in 1939: 'The Bemba constantly talk about "hunger months" as distinguished from food months. At the end of the rainy season they regularly expect a shortage.'[10]

Hunger is unpleasant but seldom fatal. People who are not getting enough to eat suffer the pangs of hunger, cannot do much work, lack energy and resolve, but by conserving energy and curtailing their activities they can usually survive, even for long periods. What is more, in such societies people know this, and act accordingly. They may even choose to go hungry rather than eat the seed-corn and render themselves destitute. They may adapt, for example, by eating more wild foods such as roots and berries, sometimes with positively beneficial effects on their diet. Only in extreme cases do people die of starvation. People do die in famines (however defined) but arguably more often from other causes.

Drought, resulting in crop failure, is the prime cause of many famines. Drought may also kill people directly, for though people can go short of food for long periods they cannot survive more than a few days without water. Even more commonly, people desperate for water in conditions of drought may drink water that has been muddied by livestock, or is otherwise impure, and may lack the fuel to purify it by boiling. As water supplies shrink, their bacterial concentration increases, and with it the risk of infection. It is commonly believed that in famines people become ill because they are malnourished, when their resistance to disease is lowered. However, some argue that illnesses, particularly diarrhoea, reduce the body's ability to assimilate food even when it is available, so that people, particularly children, may be malnourished because they are ill.

Moreover, some deaths occur in all societies and in all conditions. To assess the effects of famines we need to consider the excess mortality, that is, the number of deaths over and above the previously prevailing death-rate, which may be high, in the populations affected.

Thus the anthropologist Alexander de Waal, who carried out fieldwork during the famine in Darfur, Sudan, in 1984–5, found that it (and probably many others like it) was a health crisis rather than a food crisis. Excess mortality occurred mainly in the dry season and at the start of the rains, before the new harvest. It affected mostly children aged one to four years; breast-feeding infants were less affected, probably because they were less exposed to infection from contaminated water. The main causes of death were diarrhoea, measles, and malaria. Emergency food distribution, organized against great difficulties by the United States Agency for International Development (USAID) and the non-governmental Save the Children Fund (SCF), had little effect on mortality. Partly this was because it came too late, for which the aid agencies were not to blame, as they acted with neither central nor local government's co-operation, while a rail strike did not help, either; partly because it did not reach those who needed it most. On the other hand, contrary to the fears of many, nor did higher than normal mortality result from exposure to health hazards in crowded relief camps. So de Waal concluded that food aid was not what was most wanted, did little to save lives, and did nothing to prevent destitution. More excess deaths could have been prevented rather by health measures: clean drinking water, sanitation, immunization especially against measles (despite the problems of refrigerated distribution), malaria control, and the supply of weaning foods.

Against that background I turn to the question of definition. According to de Waal, the English word famine as misunderstood in the past (particularly by Thomas Malthus) implied mass starvation through severe shortage of food. This was not the case of the Darfur famine, and probably not of other famines generally; as has been seen, he regarded that as a health crisis rather than a food crisis.[11]

Famines are often politically defined, and designating a particular situation as a famine commonly involves a government in political decisions: whether or not to declare a state of emergency, organize its own relief programme, and possibly seek foreign aid. Thus according to the account by Paul R. Brass of the famine in Bihar, India, in 1966–7, the central government of India at first discounted warnings from Bihar, whose politicians they distrusted, then turned the situation into a grave national crisis in order to secure the release of PL480 (food aid) wheat from the USA.[12] Equally, on the other hand, a government may *refuse* to recognize a famine precisely *for fear of* foreign meddling.

In his study of famines, the Oxford economist Amartya Sen asserted that 'food availability deficiency' (FAD) is seldom if ever the cause of suffering and death. Indeed, some of the worst famines have occurred in countries where there was no significant decline in food availability. In nearly every case, food was available somewhere, and in many cases not far away from the famine-stricken area. For example, food was exported from Ireland to England during the Irish famine of the 1840s. According to Sen, that is to be expected in a market economy: food, like other commodities, goes where people will pay most for it, not necessarily where it is most needed. What famine victims lack is *entitlement* to food: a key concept, akin to other economists' 'effective demand' or 'purchasing power', but somewhat wider in scope. People may be entitled to food in diverse ways, such as by growing it on land legitimately occupied in customary tenure or through inheritance, purchase, lease, etc.; or because they can buy it with money, legitimately earned, or from state welfare benefits; or as rations distributed by famine relief agencies. There is a possible confusion here about the word distribution: images of lorries laden with sacks of grain bumping over rough roads are not what social scientists, particularly economists, mean by such terms as income distribution. Sen's concern was with the distribution of entitlement in the second sense, which has all to do with disparities of income and wealth.[13]

Somewhat similarly, in an article published in 1935 about the widespread famine in the Roman empire under the emperor Claudius, K. S. Gapp wrote that 'In the ancient world, as in the modern, famine was always essentially a class famine', and it turned on the price of grain. The poor and improvident lacked reserves of money and food, and suffered immediately when prices rose, while the rich had reserves of both, and seldom went hungry. Though the rich might experience economic discomfort, it was the lower classes who suffered actual hunger and starvation.[14]

This general thesis was disputed by de Waal. He found that excess mortality in Darfur was due mainly to disease, which affected all classes alike, and related largely to the direct effects of drought, the restriction and pollution of water sources.

As noted in chapter 1, social scientists in general tend to be reluctant to accept that natural disasters – droughts, floods, earthquakes, etc., or outbreaks of disease among humans, livestock, or food crops – can be the prime causes of human suffering, rather than social factors such as class and exploitation. Thus a United Nations report recognized two approaches to famine. The 'entitlement' approach indicates maintaining the purchasing power of those affected by scarcity. The 'availability' approach looks at the production and consumption of food and the movement of food stocks, but does not take into account individuals' different ability to buy food, and does not explain how starvation can occur when adequate food supplies are available at the national level.[15]

Without discounting natural disasters altogether, it seems likely that, whatever their prime cause, disasters such as famines are in many cases *compounded by* social and political factors. Moreover, there seems no room to doubt that some disasters are wholly human-made (even man-made), especially wars.

Ecological concerns

Following his study of the Sahel famine in 1972–3, the geographer Michael Mortimore identified in more detail the different explanatory frameworks within which drought and famine were currently discussed. Setting these out schematically, the first division was between:

(1) those who regarded famines (however defined) as caused by drought, flood, earthquake, etc., affected very little if at all by human activities such as agriculture and cattle-keeping; and

(2) those who laid prime stress on human activities as bringing about famine, to the extent that the very idea of a natural hazard was called in question. The latter were further divided between:

(a) those who blamed practices such as slash-and-burn agriculture; over-stocking and over-grazing; deforestation; and over-population, exceeding the supposed 'carrying capacity' of the land, for bringing about droughts and desertification; and

(b) those for whom the relevant human factors included colonial exploitation and capitalist penetration, from which stemmed current differences between rich and poor. From this point of view it was axiomatic that in famines the poor die, the rich survive; and that in pre-colonial Africa there were no poor.

Ideas like those of class 2(a) had been prevalent in the past among colonial officials, especially forest officers, and were found also among latter-day conservationists. *A priori* they seemed like a case of 'blaming the victim'; and according to Mortimore's detailed assessment there was little or no evidence for them. For example, pollen core samples showed that the Sahara had advanced and retreated several times in drier and wetter periods during the past 25,000 years, indicating that desertification was not due to human activity over much shorter periods. Where environmental misuse had occurred it was more often by such activities as deforestation by 'the new class of farmer-entrepreneurs', or large-scale public irrigation projects, than by small farmers using traditional methods 'whose basic rationality emerges unfailingly from almost every field investigation'.

As for ideas in class 2(b), as already noted, de Waal in Darfur had found no difference in excess mortality between the poor and the better-off; while the view that in pre-colonial Africa there were no poor had been convincingly refuted by the work of John Iliffe.

Mortimore found equally little evidence for the population pressure hypothesis. He and others had found a general correlation between population density and the intensity of farming systems. The productivity of the land was capable of improvement by additional inputs of labour and/or capital. Small-scale farming by conservationary land-use methods was labour-intensive, therefore an increase in population would positively facilitate a transition to more conservationary land use; and this made 'sense rather than nonsense of prevailing high fertility rates'.[16]

Somewhat similarly, John Iliffe stated that in contrast to Asia, where most poverty was due to land shortage, unemployment, and low wages, Africa was 'a land-rich continent' until well into the twentieth century, when land shortages began to arise chiefly in southern Africa.[17] Although, as I have indicated in chapter 2, the population history of Africa is somewhat obscure, there seems to be reason to think that at least some areas of the continent were depopulated between about 1895 and 1920 by a series of disasters: droughts, cattle disease, and disease among, and spread by, the local men recruited into the carrier corps during the 1914–18 war. Europeans' advance into the interior took place, therefore, at a time when the population had declined and was still declining. Certainly Europeans early on the scene thought so. The demographer R. R. Kuczynski gave reasons for thinking they might have been mistaken: the population was sparse, but not therefore necessarily declining; slave raiding and trading in the mid-nineteenth century had been for internal slavery, not for export to America, so not depopulating as the slaves stayed in Africa; and the effects of inter-tribal warfare were greatly exaggerated. Nonetheless, Kuczynski concluded that at least in the then East Africa Protectorate 'there can be no doubt that the population in 1895–1920 was decreasing'.[18]

At that time, therefore, substantial areas of Africa had reverted to wilderness, presenting to those early Europeans a rich natural habitat teeming with wildlife; a paradise for rich white hunters to shoot 'big game' (while Africans were denied guns), and also an unspoiled Garden of Eden to be preserved at almost any cost.

In the 1920s population decline was arrested, and after 1930 growth set in that has continued to the present time. As already noted, this increase in the human population has always been regarded by some conservationists as a threat to the environment. It was thought likely to go beyond the carrying capacity of the land, and involve over-cultivation, over-stocking, and over-population, threatening delicately poised eco-systems. Droughts and famines, attributed to population pressure, served to reinforce fears of a general ecological catastrophe: 'Eden threaten[ed], quite literally, to dry up.'[19]

That view was challenged by R. H. V. Bell, who like Mortimore found little evidence of population pressure. Predictions of soil exhaustion and environmental degradation were seldom fulfilled, while food shortages were not density-related, and living standards were if anything higher in the more densely-populated areas. Droughts and wars were the prime causes of African famines, which were wrongly regarded as evidence of density-induced ecological collapse.

Moreover, African countries and their governments were not bad at wildlife conservation. Environmental concerns were shared by some among the urban African elites. At the level of economic calculation, too, there has no doubt been some shift of attitude towards wildlife 'from meat on the hoof to tourists on the tyre'. According to Bell, about 4 per cent of Africa south of the Sahara enjoyed protected status as national parks and the like, well up to international standards, and in some countries, including Botswana, Malawi, Tanzania, and Zambia, over 10 per cent. (An IUCN estimate quoted by Brundtland put the African average higher at 6.5 per cent.)[20] Undeniably there were problems. Some eco-systems were under-protected, and some animal species endangered, mostly in southern Africa, including some 180 species of birds along with a few wild mammals, notably the rhinoceroses illicitly hunted for their horns.

However, according to Bell, although in some African states enforce-ment was lax, in many countries normal rural life was practically impossible without breaking wildlife conservation laws. 'Most conser-vation agencies are paramilitary armed and uniformed organizations . . . armed confrontations between "poachers" and enforcement staff are commonplace and deaths and injuries on both sides are regular occurrences.'[21] In many cases the establishment and administration of national parks deprived local people of legitimate access to needed resources, as reported by David Turton among the Mursi pastoralists of southern Ethiopia.[22] Such cases could only engender hostility towards national parks and the whole idea of conservation. As Anderson and Grove put it, that was certainly not an issue above politics. On the contrary, the debate about the African environment would 'continue to be destructively one-sided until . . . African rural people participate directly in the process of decision-making that affects the environment in which they live'.[23] Conservation measures would be unlikely to succeed without support among local people. National parks, wildlife reserves, etc., must serve their needs too, in everything from joint schemes combining conservation with rural development down to simple measures like encouraging parties from local schools as well as foreign tourists to visit the reserves. Failure to win political support from the local people was likely to result in popular acceptance of illicit activities such as encroachment and 'poaching'. In the words of the OXFAM slogan, 'Only a fairer world can save the earth.'[24]

Suggestions for further reading

Paul R. Ehrlich and Anne Ehrlich, *Population, Resources, Environment: Issues in Human Ecology* (London, W. H. Freeman, 1970)

Amartya Sen, *Poverty and Famines: An Essay on Entitlement and Deprivation* (Oxford, Clarendon Press, 1981)

David Anderson and Richard Grove (eds.), *Conservation in Africa: People, Politics and Practice* (Cambridge, Cambridge University Press, 1987)

John Iliffe, *The African Poor* (Cambridge, Cambridge University Press, 1987)

Alexander de Waal, *Famine that Kills: Darfur, Sudan 1984–1985* (Oxford, Clarendon Press, 1989)

Michael Mortimore, *Adapting to Drought: Farmers, Famines, and Desertification in West Africa* (Cambridge, Cambridge University Press, 1989)

6

The social sciences and the 'Third World'

Before the Second World War, the only social scientists to take much interest in the countries later known as the 'Third World' were the social anthropologists. For them, indeed, the 1920s and 1930s represented the golden age of the classic field studies, of Tikopia and Samoa, the Bemba, the Nuer, and the Azande. Evolutionism was rejected, and the prevailing approach was functional and comparative. Here were peoples with their own ways of doing things, different from 'ours' (that is, the western societies from which most of the anthropologists came), yet viable, internally consistent, and not irrational, enabling them to meet their basic needs and survive.[1] Although changes in the cultures and social structures they studied were not always entirely neglected, many anthropologists aspired to be early on the scene in their search for what Margaret Mead termed 'untouched societies'[2] before these had been much affected by colonial administration, missions, schools, labour migration, and other outside influences.

From about 1950 onwards, however, all that changed. Political scientists, who had taken little interest in colonies and regarded their government as mere administration, not politics, suddenly became aware of the political scene in the newly independent states of Asia and Africa. Among economists there was a similar awakening; whereas in the 1930s the supreme economic problem had been seen as that of mass unemployment in the West, by the 1950s a similar challenge was presented to a new generation by 'the hideously great, and alas, ever widening disparity between the standards of living in the rich, developed countries and the poor, underdeveloped countries of the world'.[3]

The 1951 United Nations (Arthur Lewis) report

That interest was both signalled and stimulated by a report to the United Nations in 1951 by a group of experts headed by Professor W. A. Lewis (later Sir Arthur Lewis), 'Measures for the Economic Development of Under-Developed Countries'. True to the preoccupations of economists of their generation, they devoted a good deal of attention to unemployment and underemployment, and regarded their own recommendations as complementing full-employment policies in 'economically more developed countries'. Countries with lower per capita real incomes were termed 'under-developed' in the title; 'an adequate synonym would be "poor countries"'. Measures needed to be taken both by the governments of developing nations and by international action. Economic progress depended on a favourable atmosphere both in social, economic, legal, and political institutions and among the people themselves. Property institutions, for example, must be such as to create incentives, and legal institutions must protect the rights of tenants to the benefit derived from their improvement of the land. The public sector must perform all the tasks which in developed countries had come to be thought of as its traditional sphere, and must indeed perform them particularly well in underdeveloped countries, providing a sound infrastructure of roads and other communications, education, public health, and other public and social services. In addition, public action might be necessary in such fields as market research, geological surveys, and prospecting for minerals, the establishment of new industries, and the creation of financial institutions to mobilize savings and channel them into 'desirable private enterprise' notably in the form of capital for the small private farmer and artisan. The importance of education was stressed, and its scope was shown to be wider than the mere training of technicians. In general, because the market might misallocate resources, governments must be alert to intervene in fields beyond that traditionally allotted to the public sector. Some guarded but favourable remarks were made about the desirability of fertility control.

Measures to be taken by international action included, as a first priority, arrangements for stable terms of trade, favourable to developing countries. There was a good deal of criticism of the 'unfair' policies of some industrial countries in subsidizing the home production of commodities which could be produced more cheaply in underdeveloped countries. For example, subsidized sugar beet production in Europe deprived tropical countries of part of their market for an important export – a point often made in later criticisms of the economic policies of European countries. Some industrial nations were further accused of encouraging, and even subsidizing, exports of primary commodities produced in competition with underdeveloped countries. Secondly, the report called for the transfer of capital from rich to poor countries on a scale 'far beyond what is currently envisaged', thereby taking the lead in calling for what we now term aid.[4]

They make it sound so simple. Snap your fingers – Dad.

Stages of development

In 1958 Walt Whitman Rostow gave a series of lectures at Cambridge which were published in 1960 as *The Stages of Economic Growth*, a book that remains the most explicit statement of the thesis embodied in its title.[5] Basing his analysis on his earlier studies of the development of the British economy in the nineteenth century, he identified five stages or categories: 'the traditional society, the preconditions for take-off, the take-off, the drive to maturity, and the age of high mass-consumption'. The preconditions included a shift out of agriculture and an enlargement of the scale of economic relations in which the orientation of commerce and thought passed from a regional to a national and a still larger international setting. In recent history this had occurred 'not endogenously but from some external intrusion by more advanced societies'. Family limitation was at least foreshadowed, and there was a shift from ascribed status to individual ability, a disposition to invest, and a spread of rational scientific and technological ideas.

The take-off was marked by a big rise in net investment, from 5 to over 10 per cent of net national income. Rostow identified this as occurring in Britain between 1783 and 1802, the United States 1843–60, Japan 1878–1900, and India and China since 1950. But at this stage modern technology was applied only in a few 'leading sectors' – cotton in England, railways in the United States – and the requisite personal qualities of enterprise in these sectors came in many cases from a minority who formed a leading elite in economic growth. Weber's Protestant ethic is clearly relevant here, and Rostow acknowledged his insight, but remarked that other enterprising minorities besides the Calvinists had included the Samurai, Parsees, Jews, Russian civil servants, and one might add Chinese and Indian minorities overseas; I return to this point in chapter 10.

In the drive to maturity, some 10–20 per cent of the national income was steadily invested, and a modern technology extended from the leading sector throughout the economy. Finally, a mature economy could use its resources in three ways: the pursuit of external power and national aggrandizement; the 'welfare state', redistribution, the social services, and leisure; or 'high mass consumption', represented above all by the private motor vehicle.

Many criticisms have been made of Rostow's thesis. Since his book is sub-titled 'A non-communist manifesto', dissents from a Marxist analysis, and refers to communism as 'a disease of the transition', it is not surprising that Marxist critics have been hostile.[6] Some of the criticisms by radical writers seem wide of the mark. Thus, as mentioned above, Rostow did not concentrate wholly on endogenous factors in development, and he acknowledged the importance both of the colonial experience and of involvement in the international economy; while to say of so distinguished an economic historian that his work was 'a-historical' or 'denied a history to' the underdeveloped nations would plainly be absurd. Exception can be taken to his use of the term 'the traditional society'. As has been seen, radical underdevelopment writers deny that there is or ever was such a thing. From a quite opposite point of view, however, to lump together in such an undifferentiated category all pre-industrial, non-Western societies is to pay scant regard to the evidence of social anthropology showing the diversity of pre-existing cultures and their persistence despite the unifying forces at work in the world today. Non-Marxist economists, too, have been critical. Hagen suggested that the stages of growth were not really as clear-cut as Rostow made them out to be. The supposed upward surge in investment occurred in only a few countries, particularly England, the Soviet Union, and Japan, but elsewhere capital formation was a steadier process and Rostow's division into periods was 'entirely artificial'.[7] More fundamentally, Myrdal attacked Rostow for teleology, that is, for imputing to abstractions like 'history', 'society', or a 'nation' human attributes they cannot possibly possess, especially a capacity for purposive action. Thus growth once started seems automatic, and the importance of decisions and policies, especially on the part of governments, is downplayed.[8]

Balanced versus unbalanced growth

A perennial issue in development economics is that of the relative merits of 'balanced growth' on the one hand and a concentration on a 'leading sector' on the other. As long ago as 1943, Rosenstein-Rodan imagined 20,000 underemployed Eastern European peasants leaving the land to work in one large factory making shoes. Their wages would be spent partly on food, so agricultural production would be stimulated; but not much would be spent on shoes, and the shoe factory would quickly go bankrupt. If, however, a million underemployed peasants went to work in a thousand factories producing the whole range of goods on which workers and peasants spend their earnings, all would prosper. He accordingly advocated 'the planned creation of a complementary system', or industrialization in 'one big push';[9] and in this he was supported by other development economists including Ragnar Nurkse.[10] Such ideas had their critics; thus Viner thought they neglected the possibilities of international trade, through which those 20,000 shoe workers might dispose of all their products, if they were specially good, and import their other wants.[11] Youngson acidly pointed out that it might really be quite easy to think up a whole set of uneconomic, unprofitable industrial enterprises linked in supply-and-demand relations and say that one had planned a 'complementary system'. Thus an uneconomic hydro-electric scheme might look more economic if an uneconomic cement industry were linked with it. The current from the first turbines could be used to manufacture cement for the next dam, while uneconomic factories producing textiles, beer and soap could be linked with the scheme as consumers of electrical energy, and protected by tariffs on an 'infant industries' argument, so concealing the uneconomic nature of the whole.[12] (To one who lived in Uganda in the 1950s, it all seems remarkably true to life.) It was widely acknowledged, though, that poor countries were unduly dependent on primary export industries, which were precarious and had weak spread effects; and that diversification and industrialization were badly needed.

In those early controversies a leading advocate of unbalanced growth was Albert O. Hirschman. Writing in 1958 he acknowledged that export enclaves tended to let primary products 'slip out of a country' without generating much income locally, but the case was different with import enclaves. Beginning with the mere assembly of imported components, packaging, etc., these might proceed by 'backward linkages' to the local production of more and more components derived in turn from local raw materials. Import substitution industrialization, ISI, has in fact been successful in some countries, notably Taiwan and South Korea, as noted in chapter 4, and Hirschman was rather optimistic about these 'backward linkages' and 'trickle-down effects'.

Similarly, capital-intensive methods and even 'show-piece' projects might usefully demonstrate efficiency and stimulate much-needed learning, especially by inducing a 'compulsion to maintain'. For example, failure to maintain aircraft was liable to result in spectacular crashes, while neglect of roads caused little more than widely borne costs to vehicle owners and other road users, and the consequences of failure to maintain railways were liable to be more serious than in the case of roads, but less so than in the case of aircraft. So, Hirschman observed, poor countries ran their airlines well, their railways were mediocre, and their roads were mostly in a parlous state of disrepair.

Hirschman accepted that unbalanced growth was likely to lead to polarization and tension. An industrial region ('the North') might be the scene of growth in contrast to a relatively backward area ('the South'); or an innovative minority ('the Jews') might be enriched before other groups. But it was neither feasible nor desirable to suppress those tensions altogether. Emboldened by foreign aid, governments should undertake the dual task of inducing growth, with all the imbalance it caused, and of restoring balance. And economic advisers should be concerned with 'discovering under what pressures people are already operating and toward what forward steps they are already being impelled'.[13]

Modernization

The terms industrialization, development, and modernization are much confused, and their meanings overlap. In so far as it is possible to distinguish them, industrialization is the most straightforward. Like the Industrial Revolution in the history of western countries, it refers to real changes, objectively observable and statistically measurable, particularly including the shifts from agriculture to industry and from country to town. Development, as we have seen, is a somewhat more problematic concept. Growth in GNP per capita has in the past been generally taken as the criterion measure, but many economists have looked deeper in search of underlying preconditions, institutional or psychological. If in industrialization the focus is technological, in development it is economic. Modernization is one way of looking at both. It refers to a school of thought, an approach to the understanding and interpretation of industrialization and development that prevailed in the United States in the 1950s and 1960s, and whose origins can be traced much further back in the history of American political thought. Thus when David Apter wrote that 'To be modern means to see life as alternatives, preferences, and choices' there was a clear continuity with Thomas Jefferson's dictum: 'Freedom is the right to choose, the right to create for oneself the alternatives of choice.'[14]

According to that school of thought, modernization represented the change from a 'traditional', pre-industrial state or condition, the starting-point for development, to 'modernity', through an intermediate 'transitional' condition. The process affected both societies and individuals in mutually reinforcing ways. In traditional societies, most people were traditionally minded. In transitional societies there were already some modern-minded people, others whose outlook and attitudes were transitional, and many who were still traditionally-minded. It was the modern-minded people who propelled their society through the transition into modernity; equally, the institutions of a modern society encouraged and engendered modernity in its members.

Traditional societies were viewed as static and unchanging. Theirs were subsistence economies using 'Biblical' methods: the ox-drawn wooden plough, hand sowing and planting, head carrying, 'cottage industries' using little or no mechanical power.[15] Their social structures were diverse, but many could be characterized as feudal. Religious institutions were powerful and dogmatic, engendering personal attributes including submission to authority and fatalism. Fertility was uncontrolled, and there was an acceptance of 'as many children as God sends'. In such societies there was little effective choice. Traditional cultivation was the only alternative to starvation, while there was equally little alternative to submission to traditional political authority.

By contrast, modern societies were viewed as dynamically changing through innovation, technological advance, and economic development. They engendered in their members flexible, rational minds given to 'having opinions'. Modern-minded people asserted autonomy in making important decisions, notably about how many children they should have, and in rationally implementing their decisions by technically effective means. They were imbued with a conviction that we can shape our world, the very antithesis of fatalism. Religious dogma and traditional political authority alike were rejected, or at least questioned. The politics of a modern society were correspondingly based on the informed participation of citizens in the political arena. There was a choice of parties and policies, government was rationally legitimated by the consent of the governed, and in a word there was freedom.

The transition from traditional to modern was regarded as a transformation, not a transfer. It was not just a matter of transferring the capital or the technology, nor even the outward forms of social and political institutions, from one set of countries to another. When their ideas were first formulated in the 1950s, the modernization school clearly supposed that the process would be irreversible, and that once people had tasted freedom and participated in the political arena there would be no getting them out. By the 1970s it was clear that that did not always happen, and contrary evidence of 'departicipation' in some countries prompted a reassessment of the whole concept of participation and its relation to modernization; I take up the question in chapter 12.

If the stages of development thesis was most explicitly articulated by Rostow, the modernization approach was pre-eminently that of Daniel Lerner, whose book *The Passing of Traditional Society* was published in the same year that Rostow lectured in Cambridge. Based on field observations in Turkey in the 1950s, it opens with the parable of the grocer and the chief in Balgat, a village not far from the capital. While the chief represented traditional authority, the grocer, who had seen American films in Ankara, had images of a wider world including a well-stocked supermarket. What distinguished him, according to Lerner, was 'empathy', a capacity to imagine things otherwise than as they are, and to project oneself in imagination into other social roles and other states of society. Thus the chief, when asked what he would do if he were president of Turkey, replied, 'I am hardly able to manage a village, how shall I manage Turkey?' But the grocer had a ready answer; he would make roads so that people could travel to town and see the world, not stay in holes all their lives.

'Empathy', then, was related to mobility. Physical mobility through ease of travel led to urbanization as people moved to towns and became more involved in the modern cash economy. 'Psychic mobility' resulted from literacy and exposure to the mass media of communication. The modern style of life was 'distinctively industrial, urban, literate, and *participant*'. It involved 'having options', and culminated in voting 'in elections which actually decide among competing candidates'.

Extending his analysis to the statistics then available from UNESCO and other United Nations sources for some 54 countries, Lerner found that urbanization, literacy, and media exposure were indeed correlated, and he concluded that 'In these countries the urban literate tends also to be a newspaper reader, a cash customer, and a voter.'[16]

In such a view modernization seems to mean becoming more like the United States. While the Jeffersonian ideals may indeed represent for many a model worthy of emulation, it seems plain that we have here not just a social science theory or set of explanatory ideas helping us to understand what is happening in the world, but also a set of evaluative criteria by which to judge the policies and performance of 'Third World' countries and their governments. Perhaps this analysis may have been addressed, among others, to modernizing elites in those countries, of whom Riggs has succinctly written that 'A transitional society, however contemporary, is one whose leaders have an image of themselves as molders of a new destiny for their people, as promoters of modernization, and therefore as initiators of industrialization.'[17] Perhaps, too, it was intended to encourage those whom Lerner termed 'moderns' and others might designate as 'innovators' or 'change agents', such as teachers, business managers, and agricultural extension officers.

The modernization school long continued to influence social thought about the 'Third World' and development studies, especially in the United States.[18] In particular it afforded the main orientation for psychological studies of individual change, which I summarize in chapter 11. Naturally it stimulated criticism and debate. Besides the counterblast of radical theories of underdevelopment and dependence, mentioned in chapter 1 and discussed in more detail below, there was debate about 'internal' and 'external' influences in which it was not clear what units the supposed influences were internal or external to: what is internal to a country or society may be external to an individual, but international influences are external to both. Lerner's analysis spanned the individual and societal levels, but failed to distinguish between societies and countries; and apart from American films he had little to say about the international influences changing countries, societies and individuals.

Against that background, Reinhard Bendix pointed the way towards a rehabilitation of the modernization approach.[19]

According to Bendix, the 'societies of the original breakthrough' into modernity were 'England' (i.e. Britain) and France. From Britain the rest of the world learned that modernity involved industrialization; it was a matter of coal, iron, railways, steamships, textile mills and the like. From France, the rest of the world learned a different lesson; modernity involved a united nation-state with a common language and a common citizenship. In the powerfully evocative words of the Marseillaise, 'Allons, enfants de la patrie . . . Aux armes, citoyens!'

In the decades around 1800, their 'original breakthrough' put Britain and France into the positions of world leadership, and all other countries into the position of 'backwardness' or 'follower' status in an international system of social stratification, a key concept that Bendix approvingly derived from Nettl and Robertson.[20] Just as individuals low in the social scale within a country experience relative deprivation or *atimia*, so do countries in an international system of social stratification – or, to be more exact, so do their ruling elites. Smarting under the stigma of backwardness, they strive to catch up. In Europe around 1800, that aspiration was immensely sharpened by the imminent threat of conquest as Napoleon's armies, inspired by revolutionary and patriotic zeal, overran Europe from the Peninsula to Moscow, only to be defeated largely by the industrial and naval might of Britain (allied, it must be said, with Russian numbers and the Russian winter). It seemed like a case of modernize or go under.

There accordingly followed successive waves of catching up by follower countries: in the early nineteenth century, Germany, Belgium, Scandinavia and Italy; after about 1860, Russia and Japan; after about 1890, the United States. Of the later-industrializing countries, only the United States wholeheartedly followed the British private-enterprise model of development epitomized in the work of the Scottish economist Adam Smith. In virtually all others, including France, much greater initiatives were taken and control exercised by the state.

In the process of catching up, too, it was not always clear what were the essential elements in modernity and what were merely adventitious traits that happened to be characteristic of the early modernizing countries, or societies. Thus the high prestige of the French language throughout Europe, and its value in France itself as a source of national unity and pride, long antedated the 'original breakthrough' around 1800 and can be traced back to the age of Richelieu if not even earlier. Yet the model of the nation-state with a common language and a common citizenship, as has been noted, has been accepted without much question as part and parcel of modernity. It was energetically pursued in Italy after the Risorgimento and the reunification; and it has been adopted in more recent times by many 'Third World' countries with even more diverse languages and cultures.

Accordingly, as Bendix contended, one model of modernization will not do, and we need several. He was distinctly sceptical of arguments that a 'logic of industrialization' prevailed to such an extent that the process was likely to follow the same pattern or stages of development in each country. On the contrary, he asserted, at least as good a case could be made for the converse proposition: 'Once industrialization has occurred anywhere, this fact alone alters the international environment of all other countries . . . Industrialization cannot occur in the same way twice.' Scientific and technological progress, painfully slow in the 'societies of the original breakthrough', could be drastically telescoped and their lead-times shortened in later-developing countries, most notably perhaps in the field of death control. Awareness of the gap between advanced and backward countries 'puts a premium on ideas and techniques which "follower" societies may use to "come up from behind"'. Educated elites were thus in positions of strategic importance; the gap between educated and uneducated widened; education was seen as having instrumental value as a source of income, prestige, and security, rather than an intrinsic or consummatory value in itself; and there was a corresponding tendency to invest too much in educating a bigger elite than a country needed or could afford.

Underdevelopment and dependence: the counterblast

During the 1960s, many writers on development and related subjects expressed a radical dissatisfaction with the prevailing ideas of the orthodox, mainstream social science tradition.[21] Among the first to debate different ways of looking at the problem of underdevelopment were certain Latin American economists, some of them associated with the United Nations Economic Commission for Latin America, or ECLA,[22] and it seems that the sequence of their thought ran somewhat as follows. It had been widely agreed during the 1950s that poor countries were unduly dependent on a few primary exports. That state of affairs could be attributed to the international division of labour that was first enforced under colonial rule, according to which the colonies were to be raw material suppliers while the metropolitan countries specialized in manu-factures. Although it might have been expected that in that role they would have shared in the great surge in prosperity that followed the Second World War and made the industrial nations into affluent societies, that had not occurred. Although western consumers were able to pay, and were paying, much more for coffee (for example) than they had in the past, much of the increased price was due to the greater value added in processing, packaging, and marketing the instant coffee products sold in the supermarkets, and little of it went to the original growers of coffee in countries such as Brazil. Clearly the remedy was to do more of the processing and packaging in Brazil; and indeed there was general agreement about the need for the diversification of the economies of poor countries and the development of industries there. But how was that to be achieved? And, in particular, how was the capital to be raised? In order to earn the foreign exchange they needed to buy the machinery and other capital imports, the underdeveloped countries had to depend even more in the short and medium term on their primary exports, thus intensifying their problem. Moreover, world markets for their products were readily glutted, so that increased production for export only led in many cases to such a drop in price that total receipts were reduced rather than increased; quantities of Brazilian coffee, indeed, had sometimes had to be destroyed to maintain its price. Some economists recommended solving that dilemma by means of what they called 'industrialization by invitation'; rather than attempt to raise the capital for industrial development themselves, the underdeveloped countries should let the transnational corporations do it for them, even offering them inducements through tax exemptions and the like. But that strategy too had adverse consequences. While it was not denied that something worthy of the name of development might occur in that way, the subsidiary enterprises the multi-national corporations set up in poor countries created only small enclaves of prosperity with limited spread effects. Much of the profits and some of the personal incomes generated by those enterprises was repatriated to the metropolitan countries. Thus not only were the poor countries denied a full share of the proceeds, but their dependent status was also enhanced by the fact that the important decisions were taken out of national hands and made elsewhere.[23] And the interests of the big international firms might be the occasion, or even the pretext, for diplomatic and political pressure from other governments – especially, of course, the United States – constraining the host country from pursuing its own policies and making its own decisions. Even aid was suspect from this point of view. Bilateral assistance from one donor country to another recipient country could be used by the former to exert 'leverage' on the latter; while multilateral aid was channelled through agencies, in particular the World Bank, which were seen as dominated by the rich non-communist countries and responsive to their point of view and their interests.[24]

Whatever the poor countries might try to do to break out of their poverty trap and promote their own development, it seemed as though their efforts would be thwarted. The rich industrial countries, their transnational corporations, and the international agencies they dominated, would always somehow manipulate the world economic system in their favour and to the detriment of the poor countries. There was only one remedy: opt out of the world system altogether, sever all links with the West, and pursue a Spartan policy of self-reliant development, perhaps in co-operation with friendly socialist countries. If that meant revolution, so be it. Much of the voluminous literature of the school of thought associated with the terms underdevelopment and dependence seems to be inspired by that conviction.

The early debates of this school of thought were conducted largely in Spanish, and it was not until 1967 that it became widely known in the English-speaking world through the outspoken advocacy of A. G. Frank.

Brought up in the United States, Frank studied economics at Chicago. Later he rejected the whole approach he was taught there, especially as applied to Latin America, and changed to a radically different view according to which economic development and underdevelopment were parts of the same process. They were attributable neither to structural differences, nor to different stages of economic growth. In grammatical terms, to underdevelop was a transitive verb. It was what rich countries do to poor countries: they actively underdevelop them. Both development and underdevelopment were generated by world capitalism; hence 'the development of underdevelopment'.

That process had a geographical aspect as the metropolitan centres of world capitalism were linked with peripheral satellite countries from which they extracted surplus value. Within satellite countries, the local metropolises likewise exploited the regions, and their towns and industrial centres exploited their agricultural districts right down to the level of local communities.

Frank's analysis, along with his polemical criticisms of mainstream development theories, was published in 1967 at a time of unrest in western universities, and merged with other streams of thought then current with which it was generally congenial. The very idea of a social science was being repudiated, and objectivity was regarded as neither possible nor desirable. Radical social thought was extolled as fusing theory and practice in revolutionary action. It was hailed as emancipatory, whereas mainstream social science was condemned as justificatory of the existing social order. Characterized as 'positivist' and 'empiricist', social science was said to represent merely the rationalization or intellectual camouflage of the status quo, and was dismissed as 'bourgeois'. At that time, too, the United States government was unpopular among intellectuals and students both at home and abroad, largely in relation to the war in Vietnam. There was sympathy with revolutionary movements in Third World countries, and leaders such as

Fidel Castro and Che Guevara were idolized. At such a time there was a ready hearing for a radical analysis that wholeheartedly rejected orthodox social science and pointed to revolutionary action – the kind of actions and policies, indeed, that had already been taken by the regime in Cuba.

As already noted, it was of the utmost importance for this school of thought to establish that Latin American societies had never been feudal, and that the world system established from *c.* 1500 onwards was capitalist from the outset. Not to do so would have been to accept the mainstream ideas about dual-sector economies, part traditional and part modern, and about stages of development, that had been so decisively repudiated. But there were difficulties about that position. It was a widely accepted view among Marxist and non-Marxist authorities alike that the Spanish and Portuguese conquests in the Americas had occurred when feudalism prevailed in Europe, and no societies were more feudal or 'seigniorial' than those of Spain and Portugal. It seemed obvious that the institutions implanted by the conquistadores were feudal in nature; and indeed the kind of landholding with servile peasants and a wealthy landed class that characterized many Latin American countries could without difficulty be recognized as resembling that of European feudal society.

Radical underdevelopment writers accordingly found themselves at odds not only with those whom they could dismiss as 'bourgeois', but also with much orthodox Marxist thought including that of Marx himself. Thus Frank controverted not only the 'bourgeois thesis' that Latin America began its post-discovery history with feudal institutions which survive today, but also 'the traditional Marxist theses' that feudalism predated capitalism, coexisted with it, and was invaded or penetrated by it. Both analyses were 'metropolitan born', and were alike in wrongly visualizing society as divided into two largely separate sectors, a progressive capitalist 'modern sector' and an 'agrarian sector' whose progress was held back by a persisting feudalism.[25]

Immanuel Wallerstein devoted monumental scholarship to establishing that all-important thesis that the European overseas expansion of the fifteenth and early sixteenth centuries brought about a world economic system which was capitalist from the start. This involved an explicit rejection of the idea, taken for granted by many Marxists and other socialists, that the rise of capitalism was associated with the industrial revolution of the late eighteenth and early nineteenth centuries. Indeed, Wallerstein noted an 'intra-Marxist debate' about the 'periodization' or dating of Marx's stages of development. Wallerstein's usage of the term capitalism was much wider, for he asked why there could be 'different modes of organizing labor – slavery, "feudalism", wage labor, self-employment', simultaneously within the single world economy. Even slavery in the Roman Empire was 'preeminently a capitalist institution, geared to the early preindustrial stages of a capitalist world-economy'.[26]

Radical underdevelopment writers taking this view have been criticized for confusing capitalism as a system of exchange with capitalism as a mode of production.[27] For a Marxist, no doubt, wherever there is capitalism there is exploitation. But the converse is not necessarily true; where we find exploitation, as in the Spanish and Portuguese American colonies in the sixteenth and seventeenth centuries, it is not necessarily attributable to capitalism. Exploitation occurs in all societies in which men are divided into two antagonistic classes, whether as masters and slaves, as lords and serfs, or as capitalist proprietors and wage labourers. Linked with this criticism has been the accusation that the radical underdevelopment school neglect the whole subject of class.

It seems that different writers have, so to speak, taken different leaves out of the Marxist book. The radical underdevelopment school have looked at the one on which are inscribed the words surplus value, its expropriation from the original producer (worker or peasant), its appropriation by the capitalist, exploitation, and the accumulation of capital. Their critics have taken another, on which appear the words productive forces, mode of production, means of production, social relations especially class relations, classes and class conflict, base and superstructure, and class consciousness.

Among the latter, some of the intellectual exercises which the debate has stimulated seem to an outsider to be of purely scholastic interest. Thus there has been much debate about the status of pre-capitalist modes of production,[28] and attempted elucidation of what Marx really meant by the Asiatic mode of production. However, in their acknowledgement that other modes of production coexist with capitalism, and are penetrated by it, writers of the latter school seem to have moved to a position not far from that of mainstream theory with its dual-sector model. Perhaps, too, the concept of the articulation of modes of production recalls that of culture contact in the older anthropology, though no doubt with a much more materialist bias.

And there have been attempts to synthesize the radical perspectives, most notably perhaps by Samir Amin. He distinguished five modes of production, different from those of Marx: the 'primitive communal' mode, anterior to all others; the 'tribute-paying' mode; slave-owning; the 'simple petty-commodity mode'; and capitalism. His analysis of underdevelopment as 'extraversion' or dependence on primary exports, was rather like Frank's. However, in his consideration of 'the contemporary social formations of the periphery', Amin proceeded to a detailed delineation of the class structures of underdeveloped societies.[29]

From the late 1960s onwards, theories of underdevelopment and dependence constituted the main intellectual opposition to modernization, and succeeded in persuading some of those engaged in development studies to change their outlook and cross over to a radically different school of thought.[30] Writing in 1990 the Leeds sociologist Aidan Foster-Carter remarked that although it was more than twenty years since Rostow and Gunder Frank wrote their definitive works the essential issues remained much the same. In his view the debate still centred on whether the major factors in underdevelopment were *internal* to 'Third World' societies (their cultures, their social structures, their governments' policies), as the modernization school presumed; or *external* or imposed (the colonial past, unequal trade, debt). Wallerstein, 'relentlessly externalist', had discounted 'countries' as units of analysis, and denied that their internal structures, policies, etc., made any difference; all states, even the then USSR, were ineluctably linked into the world system. Other radical writers, however, had disputed this assertion.

Foster-Carter further pointed out that while radical underdevelopment ideas had been highly influential intellectually, especially in Latin America, their policy implications had amounted to little more than a vague notion of 'de-linking' from the world capitalist system. The one regime to try that wholeheartedly was Pol Pot's Khmer Rouge in Kampuchea, and it led to the genocide of the 'killing fields'. Meanwhile some other East Asian countries were doing well by following the opposite policy and increasing their involvement in the world economy.[31]

The Neo-Institutionalists[32]

Summing up the foregoing debate, Paul Streeten recalled a litmus test attributed to Sir Arthur Lewis, which I paraphrase: if the rich countries were to sink into the sea, given time to adjust would the poor countries be better or worse off? Worse, say the Blues; Better, say the Reds.

For the Blues, development was a linear path through Rostow's stages. Aid from rich countries was needed to break open bottlenecks and overcome obstacles until self-sustained growth made aid unnecessary.

For the Reds, following A. G. Frank, the rich actively underdevelop the poor. Developing countries should try to de-link from rich countries' trade, technology, transnational corporations, educational and ideological influences. Paradoxically, though, there was a continuing need for aid as a kind of international redistributive income tax.

As already noted, Blues looked for spread effects and trickle-down; Reds for polarization, backwash, domination, and immiseration.

Streeten himself, however, sought a reconciliation between these opposed perceptions in a detailed assessment of the benefits and harm respectively experienced by the poor countries from the various impacts of rich countries and transnational corporations.[33]

Such an approach was characteristic of a third school of thought among development economists, notably including Streeten, Gunnar Myrdal, and Dudley Seers.

They were much concerned about the fundamental problem of value in social science. Myrdal maintained that social science was not as objective and value-free as its orthodox practitioners represented. Choice of research subject, concepts and analytical approach were alike value-loaded. Rather than permit the intrusion of tacit value-premises under the guise of objectivity, scientific integrity demanded that the investigator's value-premises should be made explicit. Streeten too was concerned about 'value-seepage' in a subject such as development economics in which it was not always to separate prognosis from programme. However, it did not follow that social science was impossible, a mere rationalization of social scientists' value-judgements and ideologies. To be both truthful and useful, 'the social scientist, and particularly the economist, should start with the actual political attitudes' of the people he or she was studying.

Secondly, they were sceptical of theories that suggested that economic growth – or indeed economic activity in general – was automatically generated or regulated by impersonal forces such as those of the market. In particular, Myrdal as a Swedish social democrat saw nothing wrong with state intervention in the economy, and it was to justify that interventionist position that he broke with classical *laissez-faire* market economics. Similarly, Rostow's metaphor of an aircraft gathering flying-speed in a 'take-off into self-sustained growth' seemed mechanistic, even deterministic. Myrdal consistently stressed the importance of attitudes, institutions and policies. The course of economic development was not to be understood as the outcome of blind impersonal forces, but was largely determined by conscious choices and decisions, particularly on the part of governments.

Gunnar Myrdal came to the study of 'the poverty of nations' while Fru Alva Myrdal was Swedish ambassador in India from 1957 to 1961. He had already carried out a massive survey of race relations in the United States, and then as head of the Economic Commission for Europe had become aware of the cumulative nature of regional disparities. That led him to formulate his analysis of 'backwash effects': centres of economic activity could attract resources of people and capital from retarded or depressed areas, leaving the latter trapped in a vicious circle of low expectations and with an undue burden of dependants. Within rich countries, governments could intervene to redress regional disparities, but to do so made great claims on public funds, which governments were likely to sanction only in response to the thought that even unemployed workers and depressed peasants had the vote. While Myrdal also saw 'spread effects' from the growth poles, like Hirschman's 'trickle-down', he was less optimistic that they would prevail.

Backwash effects were compounded by international boundaries. Clearly the poor in poor countries can exert no political leverage on the governments of rich countries, and not always much on their own. International trade had had strong backwash effects, undercutting traditional handicrafts like the weaving and metal-working industries of Asian countries. In the colonial past, some capital from Europe had gone into the export enclaves of countries such as India, and also into their public utilities such as railways, but much more had gone into setting up areas of European settlement in empty lands in the temperate zones. Compared with internal migration within countries, international migration was very limited in scale, being hampered by nationality laws, immigration controls, and in some cases colour bars. Differences in law, administration, *mores*, language and values made national boundaries 'much more effective barriers to the spread of expansionary momentum'.

Turning to the institutions of India and its neighbours, Myrdal conceded that colonial rule had brought many benefits including roads, ports, railways, political security, law and order, a civil service, sanitation, education, and contacts with the outer world. On the other hand it had also brought restrictions on the growth of their industries; for example, the indigenous Indian textile industry before 1860, as narrated in chapter 3. 'Enforced bilateralism', sometimes politely called 'close economic and political ties', between metropolitan countries and their colonies had restricted the markets open to the latter. Racial and cultural differences between European and native people had been associated with practices of segregation that had hampered the transfer of cultures, especially technical skills and a spirit of enterprise. The end of colonial rule had left some countries, notably India, with a genuine sense of national identity, but others remained artificial states with little unity or common purpose.

Myrdal conceived of the situation in each south Asian country – as in any country – as a *social system* consisting of causally inter-related *conditions* in six broad categories: output and incomes; conditions of production; levels of living; attitudes toward life and work; institutions; and policies. Data on output and incomes were useful as an index, but not as a definition of development and underdevelopment. It was an upward movement of the whole system that was desirable, and which alone counted as development. Resistance to change in the social system stemmed from attitudes and institutions that were parts of an inherited culture.

Many previous writers had analysed conditions in poor countries in terms of 'vicious circles'. Poor people do not eat enough, cannot work hard, and so are poor. The process can be reversed and turned into a 'virtuous circle': poor people are given more to eat, their health improves, they can work harder and get more to eat. While Myrdal did not dissent from that analysis, he recognized its somewhat tautological nature (poor countries are poor because they are poor) and regarded it as far too limited in scope. Rather, a 'low-level equilibrium' represented the stability of the social system.

'The great bulk of historical, anthropological, and sociological evidence and thought suggests that social stability and equilibrium is the norm.' The real mystery was how any society can break out of the low-level equilibrium and develop. The western experience might well be unique.

The 'decolonization hurricane' had deservedly swept away many of the old ideas about 'backwardness', especially racialist myths. But institutions were still important, and the honest economist had to point out that many of the institutions of many underdeveloped countries were not conducive to development. Their social structures were highly inegalitarian, and Myrdal firmly believed that 'policy measures leading to greater equality could lead to more rapid growth'. Land reforms were urgently needed, and though countries embarking on them would have done themselves no harm in the eyes of United States official opinion, few had actually done so, while some had enacted land reforms on paper but had not put them into effect. Educated elites whose emergence had been encouraged under colonial rule now had a vested interest in maintaining the gap between the educated and the masses. 'In no other field is there greater inequality in these countries than in the availability of health facilities. These are mostly monopolised by the upper classes.' Ill-health, ignorance, and lack of incentives contributed to a massive under-utilization of human resources.

Prominent among the political institutions of underdeveloped countries was what Myrdal termed 'the soft state'. By this he meant 'a lack of social discipline'; deficiencies in law enforcement; disregard of the rules by public officials at all levels, and their collusion with powerful persons whose conduct it was their duty to regulate. In particular, 'tax evasion by the affluent is colossal'. Paradoxically, although in one sense the soft state was systematically lenient and let individuals do as they pleased, it was also capable of displaying much harshness towards individuals and groups, especially in military dictatorships. Corruption was an integral and important part of the soft state, and one generally neglected by economists despite its bearing on the whole structure of economic incentives and the irrationality it introduced into the situations in which individual and collective decisions and plans were made. It hampered growth and development, and was a major contributory factor to inequality.

The soft state and corruption were linked in turn with an elitist conspiracy in which landowners, moneylenders, local officials in collusion with them, industrialists, higher officials, legislators, and the educated elite acted together to hinder reforms, manipulate them in their own favour, and obstruct their implementation. Despite their lip-service in many cases to the egalitarian ideals of a classless and even a socialist society, such elites were not willing to give up the advantages they enjoyed. Pressure from below was needed. And it was the elite with whom the outside world had to deal, just as in colonial times the metropolitan powers and their officials found it expedient and even necessary to deal with their subject peoples through the latter's established traditional authorities. Today it was members of the elites in underdeveloped countries who turned up at international conferences to plead for a new world economic order. 'They certainly did not find it opportune to stress or even mention the need for a new economic order at home.'[34]

Dudley Seers, like Myrdal, regarded the developed industrial economy as a rare and special case. Such economies had existed for little more than a century, and they covered only a small part of the earth's surface and included only a minority of its inhabitants. Yet conventional economics treated the special case as if it were the norm. Textbooks and lecture courses with titles like 'Economic principles', 'Banking', and 'Public finance', turned out on inspection to be analytical and somewhat theoretical descriptions of those aspects of the economy of the United States, Britain, or other advanced industrial countries. Worse, those textbooks were being used in the universities of non-industrial countries, translated into languages such as Spanish for the purpose, despite the manifest inappropriateness of much of their empirical content quite apart from their theoretical perspective. The case was not much better with books written for use in the Soviet Union and recommended, again in translation, in the universities of a country such as Cuba. Some Marxist analysis was highly relevant, for example, 'the "industrial reserve army" of the unemployed is after all to be seen in the streets' in many a Latin American country, while the attitudes of the landowning classes confirmed Marx's analysis, and foreign-owned plantations exemplified imperialism. But there was no attempt to adapt the analysis or content to underdeveloped countries as they are today, nor was there any scholarly analysis of the growth process.

Seers spelled out in detail the characteristic features of the special case, the developed industrial economy, and showed how special they were. He conceded that it should be studied; many economists would spend their whole working lives in economies of that kind, while others in non-industrial societies should study their characteristics if they were to understand their impact. For, as he emphasized, 'non-industrial economies cannot be understood unless studied in the context of the world economy'. Above all he argued for a comparative approach, perhaps with the slogan 'Economics is the study of economies.'[35]

Paul Streeten too criticized the limitations and biases of orthodox economics in dealing with the problems of development. 'One-factor analysis' or 'single-barrier theories of development' referred to different schools of thought, ideologies, and even changes of fashion among economists singling out first one particular factor and then another in their efforts to diagnose the root cause of underdevelopment and recommend measures to remedy it. In the history of economic thought, prime attention was given first to Land, then Labour, more recently Capital. 'Research and Development' was currently to the fore, while economists were studying aspects of 'investment in human beings': Education, along with pre-school child care, the kind of upbringing that encourages innovating personalities, and also the costs and benefits of not having children. But the removal of any one barrier had not proved to be a sufficient condition for development, while development had taken place in some countries despite the presence of unfavourable conditions, and had failed to take place in others despite their absence. Single-barrier theories were suspect. The world was more complex.

For example, while he suspected that a breakthrough in agriculture might be urged by some with an urban-industrial bias to squeeze surplus workers, food, and savings out of the rural sector into industry, Streeten saw the prerequisites for such a breakthrough largely in institutional terms. As well as an adequate infrastructure of roads, irrigation, etc., it was necessary to improve farmers' skills by training, and for the farmer and his family to have a minimum level and the right kind of education, health, and nutrition. It was necessary to increase the availability of incentive goods, which farm families would work harder to get, while resistance to work in the country on the part of urban youth and technicians had to be broken down. There had to be a system of land tenure which permitted the farmer to reap the benefits of his efforts. Credit had to be available at low interest, and marketing arrangements had to prevent middlemen from creaming off so much as to leave the farmer inadequate incentive to switch from export crops to domestic food production. Prices must be stabilized, and technical assistance available.

Conventional economists were prone to lump together for analytical and statistical purposes things that were really diverse, a tendency which Streeten termed 'misplaced aggregation'. For example (as has already been stressed) a country's 'average income' may rise because incomes in an industrial enclave are rising, while the real incomes of the rest of the population stagnate or decline. Similarly, if the notion of a single labour force did not make sense, then concepts such as unemployment, under-employment, and disguised unemployment were inapplicable.

A converse tendency to separate things that were really inter-related Streeten termed 'illegitimate isolation'. For example, it was false to separate expenditure on education on the one hand from investment in physical assets on the other. Particular kinds of education presupposed and were linked with investment in particular kinds of physical assets – agronomy with agricultural implements, engineering with industrial equipment. Likewise, much expenditure that in western countries would be classed as consumption, especially on the social services of health and education, could be regarded in poor countries as investment, since it had the direct effect of raising output and incomes. It was misleading to separate investment in agricultural improvement from expenditure on health and even from institutional reform. For instance, much of the benefit from an irrigation scheme was lost if it resulted in a spread of schistosomiasis, or if the land tenure system gave small farmers no incentive or opportunity to make use of the water to increase yields.[36]

The autonomy of the political

In a parallel development in the 1970s and 1980s, some American political scientists too rejected reductionist and determinist explanations of 'Third World' politics and asserted 'the autonomy of the political'. Like the neo-institutionalists, they viewed political structures and processes as relatively independent forces, and highlighted the diversity of 'Third World' state structures, and the different capacities of those states to promote development.[37] I take up the point in chapter 12.

Indigenous economics and rural development

Dr Polly Hill carried out a pioneer study of migrant cocoa farmers in southern Ghana and went on to a series of studies of 'grassroots' economic development in West Africa and India by methods combining economic analysis with the field techniques of the social anthropologist. In a plea for indigenous economics, as she named this approach to 'the basic fabric of economic life', she pointed to economists' earlier interest in the points of contact between West African and European economies – external trade, and organization of exports and imports – rather than with the production of crops or internal distribution. Such important matters as land tenure were neglected along with the ways in which native producers raised capital and managed labour, and myths grew up about West African economic behaviour, a kind of 'economic folklore', which became accepted by sheer reiteration in books and official publications.

The neglect of indigenous economics during the colonial period had not been rectified since independence; on the contrary, it had taken hold of the attitudes of modern West African governments and their economic advisers, who deplored the inefficiency they attributed to 'peasant' cultivation and were apt to initiate large-scale mechanization projects without adequate consideration of the consequences. Furthermore, the whole ideology of economic development planners was opposed to indigenous studies. They were reluctant to introduce into their models ideas drawn from anthropological research, to look at the humdrum problems involved in the collection of the statistical data they so finely manipulated, and to reserve judgement in cases where their knowledge was inadequate.

Although the 'indigenous economist' was in some ways opposed to the 'development economist', both were concerned with the processes of change and modernization, though perhaps the former tended to regard them more from a non-governmental standpoint. Indigenous economics resembled conventional western economics in its general approach, but those who guessed on the basis of western experience were apt to go wrong even on fundamentals. The economic behaviour of West Africans was basically rational, but the structure of that rationality required studying in the field.

In a later work Dr Hill renewed her criticism of development economists for applying inappropriate ideas; giving undue credence to bad official statistics, particularly agricultural statistics; and ignoring the findings of economic anthropologists, with their special knowledge of qualitative economic trends in rural areas.

She was strongly critical of the 'prevailing orthodoxy' about 'peasants'. The very word was misleading, and had obscured the diversity of tropical agricultural systems. Moreover, the associated notion of a peasant community made up of relatively self-sufficient peasant households, more or less equal, had seriously obscured the reality of poverty and inequality in rural societies. There had been 'a premise of equality at the base date' (that is, before modern changes) where there should rather have been a premise of inequality. There was always inequality in any society where cash circulates, and current inequality had not all been engendered by modern changes.

Inequality was much wider and more widespread than development economists generally realized. It was not only among rich and poor households, but also within households (a slippery term, but unfortunately unavoidable). Shared resources were not necessarily shared equally; for example, in many societies women and children eat separately from men. Development economists neglected women for all the usual reasons: 'statistical invisibility', unpaid work at home. But there were wide regional contrasts. In West Africa some wives were farmers in their own right, whereas in India farm families conformed more closely to western stereotypes of 'peasants'. As for poverty and inequality, compared with West Africa where there was still no landlord class, India was 'on another planet': the unequal distribution of farm land and the rigidities of the caste system made poverty among rural Harijans one of the world's greatest and most intractable problems.[38]

In a similar vein, Robert Chambers wrote of 'rural poverty unperceived' because of six biases: it was easier to visit and carry out field studies in urban areas, or areas on or near a hard-surfaced road, in the dry season, or in the northern-hemisphere long vacation. There were also diplomatic constraints, not to offend powerful people who could help or hinder research; and professional biases due to specialization. Thus a hydrologist would enquire about the water-table, a soil scientist and agronomist about soil fertility and crop yields, an economist about wages and prices, a nutritionist about diet, a demographer about mortality, fertility, and preferred family size; none would be likely to put the pieces together.

Furthermore, just as there were two schools of thought about famines and environmental concerns, so Chambers wrote of 'two cultures of outsiders', partly coinciding with two 'clusters of explanation'. Social scientists, particularly political economists, viewed rural poverty in terms of disparities of wealth and power, and exploitation at international, national, and local level; while 'physical ecologists' and practitioners trained in the natural sciences related it to such factors as disease, malnutrition, and natural disasters. But both schools of thought could hardly fail to recognize the human-made disasters of war and political persecution, refugees and displaced persons.

Both kinds of research, too, were outsiders' research, seeking to extend and apply a central body of organized knowledge of universal validity. Knowledge of this kind was often at odds with rural people's knowledge (indigenous knowledge, local knowledge, people's science); and sometimes one was right, sometimes the other. For instance, in many cases traditional African farming practices had been vindicated against the initially unfavourable opinion of outside experts. On the other hand, especially in health and nutrition, it was not sheer prejudice when outside professionals saw that rural people's beliefs and practices were harmfully wrong, and helped them with inoculations against human and animal diseases, oral rehydration, and the like. 'Both outsiders' knowledge and the knowledge of rural people can be wrong. The key is to know which is wrong when': an epistemological poser if ever there was one!

Chambers' central theme was that of reversals: bottom-up rather than top-down, from periphery to centre, putting the last first. The vital point was that communication should not be one-way, from centre to periphery, with the world of science representing the centre, but two-way, with a balancing flow of information and influence from the periphery, represented by local knowledge. Rural development practitioners should keep an open mind, and think *as if* the world of the rural community *were* the centre, to which the metropolitan world including the capital city and organized science was peripheral.[39]

Suggestions for further reading

Daniel Lerner, *The Passing of Traditional Society* (New York, Free Press, 1958)

Gunnar Myrdal, *Asian Drama: An Inquiry into the Poverty of Nations* (3 vols., New York and Harmondsworth, Twentieth Century Fund/Random House/Penguin, 1968)

Reinhard Bendix, *Embattled Reason* (Oxford, Oxford University Press, 1970)

Paul Streeten, *The Frontiers of Development Studies* (London, Macmillan, 1972)

Ian Roxborough, *Theories of Development* (London, Macmillan, 1979)

Gerald M. Meier and Dudley Seers (eds.), *Pioneers in Development* (New York, Oxford University Press for the World Bank, 1984)

Peter L. Berger, *The Capitalist Revolution* (New York, Basic Books, 1986; Aldershot, Gower, 1987)

Aidan Foster-Carter, *The Sociology of Development* (Ormskirk, Causeway, 1986)

Aidan Foster-Carter, 'Development', chapter 3 in M. Haralambos (ed.), *Developments in Sociology: An Annual Review*, no. 6 (Ormskirk, Causeway, 1990)

7

The rise of towns

Town life is not new; indeed, it is more than just a play on words to say that it is as old as civilization. However, while hunting and food-gathering people had no towns, and the neolithic culture which was the basis of the pre-industrial civilizations supported an urban minority, the rise of industry has been associated with a process of urban growth in which most people in developed countries have come to live in towns. Although in the present-day poor countries the urban population is smaller, it is growing, and indeed one of the most obvious changes that is taking place in these countries is a worldwide movement of people from the country to towns which are experiencing rapid, even headlong growth. But in a world in which the dominant technology is capital-intensive, that migration is not generally matched by a corresponding expansion in modern-sector employment. It is this which gives contemporary urbanization in the poor countries its special character, and many of its special problems.

Urban development in historical perspective

The first towns, such as Ur of the Chaldees and Mohenjo-Daro in India, seem to have arisen before 4000 BC, and their life was clearly related to aspects of neolithic technology. Agriculture made it possible to accumulate stores of food, and this enabled some people to live by working at crafts other than agriculture and selling the products for food. At the heart of every town, indeed, then as now, is a food market. Stocks of food could, in particular, be accumulated by persons or groups possessing political power; taxes or tribute from the surrounding countryside stimulated the development of writing and counting, and enabled the rulers to employ bureaucrats, soldiers, and servants, as well as to pay others to build their palaces and temples, dress them in fine clothes, and deck them with jewels traded by caravans across the deserts from distant places. And so the 'services' which the town 'exported' to the surrounding countryside, in exchange for food, included political services or administration, and also religion; for it seems likely from the excavations that have been made of ancient cities that their rulers in many cases owed their power at least in part to beliefs that they were of divine origin, or priest-kings uniquely able to perform ceremonies thought vital for the fertility of the land and the survival of men. Thus among the contributions to human culture of the neolithic cities must be counted organized religion, bureaucracy, and organized military forces, the last being necessary to keep order within the city-state and repel the envious nomads prowling round its outskirts. As Keyfitz has pointed out, the relation between these early cities and the surrounding countryside was probably highly exploitative, based as it was on force, bureaucratic organization, and legitimate power. In later civilizations there was more of a balance, with the city dominating its region in an ecological and cultural rather than a political sense, the scene of an uncontrolled market exchange of goods and services which find their own price. Later still, in the most advanced civilizations, cities' taxes may actually subsidize the countryside through agricultural price-support schemes and the like. In the non-industrial societies today, however, it is more likely that the taxation of the rural population generates the capital for industrial development, for example through import duties on consumer goods. Eventually the country-dwellers may be expected to benefit, but after how long?[1]

The greatest cities of the ancient world had populations of as many as a million, and in the most highly developed pre-industrial civilizations between 10 and 20 per cent of the population lived in towns. Rome at the height of its power around AD 150 had a million inhabitants, and of its empire's total population of 50–100 million some 10 million lived in cities. With the decline of the Roman empire these cities decayed; by the ninth century Rome's population is put at 17,000, and it is only in modern times that Rome has again reached the million mark – still depending, incidentally, on the sewers laid down in the classical period.[2] Similarly, according to Kracke, in China there were cities of well over a million in the thirteenth century AD, far bigger than any in Europe at that time, and in the prosperous eighteenth century as many as 20 per cent of China's population lived in towns.[3] Such estimates accord well with early modern censuses of pre-industrial and early industrializing societies. In 1801 nearly 10 per cent of the population of England and Wales lived in London, while just over a further 7 per cent lived in other towns of 20,000 or more.[4] In India the urban population was between 9 and 10 per cent of the total according to the British censuses from 1881 to 1921, rising thereafter to 20 per cent in 1971 and 26 per cent in 1992.[5]

Rapid increases in the size and importance of towns first affected the early industrializing societies; as Kingsley Davis put it, 'Before 1850 no society could be described as predominantly urbanized, and by 1900 only one – Great Britain – could be so regarded.'[6] The 1851 census, which for the first time showed more people living in towns than in the country, was a landmark in human history, not merely that of Britain. Here the proportion of the population classed as urban went on rising till it stabilized at 89 per cent in the 1970s and 1980s.

Comparisons between countries and the assessment of trends over time encounter statistical difficulties because different countries define towns differently according to the way they organize local government. In the past there have been attempts to standardize, but the most recent sources give figures based on national definitions of the term urban. There can be no doubt that the world's urban population has risen dramatically, and much faster than the population as a whole. Thus according to data assembled by Breese, in 1800 2.4 per cent of the world's population of 906 million lived in towns of 20,000 or more, and in 1900 the proportion was 9.2 per cent of 1,608 million. By 1960 it had risen to 27.1 per cent of the world's population of nearly 3,000 million. Thus between 1900 and 1960, while the world's population as a whole had not quite doubled, the urban population had increased some five-and-a-half fold from under 150 million to over 800 million.[7] And that trend has continued. According to the World Bank, in 1992 the proportion of the world's population classed as urban in each country was 42 per cent. In high-income countries 78 per cent of the people lived in towns; in low-income countries 27 per cent. By far the fastest-growing cities were in the 'Third World'. In low-income countries the urban growth rate was 4.7 per cent a year, compared with 3.2 per cent in middle-income and 0.8 per cent in high-income countries.[8]

In terms of actual numbers, according to UNDP, between 1950 and 1985 the urban population in developed regions almost doubled from 450 to 840 million, while that in the developing regions increased fourfold from 285 to 1,150 million. Some cities, including Nairobi, Dar-es-Salaam, Lusaka, Lagos, and Kinshasa, had grown sevenfold in thirty years. Poverty, unemployment, malnutrition, and disease had not discouraged people from moving to towns to take advantage of higher income opportunities, better schools and social services, and other amenities. The World Fertility Survey found that in most countries infant and child mortality rates were lower in towns than in rural areas, and lowest of all in metropolitan areas,[9] though this lower mortality was more closely associated with the generally higher social status of town-dwellers than with urban residence itself.[10]

Attempts to slow down, halt, or reverse urban growth had failed, including drastic measures in China between 1961 and 1976, and the depopulation of Phnom Penh by the Khmer Rouge in 1975; expulsion of the unemployed from towns in Congo, Niger, Tanzania, and Zaire; and regulation by permit in Indonesia.[11]

Urban bias

As mentioned in chapter 4, urban bias was identified by Michael Lipton as the chief reason for what he termed 'non-disimpoverishing development', the failure of aid and economic development to better the lot of the rural poor who, according to Robert McNamara, made up the poorest 40 per cent of the population of the poor countries, some 20 to 25 per cent of that of the world as a whole, and whose living standards had been stagnant or worsening.

> The most important class conflict in the poor countries of the world today is not between labour and capital. Nor is it between foreign and national interests. It is between the rural classes and the urban classes. The rural sector contains most of the poverty, and most of the low-cost sources of potential advance; but the urban sector contains most of the articulateness, organization, and power. So the urban classes have been able to 'win' most of the rounds in the struggle with the countryside; but in doing so they have made the development process needlessly slow and unfair. Scarce land, which might grow millets and bean-sprouts for hungry villagers, instead produces a trickle of costly calories from meat and milk, which few except the urban rich (who have ample protein anyway) can afford.

Scarce resources went into urban motorways rather than water-pumps to grow rice, into show-piece stadia rather than clean village wells and agricultural extension services. Resource allocations reflected 'urban priorities rather than equity or efficiency'; while a key role was played by 'the town's success in buying off part of the rural elite'.

Lipton stressed that his was not a conspiracy theory, but rather an analysis of convergent interests.

> Industrialists, urban workers, even big farmers, *all* benefit if agriculture gets squeezed, provided its few resources are steered, heavily subsidized, to the big farmers to produce cheap food and raw materials for the cities. Nobody conspires; all the powerful are satisfied; the labour-intensive small farmer stays efficient, poor, and powerless, and had better shut up.

So, rather like Keyfitz's analysis of early civilizations, the towns exploited their rural hinterland; and rather like the Soviet Union under Stalin, it was a case of squeezing the peasants to concentrate resources on industrial development.

One aspect of urban bias was the rural skill drain. According to Lipton, a case could be made out that because the content of schooling was largely irrelevant to rural life, and to enable rural areas to keep their intelligent young from draining to town, poor countries would be better off without rural education altogether. Lipton made it clear that he was not recommending so drastic a measure, which would limit opportunities and hurt talented village children and their parents. His concern was rather about the poor quality of rural schooling ('bad schools for ignorant rustics'). Bright children went to towns to seek better schooling, while better teachers too, especially secondary teachers, went to town to seek better career prospects. It could be argued that rural areas got both too little and too much education. Too little, because able people were unfairly denied life-chances by accident of rural birth; too much, because limited opportunities for school-leavers in rural areas made it necessary for many young people to move to town, from which only failures returned.

Urban bias operated too against agricultural research and training. Fewer than 10 per cent of graduates in most poor countries specialized in agriculture, while in some of the biggest including India the proportion was less than 3 per cent. Likewise there were gross disparities in medical provision. In India, rural areas with 80 per cent of the population were served by 35 per cent of the country's male doctors, and under 13 per cent of the women doctors, a crucial constraint on family planning. As for taxation, although tax rates generally in poor countries were modest, rural people were more heavily taxed than urbanites, and got far less benefit from public expenditure.[12]

Urban bias and the problems associated with it were vividly illustrated in Guinea-Bissau, according to Patrick Chabal. When the war of independence ended in 1974, the population of the capital Bissau had been swollen to one-seventh that of the country as a whole by an influx of people who had fled from the fighting, along with officials and others who had done well under colonial rule and were opposed to the new revolutionary regime whose strength was in the rural areas. The influx into Bissau was still continuing, and the city could not cope. One obvious solution was to disperse many of the city's inhabitants to, or back to, the rural areas; but there seemed no way of doing this by persuasion, and not being the Khmer Rouge the new regime shrank from achieving it by force. But to overcome the city's rapidly worsening urban problems, and to try to gain consent among its inhabitants, the new regime had to divert to the city resources that they had hoped to devote to rural development. Paradoxically, because of urban bias the regime ended the war favouring their urban opponents at the expense of their rural supporters.[13]

Sectors in the urban economy

As already mentioned, from the 1970s onwards a distinction was drawn between formal and informal sectors in the economic life of 'Third World' towns, and a state sector was also identified.[14]

According to this view, the formal sector was characteristically made up of a few large firms in corporate ownership, many of them foreign-owned, relying on capital-intensive imported technology. Entry to this sector was difficult as these firms dominated the markets for their respective products, markets in many cases protected by tariffs, quotas, and the like. They employed a small number of highly paid, highly skilled workers with formal training, many of them expatriates. Local staff too tended to be rather well-paid by local standards, while working conditions were good, partly because it was in such firms' interest to secure a healthy, contented labour force, partly to forestall criticism locally and in the firm's home country.

The state sector was not particularly capital-intensive, and employed many workers at or near the local market rate as sweepers, office cleaners and messengers, construction workers in public health and housing schemes, and the like. State bureaucracies and those of public corporations embraced a wide range of grades and incomes, and were as much a source of disparities as those in which market forces prevailed.

By contrast, the informal sector was made up of many small enterprises including self-employed individuals and those employing a few workers. These supplied both goods and services, for example as hawkers and street traders, repairing bicycles, making footwear out of old car tyres, in many cases combining and adapting local and imported materials and technology in highly labour-intensive ways. Individual or family owner-ship of these enterprises predominated, and there was ease of entry into free and highly competitive markets.

In his presidential address to the World Bank in 1975, Robert McNamara pointed out that the informal sector provided nearly half of all the jobs in Lima, more than half in Bombay and Jakarta, and over two-thirds in Belo Horizonte. 'And yet, the fact is that governments tend to view the informal sector with little enthusiasm. They consider it backward, inefficient, and a painful reminder of a less sophisticated past.'[15] His remarks represented a change in the attitude of organizations such as the World Bank and the ILO, and in the 1980s the informal sector came to be regarded more favourably by governments and aid agencies. This was nowhere more apparent than in the field of urban housing, to which I turn below.

However, the analysis in terms of sectors has been criticized as too simple, and for implying that the sectors are more self-contained than they really are. There are many complex interactions as people and money circulate among the urban sectors and between them and the countryside. The lure of high wages in the large-scale formal sector may draw migrants from the country, but not all regard employment there as a job for life; rather, their object may be to save enough to start up in business as, for instance, a photographer. Many craftsmen and traders in the informal sector buy tools, spare parts (e.g. motor spares), and supplies (e.g. motor fuel) from wholesalers in the large-scale formal sector. Successful local entrepreneurs in the informal sector may go on to become retail outlets, agents, or subsidiaries of the big firms including the transnational corporations.

Moreover, the well-to-do and those working in the formal sectors, public and private, enjoy the benefits of cheap goods and services from the informal sector: domestic servants, goods brought to the door by hawkers, and the like. On the one hand, such transactions reflect disparities of income; on the other, it may be through them that the higher rewards of the formal sectors spread outwards to the poor.

Entry into much of the informal sector is not always as easy as had been suggested. This is particularly the case when the would-be entrant finds the market already dominated by an exclusive group such as a craft guild, an ethnic association, or even a criminal gang.

Finally, the sectoral analysis is not universally applicable in all 'Third World' towns. As mentioned in chapter 4, Rakesh Mohan in his study of Bogota and Cali found a labour market more or less in balance, no protected formal sector, and no discernible informal sector.

Urban housing policies

It has been well said that if housing standards are bad in 'Third World' towns, they are even worse in the country.[16]

Changing official attitudes towards the informal sector have been reflected in a changing terminology: from 'slums', 'squatter areas', and 'shanty towns' through 'irregular settlements' to 'self-help housing'. According to the geographer David Drakakis-Smith, 'squatter' housing tended to be illegally built on out-of-town sites, either without the landowner's permission, or not up to official standards, or both. 'Slums', however, tended to occur in or near the city centres in once-permanent buildings that had deteriorated from age, neglect, and multiple occupation. In his opinion, slums made as great a contribution as squatter settlements to meeting the housing needs of the poor. Migrants tended to find homes first in inner-city slums and move out later, in response to growing family size, to the more spacious areas of squatter settlement. Terms such as 'temporary', 'uncontrolled', and 'spontaneous' were misleading. Many such settlements had been there for a long time, their growth as carefully watched by the people who already lived there as by the local authorities, who could use the illegal nature of the housing or the residents' activities as pretexts to evict and demolish at any time.

Governments' policies had varied along with the terminology. At one extreme was the demolition of popular housing and the eviction of its inhabitants. (But many soon came back.) Secondly, there were token responses in the form of limited but highly visible projects to disarm criticism and impress foreign visitors. Thirdly there were extensive public housing schemes, intended to be low-cost, but in the event not so as a result of unsuitable design and imported materials and even labour. These tended to be affordable only by middle-income families, who, characteristically, were the chief beneficiaries of schemes intended for the poor. Fourthly, there were 'new towns' on the outskirts of cities, the sites of industrial estates and middle-class suburbs. These were linked to the city by roads thronged with two-way traffic each morning as workers from low-cost housing in the city centre travelled out to work in the industrial estates while the middle-class suburbanites made their way in to work in the city, and vice versa in the evening.

A more favourable attitude to the informal sector, and an acceptance that the poor know their own needs better than architects and city planners, had led to policies of aided self-help. Up-grading squatter settlements by installing water and sewage was popular with residents; far better than evict-and-demolish, anyway! But there were some problems. Installing main services to existing houses was expensive (though preferable, one would think, from a public health point of view), while up-grading the buildings themselves was cheaper. Governments accordingly tended to do the latter, but they were still reluctant to grant tenure rights.

In 'site and service' schemes, water, drains, and in most cases electricity were installed first, possibly with a small core house for immediate occupation, and residents were encouraged to 'self-build' or employ local contractors. Such schemes were popular in principle, most of all because residents had definite rights of tenure. However, they tended to be sited in less desirable areas, far from city centres, where land was available and cheap. Another drawback was sub-letting by poorer residents, re-creating the overcrowding it had been the object to overcome.[17]

Suggestions for further reading

Michael Lipton, *Why Poor People Stay Poor: A Study of Urban Bias in World Development* (London, Temple Smith, 1977)

Peter Lloyd, *Slums of Hope? Shanty Towns of the Third World* (Harmondsworth, Penguin, 1979)

Alan Gilbert and Josef Gugler, *Cities, Poverty, and Development: Urbanization in the Third World* (London, Oxford University Press, 1982)

David Drakakis-Smith, *The Third World City* (London, Methuen, 1987)

Caroline O. N. Moser and Linda Peake (eds.), *Women, Human Settlements, and Housing* (London, Tavistock, 1987)

United Nations Development Programme, *Human Development Report 1990* (New York, Oxford University Press for UNDP, 1990), chapter 5, 'Urbanization and human development'

8

Family life in a changing world: two studies

W. J. Goode: 'fit' and 'convergence'

In his wide-ranging study *World Revolution and Family Patterns*,[1] the American sociologist W. J. Goode advanced two main theses. First, that there was a 'fit' or congruence between the conjugal family and the modern industrial economy. Goode used the term conjugal as a shorthand expression for the whole complex of characteristics of the western family: an emphasis on the nuclear family household as the normal residential unit, bringing up children and managing its own affairs in relative financial independence; monogamy, relatively free choice of marriage partner, egalitarianism in relations between spouses, some provision for divorce in case of marital breakdown, though with checks and safeguards for the interest of dependent children; bilateral descent, an absence of clan or lineage structures and of joint family systems giving other kin (the 'elders' as he called them) the right to interfere in the choice of marriage partner or the management of the nuclear family household.

Western family life had 'always' approximated to the conjugal model, certainly for many centuries before the industrial revolution. It was not a response to industrialization, the result of a breakdown of an earlier extended family system. 'The classical family of western nostalgia' was a myth. A form of the family emphasizing the husband–wife–child unit might very well have been 'a facilitating factor for industrialization, rather than the other way round'.

According to Goode, the conjugal family system facilitated both geographical mobility and 'class-differential' mobility. It encouraged achievement orientation, making one's own way; and it afforded fewer opportunities for nepotism. It may be suggested that Goode could have advanced stronger arguments here, such as the tradition of young adults leaving home and going into service; while the concentration of resources in nuclear families facilitated the accumulation of capital in the family firm, and also the education of children.

Goode's second thesis was that as other societies become industrialized their family patterns may consequently be expected to converge on the conjugal type. That put him in the company of writers such as Clark Kerr who maintained that there is a logic of industrialization impelling all industrial societies towards similar institutions – a point of view broadly in line with that of the modernization school.[2]

Goode investigated those hypotheses in a monumentally comprehensive review of the available evidence from most of the major continents and culture areas of the world: the West, Arabic Islam, Africa south of the Sahara, India, China, and Japan. His coverage was not quite worldwide, and he noted with regret the paucity of studies of eastern Europe and of Latin America, while the Islamic world outside the Arab states was also omitted. In considering India, China, and Japan he dealt with the material from one large state, while his other areas consisted of a number of states, as in Europe, Arabic Islam, and Africa. From each area he amassed a wide variety of evidence, including laws (together with the reports of government commissions on family law and related topics), official statistics (of much of which he was properly sceptical), social surveys, and the field reports of social anthropologists. This evidence he analysed under similar broad headings, adapted as necessary. They included practices relating to the choice of mate, plural marriage (polygyny or polyandry), marriages with relatives, age at marriage, the birth-rate and fertility along with related factors such as infanticide, abortion, and contraception; the extended family, household, clan, and kin network beyond the nuclear family; divorce and the remarriage of widows and divorced persons; the position of women in the wider society, women's work and rights, the equality of sexes; and relations internal to the family, especially those between spouses. Sometimes it proved difficult to separate material under these heads. For instance, the marriage or betrothal of children obviously came under 'age at marriage', but it also affected choice of mate, and had a bearing on the power of parents and other elders in a wider kin network to exercise that choice on behalf of dependent minors.

From that study of the literature, Goode concluded that where changes in the family were taking place at all there was indeed a convergence. In many countries laws had been enforced prohibiting such traditional practices as infant marriage and betrothal, and bringing legal minimum ages into line with internationally accepted standards. Arranged marriages had declined and there had been a general trend towards individual choice of marriage partner. Very large 'extended family' households were more of a myth than a reality in most civilizations, yet modern changes had tended towards nuclear family households as the norm. Relations with wider kin were of continuing importance, no less in the West than elsewhere, but the power and indeed the inclination of kinsfolk to interfere in the running of, or share the benefits of, the nuclear family household had been reduced. Where divorce had been easy and divorce rates high, it had become more difficult in some cases with the interposition of a judicial process, and rates had fallen; where it had been hard, shameful, or even quite impossible, it had been legally instituted and tended to lose some of its former stigma. It was in this respect that convergence had been most striking, with a movement in contrary directions from the two extremes towards the middle position of most western countries where divorce is possible but not easy, with checks and safeguards for the children.

However, change had been neither uniform nor rapid. Thus in India, though infant marriage had been abolished, it was not yet generally accepted that young adults had the right to meet, engage in courtship, and decide whom and when to marry. Arranged marriages were still normal and girls were strictly chaperoned. Caste endogamy was generally observed, most people supported the joint family at least in principle, and though divorce had been legalized it remained hard and shameful. Contrary to Hindu traditions most people favoured the remarriage of widows, but women did not yet mingle freely with men in most walks of life. Similarly in Africa little or no change had taken place in such institutions as polygyny, clan and lineage structures, traditional courtship, or divorce.

The qualifying phrase 'where changes were taking place at all' was an important one, therefore, and in a good many areas of family life no change was to be discerned. But the strongest point in favour of Goode's thesis was that according to his evidence there were no contrary changes. Nowhere, for example, had there been a tendency for parents to exercise *more* control over their children's marriages, for the wider kin network to be *strengthened*, for *more* men to take plural wives, or for hard and shameful divorce to become even harder and more shameful.

As has been seen, there are reasons for agreeing with Goode that the particular forms of the family that prevailed in the West were such as to facilitate industrialization in those countries.

If that is the case, then change in the family may be expected to be more radical in societies with other kinship systems. While there may well be a convergence, and the kinship systems of those countries may come to resemble those of the early-industrializing nations, nevertheless the discontinuities are likely to be sharper. For a time at least, the transitional forms of the family in developing countries may differ substantially from those of industrial societies, in relation to the widely different traditions that were their starting-points for change.

John C. Caldwell and Pat Caldwell: a theory of fertility decline

Between 1959 and 1981 the Australian demographer John C. Caldwell with Pat Caldwell carried out a number of field studies of small-scale rural communities in Africa and south Asia, mostly by methods like those of social anthropologists.[3]

For demographers, as seen in chapter 2, the all-important question was that of fertility decline. Caldwell and Caldwell's first aim was to construct a theory 'congruent with Third World experience' of the conditions that made for stable high fertility in the first place, and why those conditions were destabilized.

In doing so they went deeply into the difficult and sensitive field of economic and social relations among the members of family households, analysing the flow of resources (or in their terms 'income' or 'wealth') within families.

Two modes of production

In 1992 Caldwell and Caldwell put forward the thesis that 'there have been only two modes of production . . . familial production . . . [and] labour-market production'; and 'that these determine the two very different types of society that exist'. Against the grain of much social anthropology, they were impressed, not by the diversity of traditional family systems, but by how much they had in common. They felt 'a certain unease', too, about finding themselves thinking in terms like 'the traditional family' and 'modernization',[4] especially as J. C. Caldwell had previously criticized earlier theories of fertility decline for their over-emphasis on modernization.

The archetypal form of familial production was, of course, subsistence farming. In this mode of production, work was allotted, directed, and supervised, and rewards assigned, by family members. Characteristically it was men who made the decisions and gave the orders: fathers to sons, elder brothers to younger, husbands to wives.

By contrast, in the labour-market mode of production individuals were employed, directed, supervised, and rewarded impersonally by individuals or organizations outside the family.

The familial mode of production: 1. Work

In rural societies of north Africa and south- and south-west Asia, Caldwell and Caldwell found that everybody worked hard, adults typically 70 to 80 hours a week; but not equally hard. Adult sons worked harder than their fathers. Women worked longer hours than men, and their work was consistently down-graded. For example, ploughing was easier and pleasanter than cultivating with a digging-stick, as women did; but by defining it as men's work men were able to contend that it was they who did the real work. In fact, though, the most hard-working family members were the daughters-in-law, brought up in other families to be submissive and accept their lot.

Children too worked long hours, starting at about five years of age, and reaching adult levels by about 14 years. There was little opportunity for play. Only about 3 per cent of all family work inputs was devoted to child care, most of it by the infant's sisters.

2. Resources, rewards, and advantages

While family resources were shared among family members, they were not shared equally, nor according to their need, nor according to their work. The old and male were served first with food, and got most; likewise with money, clothes, house space, and access to transport. Old men chose what work they did, and how much, before they made their way to the coffee-house to chat with their cronies. They considered they had the right to be pampered, to expect small services, to be supported in danger or disputes; and on the whole their claims were accepted.

Other advantages were distributed similarly, to males before females, the old before the young. For example, in Middle Eastern countries many baby boys were breast-fed for twice as long as girls. In rural Bangladesh female mortality at ages 0 to 30 was almost 50 per cent higher than among males. Infant and child mortality rates were high in these societies, mainly for lack of access to medical facilities, though Caldwell and Caldwell noted also the small proportion of resources devoted to child-care.

3. Demographic aspects

In a society based on familial production, high fertility provided labour: the more the better, up to a maximum of about ten (presumably adults or adult-equivalents). It also had other advantages, from the patriarchs' point of view; it kept women family-centred and docile, and the old liked having young grandchildren around to run errands and perform small services for them. A five-to-ten-year age gap between spouses, together with patrilocal marriage, ensured male dominance. Moreover, a young husband could look forward to having some help with the farm work in about 10 to 12 years after his marriage, and with most of the harder work by the age of 40. And even for a young wife there were rewards for child-bearing, which established her position in the family, entitled her to a little more consideration and help, and brought nearer the time when she could become a mother-in-law dominating her daughters-in-law in her turn. Everybody, therefore, had an interest in high fertility, as indeed they had in the whole system.

Clearly, in such societies, unrestricted fertility was not a matter of ignorance, or fatalism, or the unavailability of contraception. It was for these reasons that, as noted in chapter 2, J. C. Caldwell was critical of the World Fertility Survey. Asking women how many children, or how many more, they would like to have, and whether they knew about various methods of contraception, was beside the point in societies where there was no notion of an ideal family size, only 'as many as possible'. Moreover, women simply did not make decisions on any important question, whether family planning, farm management, or anything else; certainly not alone, nor even jointly with their husbands. As for family planning, there was little or no time or opportunity for serious discussion of such intimate matters, as the sexes were segregated all the working day and had little privacy at night. Contraception was highly suspect, not only because it affected fertility, but for what it implied about the married relationship. A man thought to be on intimate and equal terms with his wife would be subject to ridicule and perhaps worse in the local gossip network.

4. Stability

Caldwell and Caldwell indicated four reasons for the system's stability. First, everybody was brought up in the system and taught to accept it. Secondly, as already noted, everybody knew that their lot would improve over time if they could only survive the present. While young men in particular might labour under a suppressed sense of injustice against their fathers, they acquiesced because they could foresee being fathers in their turn; likewise, downtrodden daughters-in-law had only to endure till they became mothers-in-law. Young men's bitterness was more likely to find a displaced expression in quarrels between brothers, but rather than revealing fissures in the system these quarrels served to strengthen paternal authority. 'Sons with many siblings can hardly revolt if there are rivals for the inheritance.' Thirdly, the gossip network was all-pervasive. Fourthly, there was a massive superstructure including religion, law, conventional wisdom, and folk-lore supporting patriarchal authority and high fertility.

5. Transition

According to Caldwell and Caldwell, labour-market production was the economic base for a low-fertility society. However, the manner and timing of the all-important transition depended very largely on how and when that massive superstructure justifying high fertility was dismantled. Prominent among the superstructural elements involved was schooling. More than any other factor, the introduction of universal primary schooling affected the timing of the demographic transition, sometimes ahead of economic development, as in Sri Lanka and Kerala. Children attending school were obviously less available for traditional tasks. They were a source not of labour but of expense, directly for fees, school uniforms, books, etc., but also indirectly, for example in response to school lessons about nutrition, health, and hygiene. If they were ill they were more likely to be taken for medical treatment. In relation to the family economy they became consumers, not 'battlers in the family's struggle for survival'. In such circumstances, the traditional presumption in favour of high and unlimited fertility could not but be weakened.[5]

Suggestions for further reading

W. J. Goode, *World Revolution and Family Patterns* (New York, Free Press, 1963; paperback edition with a new preface, 1970)
John C. Caldwell, *Theory of Fertility Decline* (London, Academic Press, 1982)
Elza Berquó and Peter Xenos (eds.), *Family Systems and Social Change* (Oxford, Clarendon Press, 1992)

9

Cultural diversity, language, education, and communications

Cultural diversity

In the neolithic world of limited communications, human communities in relative isolation developed different cultures. The term culture in this context refers to a whole way of life: a complex whole including language, material culture or technology, social institutions, and religious, moral and aesthetic values. A culture is a combination of these elements in a total pattern recognizably different from other cultures, even those with which there are elements in common. Thus neighbouring societies might get their living in similar ways yet speak different languages and have different forms of political organization. There may be problems of delineation, as cultures shade over into one another; for instance, it may be a moot point whether two tongues are different languages or dialects of the same language. So we cannot say with precision how many different human cultures there are, or were, before the forces that in our time have made for the breaking down of isolation. But that should not lead us to minimize the extent and depth of cultural diversity, to which the whole science of social anthropology bears witness.

Cultural diversity, though a common characteristic of many 'Third World' countries, is not equally well marked in all. Some areas have long been exposed to the overlordship of a dominant people, whose culture has more or less heavily overlaid the indigenous folk-cultures, or even (as noted in chapter 3) extinguished them altogether. That is most clearly so in Latin America, though even there the persistence of pre-conquest cultures should not be overlooked, for instance among the Amazon forest peoples, while in Bolivia in the 1970s more people spoke Amerindian languages than Spanish as their mother-tongue, and there were four and a half million Quechua-speakers in Peru.[1] A common language, religion, and related institutions such as kinship are equally evident in the Arab-Muslim region. Cultural diversity is rather more marked in Asia despite the unifying factor of religions – Islam in Pakistan and Indonesia, Buddhism in Burma and the adjoining lands. In India, a recognition of cultural diversity and tolerance of different ways of life and worship have always characterized the Hindu attitude to life, and non-Hindu communities found an accepted place in society through the caste system. It is in Africa that cultural diversity is most marked, presumably because of the short time since, under colonial rule, government was established over wider areas than before.

As an illustration, Uganda is a comparatively small country whose population was some four million when British rule was established around 1900, and about $17^1/2$ million in 1992. That population includes some twenty-five to thirty groups, each with a language, culture, and identity recognized as distinctive by themselves and others.[2] (Under colonial rule such groups were called tribes; I discuss the word below.)

The indigenous languages of Uganda have been classified in four main groups as Bantu, (Central) Sudanic, Western Nilotic, and Eastern Nilotic (formerly termed Nilo-Hamitic). Within each group the individual languages resemble one another, though the degree of mutual comprehension varies. Thus the Bantu languages are about as alike or as different as English, German, Danish, and Dutch. Nilotic, Sudanic, and Bantu languages, however, differ much more fundamentally in grammar, vocabulary, and tone.

Though kinship systems in Uganda are not as diverse as elsewhere in Africa, being all patrilineal, there are important differences between peoples with a fixed number of clans, particularly among the inter-lacustrine Bantu in the south, and those with flexible and fissiparous lineage systems, especially in the Nilotic areas to the north. Thus the social anthropologist Christine Obbo in a study in and around Kampala in the 1970s contrasted marriage patterns among the different groups. Nilotic wives lived and identified themselves closely with their husband's lineage. Bridewealth was high, and in theory returnable at divorce, which was rare, as ex-wives were not allowed to take their children with them. In polygynous marriage, each wife and her children formed a separate matrifocal residential unit, potentially a minor lineage. By contrast, Interlacustrine wives never joined their husband's clan, and maintained strong links with their brothers and other kin. Bridewealth was low and not returnable; divorce was frequent, and ex-wives took their children with them.[3]

Different clan and lineage systems were related to differences of political organization. In the south were the highly centralized Bantu kingdoms of BuGanda, BuNyoro, Toro, and Ankole, with strongly authoritarian and inegalitarian attitudes about political relations and human relations generally. One of the titles of the Kabaka or king of

BuGanda was Sabataka or chief of the clan-heads, and the latter held traditional fiefs including county chieftainships, military commands, and courtly offices. Elsewhere political authority was weak or absent, and political relations were conducted at the level of feuds among lineages. Unlike Kenya, few of the peoples of what is now Uganda practised circumcision or organized young men into warrior age-sets, though some did including the BaGisu. Politically the area was a kaleidoscope of small kingdoms or chiefdoms expanding, conquering their neighbours, reducing them to tributary status, and establishing small empires that fell apart again after a generation or two.

Particularly under colonial rule, an individual's tribal identity was usually regarded as an ascribed status, fixed for life; and it was among the questions people were asked on occasions such as seeking employment or entering a school or college, and when a census was taken. However, people can and do learn languages other than their mother-tongue, convert to another religion, adopt different ways, etc., and so hope to gain a different tribal identity. Clearly in such circumstances much will depend on the extent to which they are accepted by the group they hope to join.

Thus according to Audrey Richards, in the early 1950s it was easy for non-Ganda foreigners to take up land in BuGanda, and many foreigners tried to become incorporated into Ganda society by adopting Ganda names, wearing Ganda dress, and attempting to pass themselves off as members of Ganda clans. Ganda landowners with large estates were prepared to grant migrant labourers plots of land as an incentive to stay and work. BaGanda tenant farmers, however, wanted them only as temporary labourers, not settlers.[4]

However, one group who, exceptionally, did accept outsiders into full membership were the Nubians, descendants of Sudanese mercenary soldiers who had served in the colonial wars at the turn of the century, and settled in towns and trading centres. With them it was a matter of learning their language and embracing Islam; and those who did so did not lose their original tribal identity.[5] The Nubians came to greater prominence under Idi Amin, who was himself both a Kakwa by descent and a Nubian.

European intervention and colonial rule had the effect of simplifying the tribal or ethnic pattern and fixing it in a more definite form. The British arrived on the scene late in the nineteenth century when one little empire, that of Bunyoro-Kitara, was in decline. The province of Toro had lately asserted its independence, and the neighbouring kingdom of Buganda was aggressively expanding. The British based themselves on Buganda and extended their rule to adjoining areas in alliance with its remarkable missionary-schooled elite, and the very name Uganda, which the British gave to the whole protectorate, is the Swahili version of the name of the kingdom.[6] Their central position, their alliance with the British, and their head start in schooling and economic development put the Ganda in a position of privilege if not hegemony over other peoples in the Uganda Protectorate. As elsewhere in Africa, the boundaries of that protectorate were settled by statesmen in the chancelleries of Europe drawing lines on a map – lines that parted like from like as often as they united unlikes under a common overrule. There is scarcely a point at which the boundaries of Uganda do not divide people who had a common language and culture, and in some cases a traditional political unity.

Uganda can thus be seen as a highly artificial and arbitrary creation. For about sixty years it was subject to British rule, with the establishment of a common official language – the completely alien English – along with common systems of taxation, justice, schooling, traffic regulations and the like, while shortly before independence the forms of representative government were set up. When it became independent in 1962, however, it was a country with no common indigenous language or culture, nor any deeply felt traditional loyalty or sense of national identity on the part of its people. Those sentiments belonged rather to the primordial groups such as the interlacustrine Bantu kingdoms; and attachments to and rivalries among those groups dominated Uganda's stormy and tragic post-independence history, to which I return in chapter 12.

In these respects Uganda is by no means unusual among modern African states. It is rather the countries with a single indigenous language and a common political tradition – Lesotho, Swaziland, Somalia and Madagascar – that are the exceptions. Elsewhere a similar diversity prevails. In neighbouring Tanzania, for example, there are not twenty-five to thirty but well over a hundred recognizable different cultural groups; while rivalries between such groups in other countries too, notably Nigeria, have led to devastating civil wars.

A question of terminology

Before about 1970, particularly in Africa, a people with a distinctive language and culture, and in most cases inhabiting a particular territory, was called a tribe. Social anthropologists used the term without evaluative overtones to delineate a group under study, either in terms of culture especially language; or in terms of customary law and political organization ('within a tribe there is law'); or 'on the basis of cultural-regional criteria'.[7] In the same way President Julius Nyerere wrote of 'tribes' in discussing indigenous education in Africa.[8] Colonial government officials too recognized tribes as natural units for local administration. From the point of view of social science, one of the most important such occasions was the census. Demographic data were useful as a background to more detailed studies by social anthropologists; indeed, one of the first things the reader of a monograph about a people wants to know is how many of them there are. They were important too to geographers and economists; for example, internal migration patterns within an African country could hardly be studied without reference to census data on tribes.[9] Such data had a bearing on the planning of school systems, for example in deciding on the allocation of resources to the production of textbooks in the different vernacular languages; while by comparing the tribal composition of students at a university college (as I did at Makerere) with the population of the tribes from which they came, it was possible to lay bare the patterns of regional and ethnic disparities in the incidence of higher education.[10]

In modern times, a person's tribe became an important aspect of his or her ascribed status, and this led to inter-tribal rivalries and conflicts. In many cases some tribes came to dominate particular occupations; this arose partly from stereotyping by employers who believed, for example, that some tribes were physically strong, others quick-witted, etc.; and partly from attempts on the part of workers of a particular tribe to project a favourable image and so create a partial monopoly of the trade for themselves.

Factional rivalries over such things as employment, housing and education accordingly led to a heightening of tribal consciousness at a time when traditional tribal identity was being transferred into new, non-traditional situations. Thus Parkin traced the rivalries between the immigrant Luo and the local Ganda tenants in a municipal housing estate in Kampala in the 1960s,[11] while Grillo showed how the Luo and the Luyia-Samia factions grappled for control of the Railway African Union in Uganda at the same period.[12]

Finally, after independence, tribal rivalries have broken out in many new states over the biggest prize of all – the control of the state with all its power and resources.

It is not hard to understand why modern governments in poor countries, especially in Africa, should have come to regard factionalism and particularism of this kind as a negative force to be opposed, a danger to be checked. Tribalism got a very bad name as a result of events like the Nigerian civil war, Katanga separatism in Zaire, and Buganda separatism in Uganda. It is not surprising therefore that modern African leaders have played down tribal differences in the name of nation-building, however artificial and arbitrary the nations to which the new sentiments of loyalty are to be attached. Thus the government of Tanzania departed from the practice of its colonial predecessors and omitted any question on tribe from the 1967 census,[13] a decision which, however understandable politically, was much to be regretted from the point of view of social science. As we have seen in chapter 6, a nation-state with a common language and common citizenship has come to be regarded as the badge of modernity, while tribalism is associated with the stigma of backwardness and is repudiated by the modernizing elites. And so, as Audrey Richards well put it, some African political leaders wished to forget the different tribal polities by which Africa is inhabited, and wrote as though the colonial powers had invented tribal differences, though such a view seemed clearly disingenuous and involved turning a blind eye to the immense diversity of African cultures.[14]

As a result, the very word tribe seems to have been discredited, to be replaced by synonyms such as ethnic group, cultural group, people, or (in the context of language) mother-tongue group. To some extent no doubt this represents a case of Myrdal's 'diplomacy by terminology'. However, as Nelson Kasfir has argued, there is just one good reason for preferring 'ethnicity': since 'tribalism' has commonly been used in an African context, it has tended to suggest that there is something specifically African about it, which is misleading.[15] As W. J. Argyle cogently pointed out, there are close similarities between what is termed tribalism in Africa and what is termed nationalism in Europe, and ethnicity covers both.[16] Ethnic rivalries and hostilities erupting into separatist movements and civil wars are confined neither to Africa nor to the 'Third World' in general; they cause death, suffering, and destruction the world over, whatever word we use.

Language[17]

In most developed, high-income countries there is a national language in which everybody is supposed to be fluent. For most people it is their mother-tongue, for linguistic minorities their second language (for example in the UK speakers of Welsh and Gaelic, Arabic, Gujarati, Polish, etc.). Some countries, such as Sweden and Japan, are termed linguistic states because their language is peculiar to them and not much spoken elsewhere. In other cases, the national language of one state is widely spoken and officially recognized in other countries too, as French is in Belgium, Canada, and Switzerland; German in Austria and Switzerland; Spanish throughout Latin America except Brazil; and English in the United States and other countries. Among industrial countries, multi-lingual states are the exception rather than the rule; and though the difference may be one of degree rather than of kind, the contrast with the 'Third World' is clear and wide.

In many 'Third World' countries the diversity of languages is much greater. The indigenous vernacular languages have only limited currency, and tend to be supplemented by a widely understood lingua franca such as Swahili, and a language of wider communication, usually inherited from the colonial past, such as English or French. In employment, education, dealings with officials, and everyday communication in shop and street, people are forced to be linguists. Some indeed become remarkably adept at language-switching according to the social situation; thus hotel workers in Kenya have been heard to switch from one to another of four or five languages including their mother-tongue such as Kamba, the lingua franca Swahili, English, and German, spoken by many tourists.[18]

On the whole it is men who have hitherto been under the greater necessity to learn languages other than their mother-tongue, since (as noted in chapter 4) they have been more involved in the wider social milieux of employment, trade, and migration to towns. For example, a survey in Uganda in 1968 found that 52 per cent of men but only 18 per cent of women could converse in Swahili; 28 per cent of men, 13 per cent of women in English.[19] Local languages accordingly continue to be mother-tongues, learned by children of both sexes. Later in life, different languages may be needed for different purposes. Manual workers may need to know an oral lingua franca for work, traders for business, and town dwellers for communication with neighbours; while those who aspire through schooling to better-paid jobs in management and administration need to learn a language of wider communication as well. To give everybody a chance, such elite languages may have to be taught in schools to many who will have little or no use for them in later life.

Thus in Tanzania, although more than a hundred different vernacular languages have been recognized, nearly all of them are Bantu. That facilitated the rise of Swahili as the lingua franca spoken and understood by virtually all men, though probably to a lesser extent by women; and to its adoption as the national language. Swahili is basically Bantu in its grammar and structure, with a vocabulary enriched with Arabic, Portuguese, and English words adapted to the needs of modern life; this includes a fully developed system of number, lacked by most Bantu languages. It has been written in Roman script since the nineteenth century, and can also be written in Arabic script, in which there is a somewhat limited older literature. It was much encouraged too under both German and British colonial rule.[20] Its advantages as a national language, however, were offset by its limitations as a language of wider communication. Though spoken quite widely in neighbouring Kenya and Uganda, parts of Zaire, and the coasts of Somalia and Mozambique, it does not give access to a wider world of science, technology, literature, trade, or diplomacy. That continues to be the role of English, the legacy of the colonial period, which retains an important place in the secondary school curriculum. Educated young Tanzanians therefore have to learn three languages – their vernacular mother-tongue, Swahili, and English – unless they live at the coast or in Zanzibar, where Swahili is the mother-tongue.

In Uganda no lingua franca gained so strong a foothold under colonial rule. Many men in fact learned Swahili in trade and employment, but its use was deprecated and opposed by the people of BuGanda, who under British overrule enjoyed a privileged position of hegemony. It was a houseboy's language, they said, spoken by white bwanas to their servants in Kenya, and it was not the mother-tongue of any indigenous group in the protectorate of Uganda. It was, however, the language of the army, since under colonial government Ugandan units formed part of a regiment, the King's African Rifles, which drew units also from Kenya, Tanganyika, and Nyasaland (as they were then named), and in which Swahili was the obvious lingua franca. At the same time, fears of Ganda hegemony on the part of the other tribes of the protectorate led to resistance to any suggestion that LuGanda (the Ganda language) should become the general lingua franca there, and so after independence the only choice for an official language was the completely alien English. One advantage of this situation was nevertheless that in the education system it was possible to go straight from the vernacular to English, without the intervening step of Swahili.

Uganda in the late 1980s was accordingly described by Ruth Mukama, head of the department of languages at Makerere University, as a country without a common grassroots language. Of the 30 recognized languages, 25 were given radio air-time, though not in equal measure; LuGanda had the lion's share. The privileged position of English as a world language was secure, though English teaching in schools was quite variable, and there was no proper national syllabus. Swahili had persisted, notably as the language of the army and police; but it was not taught in schools, and not a single bookshop stocked Swahili books. But LuGanda flourished. It was firmly established in schools and colleges, radio and the press; and it was taught and used as a second language in some areas adjoining BuGanda. Vigorously promoted by voluntary associations and pressure-groups, it had gained UNESCO's approval, while a similar claim for Swahili had been rejected.

Outside BuGanda, attempts to simplify the language situation by introducing a limited number of standard 'area languages' had largely failed. For example, the unified Nilotic language Lwoo 'simply does not exist'. Acholi and Langi used different textbooks, the Alur had started writing their own, and 'what books will the Kumam use if they do not write their own?' By this standard, LuGanda was not even an 'area language'; in some districts of the Eastern Region, where it had once dominated, it was no longer taught in schools.

If LuGanda activists were in part politically motivated, hoping through language to restore Ganda hegemony over the whole country, it was clear that their attempts would meet strong resistance from other language groups. It was equally clear, however, that the activists would not consent to LuGanda's being given the status of just one indigenous language among many. There was therefore a deadlock in which, in the absence of a language policy, standard Swahili was used in the armed forces, English in the elite institutions of central government, higher education, etc., pidgin Swahili among workers and traders, and indigenous languages in the countryside and family life: surely a recipe for mutual incomprehension and distrust. To break the deadlock, Mukama herself advocated encouraging Swahili as the grassroots lingua franca. At least the 1952 policy decision that Swahili was not to be taught in Uganda schools should be reversed; people ought not to be denied the opportunity and the facilities to study any language, particularly one widely spoken in neighbouring countries.[21]

In a country with a number of indigenous languages, if one of them becomes the lingua franca or an official language the people whose mother-tongue it is will be at an advantage. For other language groups it will be an additional language to learn, taking up time in schools from substantive subjects with a bearing on entry to the professions and skilled employment. These groups will no doubt see this as an unfair disadvantage against which they are likely to be up in arms, perhaps literally, as will be seen below.

At the other extreme from Uganda, Somalia represents a country based on a single language and culture which nevertheless had language problems. When the Somali Republic became independent in 1960, there were no fewer than three languages of wider communication: Arabic, the language of Islam, and English and Italian, the legacies of colonial rule in the north and in the south respectively. There was no generally accepted script for Somali itself. It had long been written in Arabic script, but not very satisfactorily. About 1920 an entirely new script had been devised, named Osmaniya after its originator, which was championed by Somali nationalists, and did not readily give way to the claims of a Roman orthography. The language question itself was a vexed one and it was many years before an orthography could be agreed. Meanwhile written communication within the country was in English, Italian, and to a lesser extent Arabic; while rivalries between English- and Italian-speaking elites, each with their distinctive heritage of ideas about how the country should be governed, made for factionalism within the new state.[22]

As was seen in Somalia, languages are not only spoken but also written, and though scripts are not as numerous as spoken languages, their diversity adds to the complexity of the subject. Most traditional African cultures did not include writing, Swahili and Somali in Arabic script being only limited exceptions. Most African languages were committed to writing from the late nineteenth century onwards, mainly by Christian missionaries, and in the Roman script. Like other phonetic alphabets such as Greek, this assumes a sequence from the idea through the sound to the written symbol. Although Roman is not perfectly suited to every language, it can be adapted to most, and it has very great advantages. Literacy in one language can readily be transferred to another, so that though many Africans have to learn more than one language, they do not have to learn more than one script. For example, LuGanda, Swahili and English are all written in Roman. Furthermore, the comparatively limited number of symbols required – basically the 26 letters of the alphabet – make it highly convenient and economical for international use in printing and typewriting. On the other hand, since it associates shapes with sounds completely arbitrarily, it is not an easy script to learn, and many children have difficulty with it, as evidenced by controversies in western countries over methods of teaching and initial teaching alphabets. And though once learned it can be applied to other languages, it does not help people to communicate with those who speak other tongues.

By contrast, Chinese script is not phonetic but ideographic; each written symbol represents an idea, not a sound. This makes it easy to learn in the early stages, literally child's play indeed, as the symbols for 'man', 'woman', 'house', etc., consist of stylized pictures such as children delight in drawing. Its other great advantage is that people who speak different languages can nevertheless communicate with ease in writing. It is as if in Europe we used a single common ideogram which people would read variously as house, *maison*, *casa*, etc. In China, a land of several different indigenous languages, the common ideographic script has been regarded as a valuable source of national unity. On the other hand it has limitations. The simplicity and obviousness of the ideograms for commonplace objects give way to complexity and difficulty over advanced concepts, which require allusions and other conventions demanding much time and effort to learn. Thus in contrast to Roman's 26 letters, ordinary literate Chinese may know perhaps 3,000 symbols, newspapers use 6,000–7,000, and the most literate people know as many as 30,000–50,000. In traditional China that meant that the education of the elite was in the narrowest sense literary, a matter of learning thousands of symbols and their meanings and knowing how to use them in context. In modern times, too, the difficulties for printing and typing can readily be appreciated.

Among the spoken Chinese languages the one that used to be called Mandarin, named the national language under the Kuomintang republic, and latterly re-named Putonghua or everyday speech, has become more and more widely understood in twentieth-century China. Writing it in Roman script, however, runs into the difficulty that words may have different meaning according to whether they are pronounced with a rising, falling, or level tone, which is not readily represented in Roman. Various orthographies were devised in the nineteenth and twentieth centuries, and the system of conventions known as Pinyin was officially adopted in 1958 for transcribing Chinese personal names and place names into Roman in foreign-language publications. Meanwhile there has been a policy of simplifying the traditional symbols for printing and writing in China itself.

India like China has a rich and ancient heritage of literary culture, but each of the major Indian languages has its own script, and there are also ritual scripts such as Gurmukh in which Punjabi is written for the purposes of the Sikh religion. Each of these scripts, and the language and culture associated with it, was regarded as a precious heritage, and the post-independence history of India was marked by violent disputes as the country was reorganized into linguistic states. Under British rule English had taken firm root as the official language, and hence the language of opportunity for the intellectual and bureaucratic elite, so that many families at the highest social level adopted it as their mother-tongue. Ironically it was they who were the 'Anglicists' in the nineteenth-century controversies over educational development, while the British officials tended to be 'Orientalists' and included men with a deep respect for Indian culture who exerted themselves to save Sanskrit from oblivion.

The government of independent India faced difficult problems over language. While the English-speaking elite were a considerable national asset for the communication of scientific and cultural ideas with the rest of the world, as well as for diplomatic and business contacts, they were correspondingly cut off from the great majority of their fellow-countrymen, and the use of English as the official language emphasized a distance between government and people that was quite inappropriate after the departure of the British. The decision in 1963 to adopt Hindi in the Devanagari script as the official language could be said to bring government nearer to the people – but only some people. It was a contentious decision by which people in non-Hindi-speaking areas felt disadvantaged, not least because their children now had to learn an extra language at school compared with those whose mother-tongue was the new official language. Well-meaning proposals to equalize the handicap by making Hindi-speaking children learn some other Indian language seemed unrealistic and ineffective.[23] Feelings ran high and riots broke out over this issue in 1965, particularly in Madras, and the government was forced to modify its policy.

In India, too, people have to be not bi-lingual but tri-lingual, and (to coin a term) tri-scriptal as well, as they learn first the language of their state with its traditional script, then Hindi in Devanagari, then English in Roman. More time spent on language leaves less time for substantive subjects such as mathematics, science, and history, and there are said also to be indirect effects in an emphasis on memory work and rote learning which spread to the way other subjects are taught as well as the little time left to teach them, and led Myrdal to exclaim that 'people are not merely being insufficiently educated; they are being mis-educated on a huge scale'.[24]

Although India may be regarded as something of an extreme case, 'bi-scriptalism' is also called for in Arabic countries in so far as the Roman script is needed for English or French as languages of wider communication. And similar problems arise in some other south Asian countries. In Sri Lanka, for instance, there are three languages – Sinhalese and Tamil, each with its own script, and English with Roman script. In Pakistan the language spoken by the biggest number of people is Punjabi, with a script different from that used for the official language Urdu. Both regional and national languages have to be taught in Burma and Thailand. Another example of linguistic complexity is the Philippines, where there are several Malayo-Polynesian vernacular languages of which the one spoken by the biggest number is Cebuano. Another, however, was chosen as the national language since it was the vernacular language of the region of Manila, had greater prestige, and was spoken more widely as a second language; this was Tagalog, renamed Pilipino as a matter of national pride. Spanish has been used in the islands for many centuries, and continues to be taught in schools; while English has also been taught in the primary schools since the beginning of the American administration as the premier language of wider communication. At least, however, all these languages, including the vernaculars, are written in Roman script.[25]

Enough has been said, perhaps, to show the importance of language and linguistic diversity in Third World countries. That importance is particularly marked in education, politics, and the mass media of communication, to which I turn below.

Science, culture, and development

Science is a social institution whose manifest function is discovery. Scientists aim to make statements about the world that shall be true irrespective of who makes them. Scientific propositions (hypotheses, theories) are open to be tested by any competent observer against observations of the real world, and knowledge consists at any time of tested and not-yet-falsified theories. Science is accordingly the most truly international of all institutions, and the knowledge with which scientists are concerned is trans-cultural, transcending the national and ethnic cultures in which they were severally brought up. Yet there is a paradox here, for knowledge is an essential constituent of every culture. Without reliable knowledge of the world, traditional farmers, pastoralists, and the like could not survive. As Robert Chambers pointed out (and as I noted in chapter 6), in many cases rural peoples' indigenous knowledge has proved to be reliable on matters such as farming practice and animal husbandry. When indigenous knowledge is at variance with outsiders' science-based knowledge, sometimes one is right, sometimes the other; the problem is to know which is right when.[26]

While all cultures embody some science, though, they differ widely in the extent to which they have (so to speak) domesticated science, and the extent and complexity of the not-yet-falsified knowledge which they embody. Science is everywhere at loggerheads with false belief, and western societies are no exception; there seems no warrant whatever for viewing ours as in any sense a specially scientific culture. Yet it was in western countries that modern science was nurtured,[27] and overwhelmingly in developed countries that it is now pursued. Whether measured in terms of the resources devoted to it, the numbers of scientists engaged in it, or their published contributions to knowledge, something like 95 to 98 per cent of scientific activity is carried on in developed countries.[28]

Science is an intensely competitive and selective activity, and though in principle it is open to all, in practice, because of their systematic advantages, most scientists turn out to be white rather than black, men rather than women, and of upper- or middle-class social origins.[29] The centres of excellence where research of world renown is carried on are overwhelmingly located in industrial countries, where they afford apt examples of growth poles giving rise to backwash effects in 'brain-drains' and the paucity of scientific work in poor countries. At the level of applied science, too, it is often said that topics chosen for research tend to be related to the problems of industrial rather than agrarian societies, of temperate rather than tropical climates and crops, and towards capital- rather than labour-intensive technology.[30]

Education

Indications of the extent of schooling and of literacy in 'Third World' countries may be gained from United Nations and World Bank statistics. They show in general rising school enrolments of both boys and girls, though rather more of boys; rising public expenditures on schooling at all levels; and rising levels of adult literacy. Thus in low-income countries excluding China and India, between 1970 and 1991 primary school enrolments rose from 55 to 79 per cent of children of primary school age, 44 to 71 per cent of girls; while in developing countries taken as a whole, between 1970 and 1992 adult literacy rose from 46 to 69 per cent. But that still left many millions of adults illiterate, mostly women.[31]

Such developments have taken place, no doubt, in response to the perceived inadequacy of traditional education. Perceived, that is, by the modernizing elites, who in Bendix's words (quoted in chapter 6 above) 'put a premium on ideas and techniques which "follower" countries may use to "come up from behind"' in their efforts to rid their societies of the stigma of backwardness. Few questioned that it was highly desirable for the elementary skills of reading, writing and arithmetic to be widely spread among the people of a modern state, while a need was also experienced for a national elite educated at a higher level in the skills and knowledge of the modern world. The establishment and expansion of formal school systems accordingly became an essential part of the drive to modernity in the cause of nation-building. Schools contributed to that cause by spreading the use of the national language, teaching the nation's history and literature, and fostering national consciousness and pride. Few argued as E. M. K. Mulira did in Uganda for the vernacular in schooling.[32] In general, little but lip-service was paid to transmitting, still less revitalizing, indigenous cultures; the main thrust of nationalist policies was rather to break down tribal, linguistic and cultural barriers and do away with tribalism. Those perceptions accorded well enough with the aspirations of many parents in 'Third World' countries to see their children gain a foothold in the modern sector, with its high rewards and glittering prizes.

The kinds of skill and knowledge that schooling in the modern sense was intended to transmit and develop involved it, in more cases than not, in a discontinuity with traditional education. In some areas, indeed, the very institution of a school as a place where children assemble, to be formally instructed by specially qualified adults, was an innovation foreign to the indigenous culture. No society lacks the means of socializing the young and transmitting knowledge, skill, and values, but in many societies the ways in which this was done did not correspond to our preconceived notion of the school. A distinction has to be made between education and schooling; while schooling refers to the formal classroom setting, education includes all that people learn in their whole life experience. (Educationists further define formal education as schooling together with other school activities such as sport; non-formal education as organized teaching outside the school, such as adult literacy and agricultural extension; and informal education as the rest, including learning at work.)[33]

Thus in many African traditional cultures, young people learned by doing and by helping their parents and others older than themselves. Some institutions such as tribute labour had educational functions when young men and women called to work at the chief's court saw and heard what went on there. In some African societies there were initiation ceremonies marking the transition from juvenile to adult status, *rites de passage* that included tests of fortitude and some instruction in the duties of men and women; in some cases these were carried out in seclusion over a period and were therefore called 'schools'.[34] Although one or two attempts were made to reconcile the new style of schooling with these traditional initiation rites, in general the two were in conflict. For example, in Lesotho the mission schools were reluctant to accept initiated boys or to allow them to resume their studies. That resulted in a sharp division between the schooled and the initiated; the former, who had completed their formal education and attained positions of overt power and responsibility in the modern system, were nevertheless held in contempt as mere boys by those who had undergone the rigours of the initiation lodge and further proved their manhood in the mines of South Africa.[35]

Lesotho was no doubt an extreme case, but it was quite common in Africa for the setting up of schools by the first Christian missionaries to be met with indifference or hostility among the local people, who had to be persuaded to send their children to school. Adult converts were told it was their duty, while both missionaries and government officials put pressure on chiefs to set an example by sending their sons.[36] In some places initial hostility soon gave way to enthusiastic acceptance, when the advantages of employment in the modern sector came to be recognized; and colonial administrations which not long before had been with difficulty pioneering formal education were now criticized for not doing more and doing it faster.

The school was not quite so complete a cultural innovation in areas outside Africa, and in the traditional civilizations of the Arab-Muslim world and India there were institutions resembling schools in the modern sense. It might be thought that the break between old and new would be less sharp, and the possibility of building the new on the old foundations would be greater, in those areas; but on the whole that has not proved to be the case. Thus in Muslim countries the *kuttab* or Koran school generally resisted modernization, except perhaps to a limited extent in Egypt;[37] and the *madrasah* or higher college too was not very adaptable despite attempts in some countries to introduce subjects such as mathematics and the history and geography of the Arab world. In Tunisia, for example, 'it proved impossible to graft a curriculum suited to the modern age on to the traditional framework of Zitouna', the indigenous university, which despite attempts at reform continued to train its students mainly for religious positions or posts in the Islamic courts. The initiative passed to a newly founded secondary school, Sadiqi College, with a western-style pedagogical system nationally adapted to stress Arabic and Islamic studies; and Sadiqi rather than Zitouna set the pattern for development of Tunisian education.[38]

In India similarly the traditional schools (*pathsala*) and colleges (*tols, vidyalayas, chatuspathis*) were at a low ebb when British education on British lines made a fresh start in the nineteenth century. The result, as mentioned above, was that the intellectual and administrative elite adopted English as their mother-tongue, could hardly read or write any Indian language, and were thus cut off from the great mass of the people. Uneasiness about this led to movements of thought, religion and education seeking to reconcile and combine Indian and western traditions, and the foundation of experimental schools and colleges aiming to balance the two cultures. At the time of independence, then, Humayun Kabir wrote of three systems of education in India, and of 'incompatible beliefs and ideas' among, for example, Indian scientists, abreast of current scientific thought, yet also 'immersed emotionally in customs which defy all reason'.[39]

The conventional wisdom justifying the massive expansion of school systems has been expressed in phrases like 'investment in human capital'. Newly independent countries needed secondary-educated people in technical and administrative posts in their expanding economies, and to replace expatriates, while university graduates were likewise needed at higher levels. Universal adult literacy and primary schooling for all children could hardly fail to open doors of opportunity, and especially if accompanied by fair, objective selection for secondary and higher schooling would promote social mobility. Such developments must surely enhance the productivity of labour and contribute to economic development, though that was not necessarily the only reason for pursuing them, and they were fully justified as ends in themselves.

Against this has been set the 'structuralist' view that school systems conserve and perpetuate the existing social structure, especially its disparities of wealth and power. The authority structure of the wider society is mirrored in that of the classroom. So, far from liberating human potential, much of what goes on there stultifies it. Prospective failures are reconciled in advance to their future position as second-class citizens. In fair, objective assessments the children of the well-to-do always tend to achieve high scores because of the advantages they enjoy at home, both of better food and of greater mental stimulation. Such tests do nothing to promote social mobility; they only legitimate afresh in each generation the position of a hereditary elite of privileged families.

Up to a point, the conventional wisdom has been vindicated. Certainly, by and large, countries with higher school enrolment rates have higher per capita GNP. Like all correlations, though, that tells us nothing about cause and effect; perhaps schooling has contributed to economic growth, but it may just as well be that countries with greater resources have devoted more of them to schooling, viewing the latter as an end in itself according to the fall-back position of the conventional wisdom. Then there is the impressive evidence of Inkeles and Smith, detailed in chapter 11, that of all the agents of individual modernization schooling is the most effective. Not the most cost-effective; that is work in a factory, or some other modern organization. Schooling costs, but a year at school has more effect in modernizing individuals' attitudes than a year in a factory.

The World Fertility Survey found that women with more schooling were more likely to know about birth control and to be using contraceptives; they had fewer children, in some countries far fewer; and more of their children survived.[40] A study in Cali, Colombia, concluded that 'simply teaching Third World mothers to read' held out the best prospect of improving their children's nutritional well-being.[41] In Nigeria it was found that though there was widespread malnutrition in Lagos, particularly among the children of illiterate mothers, there was none among the children of mothers with some formal schooling, even though their incomes were low.[42]

If schooling really does constitute an investment in human capital, then at least in principle a rate of return on that investment can be calculated. People who have had more schooling are generally found as adults to be receiving higher incomes. Relating individuals' net incomes to how much their schooling cost them or their parents gives a private rate of return. To calculate a public or social rate of return, the individual's gross income is seen as a contribution to the gross national product, while account is taken also of the cost to public funds of his or her schooling. The findings of a number of such studies in the 1960s were summarized by John Simmons. Private returns were consistently higher than social returns because schooling is everywhere subsidized from public funds. Returns to secondary and higher education were about equal to each other and to the returns to investment in other sectors; while by far the highest returns were to primary schooling.[43]

In 1982 the World Bank reported that besides lowering birth-rates the spread of basic education tended to increase economic productivity, particularly in agriculture. It had played an important part in the diffusion of high-yielding crops, which depended greatly on farmers' literacy, while schooling beyond a certain threshold of about six years had been shown to enhance their general adaptability to changing circumstances. The rate of return on primary schooling, solely in terms of its contribution to farmers' efficiency, was between 7 and 11 per cent in South Korea, between 14 and 25 per cent in Thailand, and between 25 and 40 per cent in Malaysia.[44]

However, the survey evidence of a positive relation between schooling and agricultural productivity was described as confused and contradictory by Udo Bude of the German Foundation for International Development. Bude cited one Third-World-wide review finding that agricultural productivity increased by an average of 6.9 per cent with each year of schooling after the formal minimum of four to six years; but other studies had found nil or negative effects, particularly in Africa, among small farmers, and among those with less than minimum primary schooling.[45]

Both the UNDP and the World Bank have shown how steeply the cost per student rises at primary, secondary, and higher levels in developing countries. For example, in the early 1980s in industrial countries taken as a whole, the cost per pupil in primary school was 22 per cent of the per capita GNP, while that of a student in higher education was 0.49 (49 per cent). In developing countries taken as a whole the cost per primary pupil was lower, 15 per cent of per capita GNP, but the cost per student in higher education was 3.7 times per capita GNP. In 1990 in the least developed countries the cost per student was 5.6 times per capita GNP; in sub-Saharan Africa, 8.2 times; and in some individual countries higher still.[46] No wonder the UNDP in 1990 recommended a policy shift from subsidizing higher education to subsidizing primary and secondary schooling.[47]

But there are difficult dilemmas here. It is generally taken for granted that to be a viable nation-state in the modern world every country has to have a national elite – physicians, engineers, bankers, diplomats and other senior civil servants, industrial managers, and the like – able to cope with the modern world and communicate on equal terms with their counterparts elsewhere. So there have to be secondary schools, colleges, and at least one national university to train them. That poses the difficult question of how to select from among primary leavers the fortunate few to go on to secondary school, and correspondingly from secondary to higher education, who will have a chance of entering the elite. If it is the case that many 'Third World' countries have over-invested in secondary and higher education, to the detriment of primary schooling, the result can only be unemployment among secondary leavers and graduates. But if insufficient resources are put into secondary schools and colleges, and entry to them is unduly restricted, the result is likely to be a scarcity of skilled and qualified people.

Unemployment among school leavers was the starting-point for the sociologist R. P. Dore's diagnosis of 'the diploma disease'. It was far easier to expand the school system than to increase the number of modern-sector job opportunities.

For example, in Sri Lanka at the time of his study, there were some 100,000 young people each year completing the ten years of schooling which not so long before would have assured them of 'a decent job', competing for some 35,000 such jobs. At most one in three might be rewarded. For the other two, what was to be lost by taking the O-level examination again, for a third or fourth time, to try and improve their grades, which were all they had to commend them to possible employers? Why not try even harder to press on to the next level?

At the same time, from an employer's point of view, if there were several applicants with O-levels and one with A-levels, a quick and easy answer to the problem of selection was to take the one with A-levels. So, very soon, A-levels would become the requirement for jobs for which O-levels had sufficed before, a process which Dore termed 'qualification inflation'. In such circumstances:

It is not surprising that examinations *dominate* the curriculum, that all learning is ritualised, that curiosity is devalued, that no one is allowed to stray from the syllabus, that no one inquires about the usefulness, the relevance, or the interestingness of what is learned.

Or as they say in Ghana, 'Chew, pour, pass, forget!'

At this point it can be argued in favour of examinations that at least they are, or can be, fair, certainly more so than other modes of selection such as parental influence, tribalism, bribery, corruption, or intimidation. The more restrictive the system, the greater the pressure on the selectors from candidates and their families, and the greater the likelihood of those malpractices. Dore indeed acknowledged as much, writing of 'the equity requirement' and 'just and acceptable ways of awarding the privileges and amenities that go with different jobs', but he also put forward other suggestions: earlier entry into careers, with more in-service training; and a greater reliance on aptitude tests which, unlike achievement tests, cannot (or cannot much) be crammed for.[48]

Doubt has likewise been cast on another postulate of the conventional wisdom, that schooling opens opportunities and promotes social mobility. As Simmons wrote, 'In most countries the poor quickly learn that schooling is an escape from poverty for only a few.' They are the first to drop out of school because they have to work, or are needed at home; they fall asleep in class because they are underfed, or tired after working at home and walking a long way to school; they do less well in English or French than children whose parents speak it at home. Many studies, including mine, have indicated the selectivity of secondary and higher education and the extent to which the offspring of well-to-do families are over-represented among students, and most of all among women students. Material affluence is not always the point; in East Africa I wrote of education-minded families, in many cases the descendants of the first mission converts, while French sociologists have coined the phrase *familles educogènes*.

Two African case-studies: 1. Zambia

These problems were vividly illustrated by events in Zambia as described by Roy Clarke of the Department of Education, University of Zambia. For the first ten years of independence, 1964–74, the government were even more keen than most newly independent states to expand the school system. They were inspired alike by 'human capital' theory, by an urge to 'catch up', and by a zeal for equality of opportunity, an end to the privileges enjoyed by the white population under colonial rule.

By 1970, however, there were some misgivings about educated employment and 'qualification escalation' or 'diploma disease', and a lack of any obvious relation between expanding the school system and economic growth. Matters came to a head when Vice-President Kapwepwe argued in favour of indigenous languages in early education and against making English the sole medium of instruction throughout the school system. This set off a much wider debate about the whole subject of education and national development.

Between 1974 and 1976 a consultative paper was drawn up setting out draft proposals for educational reform. Four of the eight proposals had to do with a closer integration between school and work. All schools were to be viable economic enterprises, while all economic enterprises were to be obliged to promote workers' education. Pupils should rotate twice a year between school and community work, and the national curriculum was to be agriculture- and work-oriented. Certification was to be separated from selection, and an ideological component was to be introduced into the latter. Private schooling was to be abolished, along with parents' right to send children abroad for schooling. A subtle but vital distinction was drawn between equality of educational *opportunity* (for those able to pay) and equality of educational *provision* (for all children). And the vernacular languages were to be used as the medium of instruction for the first four years.

Exemplary provisions were made to publicize the proposals and prepare for the great national debate. The draft statement was widely disseminated in indigenous languages, serialized in newspapers, and discussed on radio and television and in meetings of the party (UNIP) at all levels. However, when it came to gauging the public response, representations were to be made mainly in writing, and about 1,500 such submissions were made, many by large groups of people. According to Clarke this method of conducting the debate strongly favoured 'the elite class', no doubt well-to-do, education-minded, articulate people adept at drafting written submissions and organizing support for them.

In the event, the proposals were overwhelmingly rejected. Without exception they would have struck at the privileges of the elite: their freedom to send their children to private schools, or abroad; equality of opportunity for those with parents able to pay, along with those from an educated home background at an advantage in selection tests; and an academic rather than a work-oriented syllabus; while English as the medium of instruction from the first favoured children from educated families where English was, or could be, spoken at home.[49]

2. Tanzania

In Tanzania great efforts were made to avoid elitism. According to Arthur Hazlewood, in 1980 in neighbouring Kenya the proportion of primary leaders entering secondary schools (Ominde's 'index of opportunity') was 40 per cent. In Tanzania it was 9 per cent, and would be only 4 per cent when that year's primary entry reached standard 7; and Hazlewood cited a UNESCO report that in relation to its population Tanzania had the smallest secondary school system in the world.

Tanzania had remained committed to manpower planning, a fashionable idea in the 1950s introduced under colonial rule shortly before independence. It accorded well with fears of over-production and educated unemployment in relation to the high cost per student of secondary and higher education; and it was believed that the country was too poor to do more than produce just enough secondary- and higher-educated people to fill the need for a competent elite.[50]

In his *Education for Self-Reliance*, one of the three pamphlets published in 1967 setting out his party's policies, President Nyerere postulated that Tanzania would 'continue to have a predominantly rural economy for a long time to come'. It followed that education should be agriculture- and work-oriented, and that 'every school should also be a farm' (very much like the proposals in Zambia, which may well have been influenced by Nyerere's ideas). Primary schooling should be 'a complete education in itself'; not a mere preparation for the competitive secondary selection examination, but a preparation for the life which most of the pupils would be leading. The only justification for secondary and higher education for a selected few was to prepare them for service to the many.[51]

However, there was some criticism of the farming practices taught in schools, which were said to take too little account of different local conditions. More generally, the whole trend of state policy was seen as creating a two-tier system, thwarting parents' ambitions for their children to get well-paid secure modern-sector jobs, and even suspiciously like 'holding Africans back', a crime of which colonial regimes had sometimes been accused. According to Joel Samoff, most people saw the central problem as, simply, too few schools. More and more parents somehow found the money to send their children to private secondary schools offering the same curriculum as for the children of the bureaucrats; and by 1986, more than half of Tanzania's secondary schools and pupils were private.[52]

Moreover, as Hazlewood pointed out, restricting so severely the entry into secondary and higher education created a scarcity of skilled and qualified people, a sellers' market for the fortunate few, 'giving rise to opposing claims of equity versus reward for education and skills'. Clearly this went against the grain of Tanzania's egalitarian incomes policy, which aimed at lessening differentials through fairly generous statutory minimum wages on the one hand and pay restraint coupled with state control of trade unions on the other, and left only 'equality by exhortation' as a last resort in the struggle against elitism.

'De-schooling society'

Schooling's shortcomings have led some to propose a drastic remedy: abolish it. 'De-schooling society' was advocated by Ivan Illich basically on the ground that compulsory schooling is an affront to individual liberty, and that it is wrong that one person's judgement should determine what another person should learn. The only learning that matters occurs when people want to learn and actively seek out knowledge. Illich envisioned education as a facilitative network in which those who wanted to learn would seek out a teacher or 'skill model', who might be paid either in cash or in vouchers of which each individual would have a life's supply. He was also concerned about the extent to which schooling perpetuates inequality, and the ways it indoctrinates people into the pernicious patterns of mass consumption that characterize modern industrial society.[53] Yet his proposed scheme seems itself to be paradoxically elitist, for it would surely be the bright, active, well-nourished children of education-minded families who would do well out of a system of market individualism in teaching and learning, and the poor who would be left behind. Dore concluded that 'Clearly, to deschool is to throw out the baby with the bathwater, for there genuinely *is* an educational baby worth preserving in the institution called school.'[54] As T. H. Marshall observed, the idea of citizenship in the modern world includes the right to partici- pate in the common cultural heritage; and the right of the adult citizen to have been educated necessarily entails the universal compulsory schooling of children.[55]

Communications

Modern means of communication are among the goods and services that are unequally distributed in the world. Mostly they represent cultural innovations, both technologically and in terms of organization. This applies both to the mass media, where the communication is so to speak 'vertical', downwards from the editorial office through the printing press or broadcasting station to the public; and to 'horizontal', person-to-person communication by letter or telephone. Where modern means are not readily available, people rely more on the primordial means of communication, word of mouth. From a rich-country point of view this tends to be regarded as slow, inaccurate, and unreliable, and mass oral communication to be dismissed as mere rumour; but it may continue to be an important means of disseminating information, however garbled, and setting the public mood.

To illustrate the disparities: according to UNDP, in 1990 in industrial countries there was more than one radio per person, a television and a telephone for every two people, and a copy of a daily newspaper shared by three. At the other extreme, in the least developed countries there was a radio for every ten people, a television for every 100, a copy of a daily newspaper for 180, and a telephone for every 330.[56] Needless to say, too, these amenities were not equally shared among the whole population. For radios there is some evidence that the north–south disparity, though wide, was narrowing somewhat. According to a BBC estimate, cited by R. L. Stevenson, between 1970 and 1980 the number of radio receivers in the 'Third World' more than doubled, from 100 million to 227 million, and increased from 15 to 19 per cent of the world total. But there were if anything fewer newspaper copies in relation to population.

Person-to-person

For 'horizontal', person-to-person communications the disparities were even wider. I have already noted the disparity in telephones, which according to UNDP widened greatly during the 1980s.[57] Obviously in countries where there are only 3 telephones to every 1000 people, they are likely to be found in the offices of government and commercial organizations, some shops, and the private homes of a very few wealthy and influential people, and they will be virtually confined to towns. For most people, including practically all country-dwellers, access to a telephone will be only at the end of a long queue in a post office, which may be many kilometres away. Similarly with letters: house-to-house postal delivery, taken for granted in rich countries, is practically unknown in many 'Third World' countries. Street names and house numbers are lacking in rural and many urban areas; letters are distributed no further than rented boxes in a post office, and in some cases even that only in the capital. As with telephones, PO boxes are utilized by businesses and official bodies, and a few private individuals. Most people have no means of receiving 'phone calls, and may receive letters only indirectly through a PO box-holder. In practice, for many people the only way kinsfolk living at a distance would hear about an event such as a death in the family would be if someone were to come and tell them.[58]

The mass media: newspapers

Newspapers are the oldest of the mass media, with a history going back for centuries in the metropolitan countries and almost as long in colonies, where papers such as the *Uganda Herald* and the *East African Standard* were printed in the languages of the white population and catered for their interests. In the latter-day 'Third World', newspapers have had some advantages for general development. The capital cost of a printing press can be quite modest, and the recurrent costs of production can largely be met by advertising. The reader incurs no capital cost, only the recurrent cost per copy, which, however, can be quite high relative to incomes in poor countries. Reading the newspaper requires literacy, of course, though this can be overcome and costs shared if one literate person reads the paper aloud to others. It can equally be argued that newspapers encourage literacy. Small newspapers, printed weekly if not daily in indigenous languages, can attract readers and local advertising in quite small language groups.

On the other hand, people who can read can generally understand a lingua franca or language of wider communication, and so become readers of a national newspaper. Such papers are at a financial advantage; they attract more advertising revenue from government departments, and for goods traded nationally, such as motor vehicles. They may be financed and equipped with foreign capital, and partly staffed by expatriates; and they are more likely to be able to afford worldwide news coverage from the international news-agencies. This means that apart from local news, which the paper can gather itself, most of the foreign news will tend to be about rich countries, above all the United States, rather than about other 'Third World' countries, even neighbouring ones.[59] Tendencies of this kind give rise to accusations of cultural imperialism. As noted in chapter 4, the activities of transnational corporations engaged in advertising and the mass media have been blamed for contributing to the decline of indigenous cultures and the spread of a homogenized, commercialized world culture.

Films

Films are generally regarded as a medium of entertainment rather than of information. However, there are 'demonstration effects' when cinema audiences are shown ways of life and exposed to value-assumptions other than their own, usually implied rather than expressed. Thus in Lerner's study, cited in chapter 6, it was in American films that the grocer of Balgat saw the well-stocked supermarket that for him symbolized modernity.

The capital costs and unit production costs of film-making are widely variable, but tend to be high where films are made in permanent studios by professionals, and to recoup those costs requires a large market. Thus notably among low-income countries India has a vigorous film industry (based in Bombay, nicknamed 'Bollywood') that smaller countries lack. As with newspapers, the consumer is involved in no capital cost, and the price of a cinema seat can be quite low, especially where as in India a warm climate permits open-air viewing much of the time. Language barriers can be surmounted to a limited extent by sub-titling, though that of course assumes an audience literate in one or another of the scripts in which the film may be sub-titled.

Radio

Radio broadcasting began in many Third World countries in the 1920s and 1930s, not long after the pioneering days in industrial countries, though in some not till after the Second World War; Tanganyika in 1951, for example. In countries that were not colonies at the time, such as Latin American countries, Thailand, and the Philippines, for the most part a commercial, private-enterprise model like that of the United States prevailed. Colonial governments tended to exercise more control, but their policies were not always very clear, and only minuscule resources were made available. In British colonies many expatriates listened to the BBC Empire (later the World) Service as best they could on short-wave transmissions giving poor reception, and some early initiatives on the part of colonial administrations took the form of re-broadcasting that service, by radio or wire, in whole or part, sometimes interspersed with locally produced news and entertainment programmes. Broadcasting for local people in local languages came later with the setting up of corporations modelled on the BBC, and staffed by seconded personnel or local people trained in Britain. However, by the 1950s there was some dawning awareness of radio's potential as a source of trustworthy news, for general development in fields such as health education and agricultural improvement, and for local cultural creativity. Colonial and independent governments alike sought through radio to spread the use of a language of wider communication, Portuguese in Brazil as much as French in North Africa. Mention should be made, too, of the radio stations set up by missionary bodies in Peru, for example, and the Radio Voice of the Gospel in Addis Ababa, which promoted literacy, health, new farming practices, and honest news as well as Christian evangelism.

Radio has many advantages and few disadvantages. The capital cost of a transmitter, roughly proportionate to its power, need not be great if only local coverage is required, while the cost of producing programmes can be very low indeed and there is ample scope for local talent. For the listener, there is the capital cost of a receiver, but that is relatively small. Cheap robust transistor radios, made in some 'Third World' countries, are everywhere among the target goods of young wage earners, while there are radios in village shops, and travellers by taxi are regaled with the output of a car radio at full volume. Radio receivers do not necessarily depend on mains electricity, though without it there was the recurrent cost of batteries before the development of 'clockwork radio'.[60] Radio broadcasting can be nation-wide in scale, but equally it can be local. Of all the media, then, it is the best adapted to the needs of small language groups, and the one that most decisively breaks through the literacy barrier. Its potential coverage is wide; and, as we are often reminded at times of crisis, radio communications are not liable to the hazards that beset surface transport, be they bad roads, floods, or riots.

Television

Television is the newest of the mass media, coming into general use only since about the 1950s. It is also by far the most costly. Katz and Wedell, in their study of broadcasting in the 'Third World', noted that in several countries it seemed to have been introduced as a matter of national prestige for curious, haphazard, and even quite frivolous reasons.[61] In Senegal, for example, after an educational experiment sponsored by UNESCO had been closed down, it was revived in 1972 on the French government's initiative for live coverage of the Munich Olympics. In Iran the special occasion that prompted the start of a television service was the coronation of the Shah; in Uganda, the Kampala meeting of the Organization for African Unity. Virtually all the equipment was made in a few industrial countries. The capital costs of transmitters and studios were of the order of thirty times as high as for radio, and so were the unit costs of making programmes, rendering it prohibitively expensive for television organizations to make much of their own output. They could hope to fill even a minimal five or six hours' broadcasting a day only by hiring imported programmes, chiefly from the United States, where the television companies made them available at very low 'country prices'. Furthermore, despite heavy reliance on imported programmes, television has tended to impoverish previously established radio services by draining them of resources of money and professional staff.

Television receivers too are expensive, costing around ten times as much as radios, and in poor countries more than an average household's annual income. They are less robust, especially in tropical countries, where repair facilities are not widely available. Battery operation is less satisfactory, and there is a greater reliance on mains electricity. The very high and ultra-high frequencies required for television broadcasts confine them effectively to visual range of the transmitter, so that unless a country is covered by a network of repeater stations – beyond the means of most 'Third World' countries – for technical and economic reasons alike the coverage of television is limited to the immediate vicinity of big cities. There it is mainly a pastime for the well-to-do, who join their counterparts all over the world in relaxing in front of the small screen to watch the same soap-opera series. The adaptability of the medium to different local languages, and its potential for encouraging local cultural creativity, have hitherto proved limited to say the least.

The politics of the mass media

In the 1950s there were high hopes that the mass media of communication could make a big contribution to development. As will be recalled from chapter 6, Daniel Lerner saw them as prime movers in modernization. His ideas were shared by many of his fellow social scientists in the United States, notably Wilbur Schramm; they greatly influenced the policies of UNESCO, and spread to the elites in Third World countries.[62] In their study of 11 low- and middle-income countries in the 1970s, Katz and Wedell found that policy-makers had consistently expected the media to contribute positively to national integration, to social and economic development, and to indigenous cultural creativity. However, those three goals had not proved readily compatible, and pointed in different directions to different policies. National unity involved the media under government control in focussing attention on the national leader, fostering national sentiment, creating a national mythology, and spreading the national language. For broadcasting it implied extending the coverage of a single national channel. Social and economic development, however, were better promoted by a quite different approach. Specialized programmes were needed to reach particular sorts of people, such as farmers and (for health education and family planning) housewives. To be effective, such programmes had to be in vernacular languages, so that the recognition of diverse ethnic groups was necessary; and their style had to be local, familiar, personal, and practical. That pointed rather to a decentralized regional organization of local radio stations. Cultural authenticity too involved encouraging vernacular languages and recognizing ethnic differences, while it also brought into sharp prominence by contrast the worldwide cultural uniformity of television programmes imported from France, Britain, and, above all, the United States.

During the 1970s, according to Robert L. Stevenson, UNESCO was the forum of a debate in which the modernization school of thought was challenged by radical underdevelopment ideas. The mass media, far from contributing to development, were seen as agents of cultural and information imperialism in the US-dominated world capitalist system, for which the doctrine of the free flow of information was merely a cover. Demands were made for a new world economic order, and with it a new world information order (NWIO). This included the concept of development news: news that promoted development, such as literacy, hygiene, family planning, and farming practices; and news that reflected development, for instance by reporting rising literacy, the opening of a factory or a school, just the kind of thing the western media ignored in favour of an earthquake or a military *coup*.

The NWIO doctrine gave a new justification for the already widespread emphasis on 'protocol news' in the state-controlled media of many 'Third World' countries. Day after day their lead story was about the doings of the head of state: ribbon cutting, cornerstone laying, airport welcomings. Everything was blandly positive, giving no hint of dissension, incompetence, or malpractice in high places. Nation-building and political development depended on presenting the image of the head of state as a wise, benign national leader.

A related NWIO demand was for a 'national right to communicate'. This went beyond a right to reply to unfavourable reports in foreign media, and amounted to state control of news coming in to a country from outside, and of reports sent abroad, so as to ensure that a favourable view was always presented of the country concerned and its development achievements.

Within UNESCO the NWIO proposals brought about an unaccustomed and uneasy alliance between western governments and their traditional adversaries western journalists. On the other side, some 'Third World' journalists privately expressed their awe of their western counterparts' freedom and independence, and their longing to be 'watchdogs, not cheer-leaders' of their political masters. Most of the debate, according to

Stevenson, was really about whether the western ideal of journalism, 'independent of government, aloof and critical', was applicable to and could be practised in developing countries. From a western point of view, NWIO seemed to entail blatant political control of the news. In the face of what seemed an irreconcilable difference of view, the United States withdrew from UNESCO in 1984, followed by Britain and Singapore.[63]

The issue of freedom is central. Even in countries where freedom of the press is written into the constitution and there is no overt censorship, informal constraints may be exerted by diverse means. Where the economy is largely controlled by the state or public corporations, an actual or threatened withdrawal of government advertising can be enough to ruin a newspaper. It has been argued, indeed, that a substantial private sector is a necessary condition for a genuinely free press for that reason alone. Withdrawal of advertising, however, is the mildest of the sanctions; more drastic ones are the destruction of a paper's premises and presses by the youth wing of the government party (a polite name for organized thugs), and the harassment, intimidation, and in the last resort the imprisonment, of its editor. In the face of such overt or covert threats, local papers inclined to criticize the government often succumb altogether; while foreign-owned national dailies, the subsidiaries of big international newspaper chains, are likely to be anxious to retain their foothold in the country, avoid giving offence, and mute their political comments accordingly.

Similarly, even in former British colonies where broadcasting was originally entrusted to an autonomous public corporation modelled on the BBC, it did not long stay that way, and everywhere governments have taken over. Throughout the 'Third World', indeed, armed guards and security checks around broadcasting studios and transmitter stations are an ever-present reminder of state control. Broadcasters have become civil servants in fact if not in name, and their accountability and loyalty lie to a government minister, in many countries the president him- or herself. They have experienced severe tensions between their professional norms as communicators and the political requirements to which they have been subject, expected as they have been to create new national myths, adjust their news values to what the government wants the people to hear, and project the personalities of national leaders. The management of broadcasting, too, has often been entrusted to people more remarkable for their political loyalty than for their managerial competence. Subordinates have become reluctant to contribute their ideas for fear of offending superiors, and at the very least being passed over for promotion. Muddle and waste have supervened as efficiency has declined.

However, according to Katz and Wedell, there has been a genuine effort in countries such as Peru and Algeria to counter cultural imperialism and make more of their own broadcasting programmes. In some countries, too, quietly successful work has been done especially through radio to promote aspects of development such as better farming. Radio has also proved effective for a once-for-all campaign, such as the change from left-hand to right-hand driving in Sierra Leone in 1971; so aware did the radio campaign make people that there was not a single road accident at that time or for a month afterwards.[64] More generally, Stevenson cited a number of studies indicating high benefit/cost ratios for investment in telecommunications.[65]

But whether the media's development potential is realized in 'Third World' countries, or whether governments regard the state-controlled media merely as useful channels for innocuous entertainment together with such information as they wish the people to hear, the media always come into prominence at a time of crisis. Then the broadcasting station becomes an all-important strategic resource whose seizure is vital to the success of a *coup*, and the announcement over the state radio and television that a change of government has taken place very largely constitutes the change of government itself.

Suggestions for further reading

W. H. Whiteley (ed.), *Language Use and Social Change* (Oxford, Oxford University Press for International African Institute, 1971)

Robin Clarke, *Science and Technology in World Development* (Oxford, Oxford University Press for UNESCO, 1985)

J. Lowe, M. Grant and T. D. Williams (eds.), *Education and Nation-Building in the Third World* (Edinburgh, Scottish Academic Press, 1971)

Ingemar Fagerlind and Lawrence J. Saha, *Education and National Development: A Comparative Perspective*, 2nd edn (Oxford, Pergamon, 1989)

John Simmons (ed.), *The Education Dilemma: Policy Issues for Developing Countries in the 1980s* (Oxford, Pergamon, 1980)

R. P. Dore, *The Diploma Disease* (London, Allen & Unwin, 1976)

John Oxenham (ed.), *Education versus Qualifications* (London, Allen & Unwin, 1984)

Roger M. Garrett (ed.), *Education and Development* (London, Croom Helm, 1983)

Elihu Katz and E. George Wedell, *Broadcasting in the Third World: Promise and Performance* (Cambridge, Mass., Harvard University Press, 1977; London, Macmillan, 1978)

Robert L. Stevenson, *Communication, Development, and the Third World* (New York, Longman/University Press of America, 1988)

10

Religion and development

Some religious movements have been seen as inspiring their followers with qualities, such as honesty, thrift, and hard work, which have enabled them not only to make a better life for themselves and their families, often after surmounting initial adversities, but also to promote general economic development. These movements have been identified ⚹ accordingly as causal agents in the development process. Some other movements have arisen in reaction to or against social and economic changes, usually for the worse, to which particular groups have been subjected as victims rather than initiators. Reaction against modern developments is a theme these movements have in common with fundamentalism, though the latter has also some unique features, as will appear.

Religion and economic enterprise

Max Weber's monumental study linking the Protestant ethic with the spirit of capitalism, to which I alluded in chapter 1, is so well known as to need no recapitulation here.[1] In support of his thesis, Weber assiduously searched the literature then available in European languages about the religions of ancient Judaism and of the East for parallels with the Protestant ethic, only to conclude that European Puritanism was unique. Thus in China, despite the high state of the arts and crafts and the great urban tradition, the currency was frequently mismanaged, the legal and customary institutions favouring business organization were lacking, and there was no adequate system of book-keeping such as would spur Chinese businessmen to allow adequately for the depreciation and replacement of their physical capital. Moreover, though there was much rationality in Chinese thought, both orthodox Confucianism and Taoism and the heterodoxies such as Buddhism tolerated magic.[2]

Turning to India, Weber analysed both the character of Hindu thought and society, especially the caste system, and the movements of protest against orthodox Brahministical Hinduism, especially Buddhism. The effects of the caste system on economic life he regarded as essentially negative. It was not so much that particular beliefs or ritual prescriptions in themselves placed insuperable obstacles in the way of economic development, for example by making it difficult for men of different castes to work together in the same factory. Obstacles like that could have been circumvented if the will had been there, just as the ban on usury was in the early development of European capitalism. 'The core of the obstruction was rather imbedded in the "spirit" of the whole system',[3] he wrote, which makes it extremely unlikely that an economic and technical revolution such as industrial capitalism could have originated from within Indian society; while if it were introduced from outside, as under British rule, then its development would be correspondingly hampered.

Although he did not altogether neglect the rise of science, Weber may not have made it sufficiently integral to his analysis. The authority of the church over men's minds, supremely symbolized in the treatment of Galileo, was broken by the Protestant reformation, and its collapse left in the end no defence for dogma against rational scientific inquiry. Not that the Protestant sects themselves espoused a scientific view of the universe and human life; on the contrary, they were in many cases as dogmatic and obscurantist as the parent church itself, as was testified in another age by the agonized mental struggles of Edmund Gosse.[3] But when sceptical rebellious scientists were struggling against Protestant dogmatism, they could in the last resort advance the unanswerable argument of freedom of conscience. The Protestant reformation of the sixteenth and seventeenth centuries can thus be seen as clearing away important obstacles to the rise of science in the seventeenth century, and hence the industrial revolution in the eighteenth.

Weber's thesis inspired continuing controversy from its first publication.[5] Among its critics was the historian Hugh Trevor-Roper, who maintained that the rise of capitalism did not depend on the advent of the Protestant ethic; on the contrary, large-scale industrial capitalism existed in the age of the Fugger, the early sixteenth century, before the Reformation. By the seventeenth century, the leading industrial and financial elite of Europe, who armed and financed Protestant and Catholic monarchs alike, were Flemings. They were also Calvinists of a sort, though nothing like as frugal as Weber had suggested; and other Calvinist societies such as Scotland did not produce comparable entrepreneurs. However, the Flemings experienced religious persecution under the Counter-Reformation in the Netherlands, then under Spanish rule, and migrated with their skills and their workmen to Protestant countries or to less intolerant Catholic kingdoms notably France; and Trevor-Roper suggested that the most important thing about them was not that they were Calvinists but that they were migrants. So the Counter-Reformation resulted in a Flemish diaspora in which they became the industrial elite of Europe, with the Jews in second place.[6] Trevor-Roper identified migrant status rather than doctrinal attachment as the critical factor in the making of an enterprising minority; the point is of wider application, and I return to it below.

Another criticism of Weber's thesis, this time in its application to India, was that of the theologian Trevor Ling. The notably enterprising character of Indians abroad in countries such as Burma and Malaya should alone cast doubt on it, though to be fair to Weber those develop-ments were only just about to manifest themselves at the time when he was recording his negative conclusion. However, at the very time in 1905–11 when Weber was collecting his material and writing his study, which was published in 1912, events were taking place in India which were to falsify it decisively, for 1911 was the very year in which the Tata Iron & Steel Company began production. The ore came from Bihar under an agreement between the Maharaja and Dorabji Tata; while the entire capital was eagerly subscribed by Indian investors, largely in response to the Swadeshi movement which was urging Indians to boycott British goods and support Indian-owned productive enterprises.[7]

Many recent studies have been addressed to the search for latter-day functional equivalents of the Protestant ethic, and contrariwise for religious beliefs and practices regarding economic development. As an example we may take a controversy about the disadvantaged position of Malays compared with Chinese and Indians in Malaya in the 1960s. Initiating the controversy, Parkinson pointed to the Malays' general resistance to change, exemplified in their refusal to follow the govern-ment's urgings to grow a second rice crop each year, use wet rice fields instead of dry upland for their rice seed-beds, and adopt other recom-mended improvements. Parkinson showed that these resistances were at least partly rational, but he thought religious and magical beliefs were also relevant, for example in waiting for a propitious day before trans-planting; and 'the Islamic belief that all things are emanations from God . . . tends to make them fatalistic in their approach to life'.[8] Wilder disagreed with Parkinson's diagnosis of 'Islamic fatalism', saying that it presents a caricature of the Malay as 'a blind, irrational slave of history and custom'. Indeed, in one respect Islam could be said to exercise a favourable influence on economic development, namely the *haj*. Saving the money to pay the fare to Mecca gave Muslims a goal to which they directed their lives and built up patterns of saving and rational forms of economic organization.[9] Parkinson, however, insisted that this was not a productive use of savings. Money being saved for the *haj* remained largely idle, and was barren and unproductive from the point of view of economic development.[10]

Another case in point was Mya Maung's analysis of state socialism in Burma (later Myanmar), first enunciated in 1947 and embodied in the national plan in 1958. The word *Pyidawtha* used for this programme carried Utopian overtones suggesting a synthesis of tradition with modernity, but Mya Maung contended that socialist planning had failed to change the cultural patterns of traditional Burmese life, especially Buddhism. Efforts to present *Pyidawtha* as a blend of old and new, ranging from the glorification of a golden past to exhortations to eat unpolished rice, merely concealed their incompatibility. So did the presentation of socialist ideas in words taken from the vocabulary of Burmese Buddhist thought, especially the use of the Buddhist term *anate-sa*, impermanency, for dialectical materialism. Burmese were unconvinced by the socialist postulate of an identity of interests between the individual and society, represented by the democratic socialist state. Indeed, state action had if anything deepened their traditional view of government as an enemy to be wooed and feared. Similarly, collective effort in a classless society was at odds with the central Buddhist doctrine of Karma or individual reincarnation. As for business enterprise, that too was distasteful according to traditional Burmese values.[11]

However, the sociologist Melford Spiro pointed out that even within Theravada Buddhism there were at least three different strands. True, some devotees were concerned wholly or mainly with attaining release, *nirvana* (*nibbana*), from the unending round of death and rebirth, causation and frustration; and this led them to renounce worldly activity. At the other extreme, many were concerned with such worldly matters as health and welfare, protection from demons, and the prevention of droughts. But for most practising Buddhists the aim was not so much release from 'the Wheel', more with improving one's position in the next incarnation (*karma*) through acquiring merit in the present. To some extent this could be done through morality, but the royal road was through giving (*dana*), and this afforded a strong incentive to worldly economic success. Spiro reported that many Burmans kept merit account books and the quest for wealth provided a powerful motivation for work. But *dana* was confined to religious giving, and was not a motive for what we should understand as 'charity' like giving money to hospitals. The most spectacular forms of *dana* consisted of building pagodas and endowing monasteries, which earned men great social prestige – expressed in the formal title of 'pagoda builder' or 'monastery builder' prefixed to their names for life, like the Muslim *Haji* – as well as the assurance of bliss in a future existence. Social prestige as well as salvation was also to be gained from lavish expenditure on one's son's ritual initiation, and another meritorious form of *dana* sanctioned by publicity was the collective offering of new robes and other gifts to monks and on monks' funerals. Spiro concluded that in a typical Burmese village something like 25 to 30 per cent of the net disposable cash income was spent on *dana* and related activities. As in the case of saving for the *haj*, such facts may be interpreted from two different points of view. On the one hand, *dana* affords a motive for work, saving, and the systematic management of resources; on the other, the methodically accumulated savings are neither invested, as Weber put it, for 'forever renewed profit by means of continuous, rational, capitalistic enterprise', nor are they well expended for social welfare. Some Burmese people thought so, too, though only a minority. A village headman told Spiro that the local community spent ten per cent of their income on provisioning monks, far less than one per cent on education. ' "If we spent, say, nine per cent on monks and one per cent on education, surely that would not harm Buddhism, and how much better off our children would be !" '[12]

Another study directly inspired by Weber's analysis was that by Bocock of the Ismailis in Tanzania.[13] The Asian population of East Africa as a whole played a notable part in its economic development, pioneering trade and small-scale manufacturing industry and dominating the world of finance and the professions, and among this population two communities rivalled each other for leadership – the Shia Ismailia Khoja and the Patidars. The Ismailis were a Muslim group owing spiritual allegiance to the Aga Khan whom they regarded as the extant Imam, while the Patidars were a Hindu community of the general character of a caste. H. S. Morris, who also studied these groups, singled out the Ismailis as the pace-making group.[14]

An important factor in the Ismailis' success was the role and personality of the redoubtable Aga Khan III, Sir Sultan Muhammad Shah, 1877–1960. Believed as he was to be the known, revealed Imam, all his words were regarded as divinely inspired, and he used his power of *ex cathedra* utterance to urge his followers to modernize their attitudes and practices. In the sphere of social welfare, for example, he opposed infant marriage and advocated modern methods of child care; he stimulated the Ismaili communities to efforts of communal self-help in health and education; and he mobilized their lavish gifts to his person to set up trust funds for investment in the enterprises of Ismaili businessmen. To all appearances the Ismailis in East Africa played the same kind of initiatory role in economic development as the Puritans in Europe, and did so in much the same kind of way and by the same kind of means – hard work, frugality, trustworthiness, and consistently shrewd reinvestment of profits. To one who lived in East Africa the comparison with the Protestant ethic has the air of a commonplace.

In a point-by-point comparison of the Ismaili faith with Calvinism, however, Bocock noted the differences as well as the similarities. Where Calvinism was positively individualist, Ismailism relied more on community self-help. On its own Bocock doubted if it could have produced the positive push towards individualism; it was only in contact with British capitalism that the Ismailis were able to adopt some rational capitalist methods, especially when urged to do so by their divinely inspired leader. There was a superficial similarity in the doctrines of predestination of both Calvinism and Islam, but the latter did not put its adherent under the same terrible strain as the former to prove that he was among the elect by his diligence in everyday work. Islam was much more relaxed, and taught that by giving alms, morality, and prayer he could attain heaven. 'Unlike the puritanical Calvinist, the Muslim, including the Ismailis, can enjoy using and consuming his wealth in this life, within reasonable limits.' Both religions were notably congregational in their forms of organization, and the local community of Ismailis who met daily in Jamat Khan, the Ismaili mosque, constituted also a community exercising moral control over its members and providing them – when in good standing – with mutual aid and credit networks. Islam generally, including Ismailism, had more room for mysticism than did Calvinism. Both encouraged education, but Islam was much more tolerant of magic and did not condemn its use by the faithful in allaying anxieties over things like illness, family and personal problems, and travel.

The development economists Cynthia Taft Morris and Irma Adelman widened the scope of the debate in their study of 55 non-communist developing countries. These were classified according to the extent to which their predominant religions emphasized the individual's responsibility and ability to influence the environment. Their nine categories extended with increasing fatalism from A-plus to D, through B, Islamic societies, and C, Buddhist and Hindu societies. A close association was found between religious configurations favourable to individualism on the one hand and industrial and urban development on the other. Much weaker was the relation between the religious factor and the westernization of political institutions. However, like all correlations this does not establish a causal relationship one way or the other. As the authors pointed out, both religious configurations and levels of socio-economic development in whole regions of several adjoining countries had been affected by common historical influences over the centuries. Examples were Catholicism in Latin America, Islam and European economic expansion in the Middle East, and the impact of European imperial expansion on African tribal societies. It may also be remarked that taking the country and its predominant religious tradition as the unit of analysis may obscure religious differences within countries, especially those of enterprising non-conformist minorities.[15]

Clearly Weber's thesis is not lightly to be dismissed; as Trevor-Roper said, it has a 'solid, if elusive, core of truth', though his reliance on so large an abstraction as 'the spirit of capitalism' makes his analysis difficult either to confirm or to refute by reference to newly discovered facts. Moreover, Weber's central preoccupation was with the original emergence of industrial capitalism, a unique historical phenomenon after which nothing could ever be the same again. As Bendix emphasized, once industrialization had occurred anywhere, that alone altered the environment of all other countries. Subsequent industrialization was either derivative, or competitive, or both; and this too makes it difficult to test Weber's ideas by reference to events elsewhere in the world after the industrial revolution in Europe.

In these circumstances there is a decided tendency to weakness in the explanations that are advanced both of economic backwardness and of economic initiative in terms of the religious and general cultural values of the group concerned. This is seen most clearly in the inconsistency between explanations of retardation in terms of the culture of a people who, when they appear outside their own country as a minority in another, abruptly become associated with innovative energy and initiative. Sometimes the contortions of the analysis in these cases can only be described as comic. For example, it was possible to explain the economic backwardness of China before the communist triumph of 1964 in terms of passivity, the Confucian ideal of the cultivated man of the world, lavish expenditure on funerals and weddings, non-rational magical beliefs, and the like; and all this seemed very plausible when applied to China itself. Yet when Chinese emigrated to Indonesia, Malaya, Singapore, Thailand, or even to Hong Kong they suddenly became the energetic innovators whose industry and enterprise stimulated the economy of the region into new life; and it does not seem to have been the case that the religious beliefs and ritual customs of the overseas Chinese were in any important respect different from those of the homeland. In exactly the same way, the economic backwardness of India has been attributed to the other-worldly mysticism of the Hindu faith, the ban on cow-slaughter, the caste system, and similar cultural factors. Yet Indians overseas have been the dynamic source of economic development, initiating industries, pioneering trade, and through kinship and credit networks maintaining financial and trading links with the world outside the countries to which they migrated – East Africa, Burma, Malaya and elsewhere. And whatever may be said about 'Islamic fatalism' as an obstacle to development among the indigenous Malays, it clearly did not constitute the slightest obstacle to the spectacular success of immigrant Muslim groups like the Ismailis in East Africa.

Clearly we must look elsewhere for explanations of the innovating energy frequently shown by migrant minorities. Here it is possible to do no more than suggest hypotheses.

First, there may be a process of selection of personality types. Migrants may possibly be the more enterprising people – indeed, the ones who show their enterprise by migrating.

Secondly, there may be demographic effects. Migrants tend to be young men, followed by young women. Migrant communities are characteristically short of older people and of teenage children, being made up of young parents and their young children. There are usually more men than women. This means that the ratio of economically active people in the community is higher than would be the case in a 'normal', settled group; or, looking at it the other way, the proportion of dependants is lower.

Thirdly, migrants may be free from some at least of the customary constraints on enterprise and initiative that are effective in the home society and culture. For example, it may be that one factor in the prosperity of the Chinese overseas in the nineteenth century was that they had not got the mandarinate on their backs. Morris reported that among Indians in Uganda it was impossible to observe the minutiae of the caste system, however committed they were to its general principles. Rules of exogamy were strictly observed – were insisted on, indeed, with special emphasis as if to demonstrate a general adherence to the Hindu way of life; but it would have been simply unrealistic to observe prohibitions such as those which would have prevented neighbouring families in a remote trading centre in Africa from accepting goods and water from each other. Morris wrote accordingly of 'the secular outlook of most of the immigrants', and quoted one of his informants as saying: 'The gods are unwilling to cross the sea. Most of them, I think, stayed in India. The women brought over a few that are important to them; but for me, it will be time to pray to God when I go back to India.'[16]

Fourthly, immigrant groups are in many cases excluded from control of the traditionally legitimate resources that go with high social prestige. These include especially land and political power. The same hypothesis, indeed, may be extended also to non-immigrant minorities like the original Calvinist and Puritan sects in England and Germany. If at the same time such groups are moved to emulation of the rich and powerful (or in the jargon of sociology if they exhibit reference-group behaviour) then success in business may be the only way in which they can rise in the world. This hypothesis would appear to fit cases like the Chinese overseas especially in colonial times, and the East African Asian groups like the Ismailis both under colonial rule, when they were largely excluded by Europeans from land and power, and after independence when it was Africans who seized both. Clearly a hypothesis of this kind assumes the general framework of a plural society.

Hypotheses such as these turn more on considerations of minority status and the effects of migration than on the specific features of the culture of the group in question; and it may be that the qualities of method, industry, thrift, and asceticism which enable such a group to survive and prosper are developed in response to a situation rather than brought in with their cultural baggage.

Religious movements as effects of profound social disturbance

In many societies and at different periods where there has been a profound disturbance of established forms of social relations, leading to large numbers of people being deprived of access to resources upon which they had been accustomed to rely, such a disturbance has been followed by the rise of religious movements of a characteristic type. These movements have been variously called messianic, millenarian, nativistic, and prophetic. The term *messianic* implies a comparison with ancient Hebrew beliefs in a saviour who should come to deliver his people. *Millenarian* and the equivalent *chiliastic* refer strictly to the doctrine among some Christian sects that Christ will return and reign in bodily presence for a thousand years; in sociological usage the same terms have been given a slightly extended meaning to cover beliefs in an impending overthrow of the present order of society by supernatural means and the coming of a new order in which 'the last shall be first and the first, last'. *Nativistic* in the colonial context referred to a movement reasserting the values and practices of the native culture as against white administration and Christian missions. *Prophetic* relates to the fact that such movements commonly have leaders who prophesy the new order and urge their followers to adopt the appropriate moral and ritual usages to prepare for it.

Hundreds of such movements are known, and they have occurred from ancient times to the present. In his historical survey Norman Cohn recalled the prophetic movements among the Jews of the ancient world, notably including the 'stream of militant apocalyptic' and the promise of a saviour, the Messiah, which marked the period from 63 BC to AD 72. In medieval Europe, Cohn traced the rise and fall of sects like the Joachimites in the twelfth century who protested against the wealth and worldliness of the church and expected the millennium in 1260, when an 'angelic pope' was to convert the world to voluntary poverty. Although there were generally few links between the fanatical few inspired by millenarian visions and the broad masses of people whose economic interests were threatened, occasionally under the stress of events the two types of movement might come together. Examples are the part played by John Ball in the English peasants' revolt in 1381, and the Taborites during the Hussite revolt in Bohemia in 1419–21.[17]

Among the factors that Cohn identified as favouring millenarian movements, singly or together, were catastrophe or the fear of it – famine, plague, massacre – along with 'the supposed defection of the authority traditionally responsible for regulating the relations between society and the powers governing the cosmos'. Another contributory factor was often 'emotional frustration in women of means and leisure but without social function or prestige'. Such movements occurred where the traditional religion included the promise of future bliss for the faithful (and not where that was absent, as in ancient Greece). That promise could be renewed by a prophet holding out hope of collective salvation, immediate and total, from frustration, anxiety, and humiliation that could not be assuaged, either by taking thought or by any institutionalized routine, and were widely enough shared to result in a collective emotional agitation.[18]

Such conditions have clearly been brought about in recent history by European expansion, colonial rule, and the new order of society related to industrial development. There is a considerable literature on the religious movements that have arisen in response to those upheavals, and most of all on anti-European and anti-colonial movements. It is salutary therefore to be reminded by Cohn that movements of this general nature are confined neither to recent history nor to those particular causes.

A pioneer work in this field was the summary and analysis by Peter Worsley of the cargo cults of Melanesia. An early cult of this type was the Tuka movement which arose in Fiji in the 1870s and 1880s, led by a man named Ndugumoi who organized his followers in a quasi-military fashion under 'sergeants' and 'scribes' with high officers called 'destroying angels'. It was mystically revealed to Ndugumoi that the ancestors were shortly to return to Fiji, the shops would be jammed with calico, tinned salmon, and other goods for the faithful, but unbelievers would die or become the slaves and servants of believers. The whites had deliberately deceived them. The bible was really written about the divine Twins of local legend, but the whites had substituted the names Jehovah and Jesus for the names of the Twins. The false Europeans were pretending to be surveying the reef with their instruments, but really they were scanning the horizon for the vessels in which the Twins were returning with the ancestors.

The Tuka cult was followed by a large number of similar movements all over the area of New Guinea and the islands to the east, in which its main themes were taken up repeatedly – the belief in an imminent millennium in which ships would bring ample supplies of the new goods for the benefit of the local people; the further assertion that the missionaries were conniving in the injustice by means of a deceit in which they were deliberately withholding part of the bible; the organization of the faithful to expel the whites and to prepare for the coming of the cargo. In later cargo cults, prophets succeeded in persuading people to stop cultivating and instead build harbours, and after the 1939–45 war in which aircraft and radio became familiar to the islanders these were reflected in cults which prepared by clearing the bush to make airstrips, putting up poles and making wooden radios.

Colonial governments were generally uneasy about such movements and in some cases acted repressively against them. This unease was prompted in some instances by a paternal concern for the welfare of people who under the influence of group hysteria neglected to make ordinary provision for themselves by cultivating. At other times the cult posed a direct challenge to law and order, as for instance when in 1923 a white plantation owner in New Hebrides was killed as a sacrificial victim symbolizing other Europeans, or when the adherents of a cult formed large crowds in a state of high emotion near police or mission stations. Many of the leaders of cargo cults were imprisoned or restrained in mental hospitals.[19]

Worsley's analysis, carried out from documentary sources, was confirmed in a field study by Peter Lawrence who described how he came upon a cargo cult almost by accident. After two months in the field, the people among whom he was working heard that he was expecting his mother and sister, and asked him to inspect a site for an airstrip for the goods they would presumably be bringing with them. Now that they had, as they put it, 'their own European', things were obviously going to change, the secret they had awaited for years would be theirs; he would 'open the road of the cargo' by contacting God, who would send their and his ancestors with goods to Sydney for onward transmission to him and them.[20]

Vittorio Lanternari's summary of the literature on 'the religions of the oppressed' traced among others the succession of prophetic cults during the nineteenth century among native Americans ('Indians') resisting the inroads of white settlers on what they had regarded as their land. These movements culminated between 1870 and 1890 in the Ghost Dance, a cult openly hostile to whites and centred on a ritual dance round a totem pole. This gained some white support from among the followers of the Mormon prophet Joseph Smith, another group at odds with the dominant white society. The Ghost Dance ended in 1890 in a last hopeless armed uprising among the Sioux, which was defeated at the battle of Wounded Knee.[21]

Following that defeat, some turned from armed resistance to a quietistic cult involving the plant peyote, a small cactus part of which when eaten has a mildly hallucinatory effect, and which was ritually used in a search for inner peace. Much of the imagery represented the revival and restoration of one near death, possibly symbolizing the desperation of individuals whose cultural identity seemed threatened by the all-engulfing civilization of white America. The tone was peaceful and conciliatory, with a playing down of inter-tribal conflicts, an amalgamation of Christian and indigenous symbols, and withdrawal from rather than opposition to the white man and his civilization.

The peyote cult was long tolerated by the US authorities, and it was not until 1964 that a Californian court ruled peyote illegal. Meanwhile it was 'discovered' by the English writer Aldous Huxley, and it was his use of the drug, which he knew as mesca (hence mescaline), that led on to 'chemical mysticism' in California in the 1950s and the use and advocacy of far more powerful synthetic hallucinogens in the 1960s.[22]

In Africa, many religious movements sprang up in reaction against colonial rule and European missions of the world churches. In 1966 the Reverend David Barrett estimated that there were more than five thousand such movements with some seven million followers.[23] But the growth of African churches did not cease with the end of colonial rule. According to a more recent account, from the late 1980s onwards there was a rapid increase both in the number of adherents of established African independent churches (AICs) and in new churches.[24]

In South Africa, pioneer studies of Bantu independent churches were carried out by the Swedish missionary Bengt Sundkler, who worked among the Zulu people from 1937 to 1942. Sundkler found that there were no fewer than eight hundred such sects in South Africa alone, and he broadly classified them into the Ethiopian and Zionist types, using names which the sects commonly and characteristically gave themselves.*

Most Ethiopian sects had broken away from white, mission churches, and aimed to be both Christian and African: as Christian as the missions

---

* In sociological usage, a *church* embraces a whole community; *denominations* compete for adherents in a tolerant secular state; a *sect* is a group united by beliefs and practices at odds with accepted norms, especially in its early stages; and the term *cult* refers to beliefs and practices not yet those of an organized group. But sometimes the term a social scientist would apply to a group differs from the name by which its members know it. In particular, the claim to be the authentic church and not a mere sect may be integral to the ideology of the group in question. Accordingly, some scholars including Sundkler adopt the terminology of the groups they study rather than that of social science.

in essentials of doctrine and practice, but self-governing and independent of white control. Ethiopia was equated with Africa, and biblical references to Ethiopia were cited as evidence of a long historical tradition; it was also identified with the twentieth-century kingdom of Ethiopia. Some of these churches had links with black American movements forged by Marcus Garvey, a Jamaican who travelled widely in the 1920s and 1930s spreading the idea of independent black churches as a means to liberation.

In contrast, Zionist sects were syncretistic, combining some Christian ideas and practices with elements such as speaking in tongues and Bantu purification rites and taboos. They combated African witchcraft and similar practices, but Sundkler wrote that 'the weapons with which they fight the struggle belong to an arsenal of old Zulu religion'. The name Zionist constituted a kind of mythical charter linking African prophets who performed baptisms with an apostolic succession embracing John the Baptist, the River Jordan, Mount Zion, Jerusalem, and in some cases Nazareth. Their identification tended to be with ancient Israel, the Holy Land, rather than with Ethiopia. There seems to have been no connection with Zionism as a worldwide political movement among twentieth-century Jews, nor with the modern state of Israel, which had not come into being at the time of Sundkler's field-work. These groups used the term Zionist in quite a different context, exemplified by the links some had with the Zion church of Zion City, Illinois. But Sundkler emphasized that no hard-and-fast boundary could be drawn between Ethiopian and Zionist groups.[25]

Following Sundkler's work, a number of East African religious movements were studied in depth during the 1950s by the Reverend F. B. Welbourn. Among them was that founded in Uganda in 1929 by two young Anglican teachers, Reuben Spartas Mukasa and Obadaiah Basajjakitalo as 'the African Orthodox Church – a church established for all right-thinking Africans, men who wish to be free in their own house, not always being thought of as boys'. Welbourn also studied the churches which grew up in association with the independent schools movement among the Kikuyu, which was in turn a part of the reaction to conquest and white settlement in the much harsher atmosphere of Kenya.[26] That reaction had its political aspects in the African nationalist parties and movements which arose during the period from 1920 onwards, most of them to be suppressed by the colonial administration in a conflict which eventually took the form of an armed revolt and guerrilla movement which Europeans called 'Mau Mau'. There has been a good deal of dispute about the character of this movement; the colonial administration at first regarded it as yet another 'dini' or religious movement, and it certainly had its ritual side in the form of oathing ceremonies. Later

interpretations characterized it as an African nationalist political movement and rejected explanations in religious terms.[27] The truth may well
be that it was both, or more exactly that it was hard to disentangle the
religious, educational, political and military aspects of a broad movement
of revolt among the Kikuyu against white settlement, Christian missions,
and colonial rule. There was in fact a large and numerous growth of sects
in Kenya, ranging from groups which, like Sundkler's Ethiopians, aspired
to be fully Christian though free from foreign control, through syncretistic
movements which admitted a good many more elements from the
traditional African cultures of the region, to cults whose predominant
character was that of a chauvinistic revival of traditional or quasi-
traditional beliefs and practices: a notable study was that by Sangree of
the situation in Tiriki, a small area of western Kenya.[28]

In West Africa, Geoffrey Parrinder's comprehensive study of religion in
the city of Ibadan included full descriptions of the separatist sects, one of
the most picturesque of which was the Sacred Cherubim and Seraphim
Society whose practices were drawn from Muslim as well as Christian and
pagan customs.[29] Another detailed study of West African religious
practices was that by the psychiatrist Dr Margaret Field, for whom they
formed a background to the detailed case-studies of mental patients.[30]
Field emphasized the continuity between Hebraic, Christian, Muslim, and
pagan West African beliefs and practices. Quite apart from the possibility
of common origins, 'Christianity has been in West Africa for five
centuries', as she put it; it was not a question of a sudden contact with a
complete cultural innovation. She rejected the notion that a supposed
conflict between Christian and pagan ideas – 'the opposing pulls of tribal
gods and the dictates of Christianity' – was responsible for neurosis or
other forms of mental trouble. In particular, beliefs in spirit possession
were common to all three of the main religious traditions in West Africa,
and it was those which were vital to the new shrines at which 'the
troubles and desires of ordinary people' found expression and solace.

In Zaire, then the Belgian Congo, Simon Kimbangu began to see
visions and was credited with the power to heal the sick about 1921, and
quickly attracted a large following, to the detriment of both the Roman
Catholic missions and work on the railway and the plantations. Within
months he was arrested, tried, and sentenced to death, which was
commuted to life imprisonment; he died in prison in 1951. Missionary
hostility notwithstanding, the movement continued to grow throughout
Belgian rule. It was legalized in 1959 and took the title *Eglise de
Jesus-Christ sur la terre par le prophète Simon Kimbangu* (EJCSK). Since
independence, with its impeccably anti-colonial origins it has grown both
in numbers and standing under the leadership of Kimbangu's sons.[31]

Joseph Booth was responsible, directly or indirectly, for starting no fewer than seven African sects between 1892 and 1910 in the country then named Nyasaland, now Malawi, an area which before the formal declaration of a British protectorate had been ruled in effect for nearly thirty years by Scottish and Anglican missions. As a Baptist and a radical, Booth incurred the suspicion of missions and government alike in his activities as a kind of freelance missionary, attached successively to parent bodies including Seventh-Day Adventists. He travelled between southern Africa and the United States, in touch with the Watch Tower movement known as Jehovah's Witnesses as well as with 'Ethiopian' sects in South Africa, and supporting African followers in both continents. One such was Elliott Kamwana, to whom Booth taught the Watch Tower doctrine which he returned to Nyasaland to preach, supplied from time to time by Booth with their literature. Watch Tower spread widely throughout colonial Africa, becoming almost wholly independent of the parent American sect, and acquiring a militantly anti-white tone in which the coming millennium was viewed mainly in terms of liberation from colonial rule. The name was rendered into Bantu languages as Ki-Tower or Kitawala, and as lately as the 1950s it was still causing alarm among missions and governments. Another was John Chilembwe, who was influenced by the National Baptist Convention (a black civil rights movement) in the United States, and returned to Nyasaland with a number of black Americans to found the Providence Industrial Mission. After they left in 1906, Chilembwe's mission became the centre for African militancy, and in 1915 he led an armed rising in the Shire Highlands.[32]

In 1953 a Bemba woman named Alice, whose followers called her Lenshina (Regina, Queen) received a call to start a new religious movement which two years later broke away from the Presbyterian church and attracted large numbers of followers from both Protestant and Catholic missions. Known as the Lumpa (Itinerating) church it spread northward into Tanzania and sent a mission southwards to Salisbury in Rhodesia. At its height the movement is said to have had a hundred thousand members. Trouble began when they refused to pay taxes, and in 1964 this led to the movement taking the form of an armed rebellion against the authority of the newly independent state of Zambia. Bloody clashes ensued and several hundred people were killed before the movement was crushed. Alice was put into restriction, and many of her followers fled to Zaire.[33]

Such movements did not spring up only under colonial rule. In Uganda in 1985 Alice Auma of Gulu believed herself and was believed by others to have been possessed by a holy spirit Lakwena, who had been an Italian doctor in an earlier incarnation. She became the charismatic prophetess of the Holy Spirit Movement with a mission to heal the sick (including in 1986 the first to be diagnosed as AIDS sufferers) by countering the witchcraft to which the Acholi, like many other African peoples, commonly attribute sickness. About a year later, however, she received fresh instructions from the Lakwena identifying President Museveni's National Resistance Movement as the chief source of evil and suffering in Uganda. She raised an army, the Holy Spirit Mobile Forces, mostly from ex-soldiers of factions opposed to the NRM and its army the NRA. Alice's forces defeated the NRA in a series of battles in the north, and advanced southwards into Busoga, where they posed a threat to the Nile dam and hydro-electric station near Jinja, which supplies not only Uganda but also western Kenya. There they were defeated in a decisive battle in which Alice was wounded. She escaped into Kenya, where she was imprisoned as an illegal immigrant but later granted asylum.

From the anthropologist Heike Behrend's account, it seems clear that the Holy Spirit Movement was characterized by a syncretism of Christian and modern military culture elements with traditional Acholi spirit beliefs and magic. It was a revolutionary movement mainly of ex-soldiers, not primarily a 'peasant' movement. There was an ethnic aspect, including bitter hatred and suspicion between the Acholi and the neighbouring Langi, President Obote's people. Moreover, the movement identified the Acholi as the chief evil-doers in Uganda (though closely followed by the BaGanda), and so in the greatest need of a movement to cleanse them from witchcraft and sorcery. The movement also had to do with internal tensions among the Acholi, especially between established authorities and young men; and it gave some women the chance to defy tradition, escape from their husbands and fathers, join an army, and fight in a real war.[34]

But perhaps the biggest of all these movements was the Taiping rebellion, the most important of a series of religious revolts in China from the eighteenth century onwards, whose suppression, according to Yang, ranked with border defence as one of the two great tasks of the imperial army.[35]

Taiping was led by Hong Xiu Zhuan, son of a poor farmer of the minority Hakka people, who studied unsuccessfully for the state examinations and became instead a village teacher. In 1837, when he was twenty-three, he came across a Protestant missionary pamphlet from which he learned the elements of Christian belief. In the following year he saw visions which he interpreted to mean that he was the son of God, a younger brother of Jesus, and charged with a mission to establish *Taiping tien kuo*, 'heavenly kingdom of great peace'. Hong later underwent two months' instruction at a mission station, but he had little understanding of Christianity.[36]

From 1847 the followers of Taiping were in open revolt, and with their homes burned and their goods confiscated by government troops they took to a sort of primitive communism. From 1852 to 1856 they extended their hold into Hunan and down the Yangtse, capturing Nanking (Nanjing), the imperial southern capital, where Hong, now styled 'Heavenly King', established his residence. Despite severe internal dissensions and fighting in Nanking, the movement held the city until 1864 when it fell to the 'ever-victorious army' of Zeng Guo-Fan, an army which included Charles George Gordon among its European and American mercenary units.

Taiping's zeal for social reform embraced common property; over and above subsistence needs, families were to hand over crops and money to a central granary and bank. It advocated land reform, with moderate taxes; the equality of women; temperance in the use of alcohol and tobacco, and the suppression of opium; and iconoclasm, which entailed the destruction of works of art embodying outworn beliefs. Foreigners were not regarded as inferior; all men were equal, and some foreign ideas were good, notably those of Christianity; but foreigners ought not to be exempted from Chinese law, and the movement expressed the resentment which many Chinese felt at what they regarded as the imperial government's surrender in this regard. After the capture of Nanking, the movement appears to have lost its moral fervour, and Franke describes its leaders as succumbing to the traditional vices of display, nepotism, and factionalism. This led to cynicism and demoralization in its army; especially when opposed by Zeng, a man of high ideals and upright character. Further, it failed to co-operate with other movements of revolt, although several peasant rebellions and one other religious revolt were going on at the same time. But it certainly shook the empire to its foundations, and both the Kuomintang and the communists may well have learned much from Taiping.

In many monographic accounts of these movements, the explanatory emphasis has been on the particular circumstances in which they have arisen. Some have been regarded as responses to the grievances and humiliations of colonial rule, or internalized colonialism as in South Africa. Thus movements among indigenous Americans arose in conflict with whites; cargo cults in Melanesia under colonial rule; and the Taiping rebellion largely in reaction against European incursions into China in the 1840s. Similarly in South Africa Sundkler attributed the rise of independent African churches to the inequities of the old *apartheid* regime, the Netherlands Reformed Churches' 'golden rule' of '*geen gelijkstelling*, no equality in church or state', and the inscription '*Net vir Blankes*, For Whites Only', figuratively but no less virtually written on many church doors.[37]

But separatist sects have arisen also under less repressive regimes. For example, under colonial rule in Uganda and Nyasaland (now Malawi) both government and missions encouraged African advancement in education, economic life, and (though more hesitantly) public affairs; yet the mere atmosphere of paternalism seems to have been enough to engender separatist movements like the African Greek Orthodox Church in Uganda and those associated with Joseph Booth, Elliott Kamwana, and John Chilembwe in Nyasaland.

True, among the African independent churches surveyed by Barrett in the 1960s, more than proportionately they were in South Africa (two thousand out of five thousand churches with three million out of seven million followers),[38] suggesting that the more forceful the white domination and the more rigid the colour bar the greater the resort to millenarian movements. But these movements have not come to an end with the advent of African political independence. As already noted, the Kimbangu-ist church has continued to attract a mass following in Zaire, Alice Lenshina's Lumpa church clashed violently with the government of Zambia, and the Holy Spirit Movement of Alice 'Lakwena' fought the nascent government of Uganda in 1986.

Another broad type of explanatory hypothesis is that which regards syncretistic, prophetic religious movements as arising from the contact (or impact, or clash) of Christianity upon an indigenous system of religious beliefs and practices. Such explanations are 'anthropological' in the sense that they consider the religious phenomena in rather strictly local terms. Thus Peter Lawrence related cargo cults to traditional Melanesian beliefs in the need for co-operation between the living and the dead, so that all important work was compounded of secular and ritual techniques, and it was natural to think of the ancestors as being involved in the production of goods for the use of the living.[39]

But to view these movements purely in terms of a local clash of cultures is to fail to take into account networks of influence, ideology, and social relations which since the early nineteenth century have been worldwide in scale. Thus the African Greek Orthodox Church in Uganda was stimulated by Marcus Garvey's Universal Negro Improvement Association in America, its original connection was with a Garveyite church in South Africa, and its later links were with the Greek Orthodox church. Or consider the networks in which Joseph Booth was involved, moving as he did between England, Australia, the United States, and southern Africa and setting up links between the American Jehovah's Witnesses and the black Kitawala movement of Elliott Kamwana, besides involving himself in 'Ethiopian' movements in South Africa and initiating half a dozen other movements in what is now Malawi. Yet another example is afforded by the links between the white Mormons of Joseph

Smith and the prophetic movement of Smohalla among the native Americans.

Among those who have taken a wider view I have already cited Norman Cohn. Another is John Milton Yinger, who has written of sects and cults arising among 'groups caught in conditions of severe disprivilege'. Yinger cited the cargo cults, the 1890 Ghost Dance, and the Jehovah's Witnesses as examples of 'attack cults', who attack the dominant society 'by downgrading its institutions and refusing to accord it final loyalty'. Such religious movements, as Yinger mildly put it, are seldom regarded with favour by the dominant group. In many different times and places the movements have been defeated in battle or otherwise suppressed, and their leaders imprisoned.

The 'attack' type of cult, however, is fairly short-lived. If hope for the restoration of the old culture and the independence of the subject group fades, then there is likely to be a transition to a more accommodative type of cult, like the peyote cult which followed the suppression of the Ghost Dance. On the other hand, if the sect achieves 'success', and more especially if its members under its influence gain improved status, Protestant-ethic-style, then what began as a militant sect becomes a denomination accepting its place as one of several alternative forms of religion, tolerated by society and accommodating itself to the existing order.[40]

Fundamentalism

To those considerations must be added another: reaction against the materialism that seems inherent in economic development and the secularism that pervades modernization. In recent times that reaction, as Talcott Parsons foresaw, has taken the form of religious fundamentalism and the reassertion of a traditional faith not as one denomination among others but as the dominant form of religion in a whole society.

Fundamentalist movements have arisen throughout the world and within virtually all the major religions, most notably in Islamic societies and among Protestants in the USA. Together they represent an ideological movement of comparatively recent origin; according to Bruce B. Lawrence, they first arose in Protestant America in the late nineteenth century, and in Islamic states mostly after these gained independence following the Second World War.[41] They have something in common with 'attack cults'; as Yinger said of the latter, they downgrade the institutions of the dominant society and refuse to accord it final loyalty. Unlike other movements, however, fundamentalism represents a directly hostile response to 'the great Western transformation'. Modernization, indeed, has become a kind of code-word for all that fundamentalists abhor and fear: the modern rational secular state, tolerant of different religious beliefs and denominations, and likewise of different moral convictions, political opinions, scientific theories, and artistic expressions; hence relativism, individualism, immorality, and depravity.

Martin E. Marty and R. Scott Appleby of the University of Chicago have set out the 'family resemblances' among fundamentalist movements. Their ultimate aspiration is to bring every aspect of society into conformity with the divine law. Their core values notably include family life, 'certain understandings of gender, sex roles, the nurturing and education of children'. They favour physical punishment, and severe penalties too for adult offenders. In general they see themselves as fighting back against encroaching modernity and secular rationality, and doing so rather effectively. In that fight they are highly selective in their choice of targets, and concentrate their attack on issues that enable them most strongly to reinforce their own identity and assert their principles (no doubt, for instance, in the USA, abortion; in the Islamic world, blasphemy). They fight against a wide range of others: not only the infidel, the agnostic modernizer, but also the friendly liberal who seeks compromise and the middle ground, and most of all the insider who would betray the movement by negotiating. As Lawrence put it, 'fundamentalists don't merely disagree with their enemies, they confront them'. Although their ultimate aims are theocratic and therefore authoritarian rather than democratic, they take full advantage of their rights in secular democracies to freedom of expression, assembly, and organization, along with related modern technologies such as television.[42]

According to James Piscatori, however, Islamic fundamentalist movements are more complex. Unlike revivalist movements, they are avowedly political. Much as they aspire to create a new order, or restore a past Golden Age, real or imagined, they are therefore involved in compromise and negotiation with the very forces they most deplore, the secular rationality of modern states. Characteristically they are split between pragmatic and radical factions, and present their leaders with difficult choices between policies aimed at attracting outside political and financial support, and appeals to popular anti-Western sentiments.[43]

Suggestions for further reading

Robert W. Green (ed.), *Protestantism and Capitalism: the Weber Thesis and its Critics* (Lexington, Mass., D. C. Heath, 1959)

Marie-Louise Martin, *Kimbangu* (Oxford, Blackwell, 1975)

Ernest Gellner, *Muslim Society* (Cambridge, Cambridge University Press, 1981)

Nikki R. Keddie, *Roots of Revolution* (New Haven, Conn., Yale University Press, 1981)

Bruce B. Lawrence, *Defenders of God: The Fundamentalist Revolt Against the Modern Age* (San Francisco, Harper & Row, 1989)

Martin E. Marty and R. Scott Appleby (eds.), *Fundamentalisms Observed* (Chicago, University of Chicago Press, 1991).

Melford E. Spiro, *Buddhism and Society: A Great Tradition and its Burmese Vicissitudes* (London, Allen and Unwin, 1971)

Norman Cohn, *The Pursuit of the Millennium* (London, Secker and Warburg, 1957)

Peter Worsley, *The Trumpet Shall Sound* (London, Macgibbon and Kee, 1957)

Bengt G. M Sundkler, *Bantu Prophets in South Africa* (London, Lutterworth Press, 1948)

11

Individual modernization: some psychological studies

From the late 1950s onwards, growing interest in development studies in economics and other social sciences was matched by studies of the social psychology of individual change in relation to development, having at least their initial orientation in the modernization school of thought.

Leonard W. Doob on 'becoming more civilized'

A pioneer study in this field was that of the Yale psychologist L. W. Doob, whose previous work had included research on public opinion and propaganda. His 'two principal questions' were why some people in less civilized societies became more civilized in some respects, and what happened to them as they did so.

Among the earlier studies of societies undergoing change, many of them the work of anthropologists, on which he drew in framing his hypotheses, were those by Lerner in the Middle East; and Doob used the terms 'less civilized' and '(more) civilized' more or less interchangeably with Lerner's 'traditional', 'transitional', and 'modern'. Doob's own field studies were carried out in the 1950s in Jamaica and three African societies, Luo, Ganda, and Zulu, by means of interviews comparing the responses of the old with the young and the schooled with the illiterate.

Some of Doob's twenty-seven hypotheses were quite specific and could be confirmed or disproved. Thus 'people changing centrally from old to new ways' were found to have longer time-horizons. People changing in other respects were likely to retain traditional family attitudes. And people changing their ways were probably apt to join new groups and put more value on traits like initiative, independence, and self-confidence.

Even among the most educated groups some respondents adhered to at least some traditional beliefs or values, possibly because these are taught at an early age, or because they still met a continuing need such as family unity, harmonizing the views of younger and more-educated people with older and less-educated kinsfolk. Doob drew a parallel here with syncretism in magical and religious beliefs and practices.

Going on to more general and less testable ideas, Doob advanced the notion of the 'piecemealness' of change: it was easier to change piecemeal than all at once. He further suggested that people were likely to change more proficiently from old to new ways when they sought a central goal that transcended specific forms of behaviour. The central goal might simply be 'becoming more civilized', or it might be more complex.

The BaGanda were cited as a case of an African people intent on adjusting to the modern world without losing their distinctive identity and cultural heritage. They had adopted western ways quickly and thoroughly when these appeared to be instrumental to that end: money, education, modern technology, even Christianity.

Distinguishing between central goals and those which are incidental, instrumental, or in his word 'segmental', led Doob to suggest that 'people who retain strong central values are motivated to learn segmental forms of behaviour that do not appear to be at variance with those values'. Such a proposition seems to indicate that tradition and modernity can be mutually reinforcing in processes more complex than those of unilinear modernization.[1]

Everett M. Rogers on the diffusion of innovations

Rogers' work began with the study of agricultural innovations in the United States and broadened to that of farm practices worldwide and of innovation in general, including medicine, education, family limitation, public health, and industry.

He defined an innovation as an idea perceived as new by the potential user, and diffusion as the process through which a new idea spreads from a source, its original invention by a creative individual, to its adoption by users. Adoption implied a decision to continue full use of the idea, as distinct from a decision merely to try it. A typical time-sequence would therefore consist of three stages: 'awareness', 'trial', and 'adoption'. The adoption period was the time between first awareness and full adoption. Individuals differed in their propensity to adopt innovations, which Rogers termed their 'innovativeness', and could be classified as innovators, early adopters, early or late majority, or laggards, according to how long it took them to adopt a new practice after first hearing about it.

From a number of studies Rogers concluded that some cultures are more favourable to innovation than others. For example, in his own research in Wisconsin he found that farmers of Danish descent were far more innovative than those of Polish descent, even though all shared in the common cultural environment of a single American state. Rogers' discussion of this finding in terms of 'traditional' and 'modern' norms was in general accord with the modernization school.

Elaborating the adoption sequence into five stages: awareness, interest, evaluation, trial, and adoption, Rogers found that early adopters not only start on the process ahead of others, but also go through each stage faster.

Not surprisingly, innovations were more readily adopted if they offered a clear and visible gain to the user; were compatible with existing practice and past experience; were simple (from the user's point of view, that is; a television receiver is a complex product, but all the user has to do is to switch it on and off); and could be adopted piecemeal, as when a new farm practice was tried out on a small portion of the available land.

Rogers found that early adopters were younger than others, had higher social status, and were wealthier, whether as a result of adopting innovations in the past, or as a factor enabling them to innovate currently because they had enough resources to fall back on if an experiment failed. They showed distinctive personality traits including less rigidity and greater rationality. Early adopters made more use of impersonal sources of information such as farming weeklies or medical journals, while late adopters relied more on personal sources, the word of mouth of neighbours and professional colleagues. Early adopters' sources also tended to be more 'cosmopolite', such as national or international journals; they were more likely to be in direct communication with the sources of new ideas, such as agricultural scientists; and they tended to travel more. Some American farmers, for example, had literally travelled the world in search of new ideas. Early adopters, too, were more likely to be opinion leaders, the first to hear news and pass it on to others.

Consequently, innovators sometimes saw themselves and were seen by others as deviant from the local social system. But though neighbours might think them eccentric they identified themselves with reference groups outside the local community; they were 'in step with a different drummer'.

Finally, Rogers drew attention to the important part played in the diffusion process by professional 'change agents', such as public health officials, teachers, and agricultural extension workers.[2]

William Ogionwo on Nigerian progressive farmers

Following Rogers' work, the Nigerian sociologist William Ogionwo studied the adoption of innovations by Nigerian farmers. His sample consisted of a thousand farmers who grew cash crops and a further two hundred who did not. Innovativeness was measured by the proportion of government-recommended practices that farmers had adopted from lists, mostly of about twelve to fifteen practices, that differed in different parts of the country according to climate and other local conditions.

Just as Rogers had found in other studies, the material circumstances most strongly associated with innovativeness were gross farm income and (presumably as a consequence) level of living. The psychological characteristic most strongly associated with innovativeness was change-proneness; in other words, people who said they were ready to try new ideas proved to be so in practice as well as in words. Also related to innovativeness though less strongly so was rationality, manifest in deliberate planning after seeking the best available advice. Young farmers were somewhat more likely to adopt new ways. Information contact, education, and social participation were positively but weakly related to innovativeness. Innovative farmers were found to be deviant rather than conformist, and more likely to agree with test statements like 'I never worry about being different from others', but this correlation too was not very strong. And there was no appreciable correlation with mobility.

More surprisingly, nor was there any significant relation with resignation, traditionalism, or familism. These findings ran counter to the tenets of the modernization school that tradition and modernity are at opposite poles, and that traditionalism, familism, and resignation to fate or to the will of God are obstacles to modernization and development. On the contrary, Ogionwo pointed out that people can adopt new methods because they are seen as more effective means to achieving traditional ends, like increasing income and making better provision for a family's needs; or because persons respected as traditional authorities are recommending or urging adoption of the new practices. So tradition and modernity could be mutually reinforcing. Institutions such as kinship should not be seen merely as impediments to economic growth. Against the oft-cited 'plague of family parasitism' should be set the family's contribution to the division of labour, the supply of skill and training, and the accumulation of capital. Pitting tradition and modernity against each other as paired opposites led us to overlook the mixtures and blends that reality displayed. It became 'an ideology of anti-traditionalism, denying the necessary and usable ways in which the past serves as support'.

Almost all of Ogionwo's sample heard the radio, and many of those who did not have a radio themselves listened to farming programmes in neighbours' houses. Not all could read, and the most effective influences were the peer group of neighbours, kin, and friends, followed by 'oral extension', the word of mouth of an extension officer. Literate farmers were not notably more innovative than non-literate, and hard technical information in print was important rather for the extension officers.

Ogionwo therefore concluded that the best medium for spreading agricultural information was the radio, with close personal-follow up by extension officers.

It was, however, a mistake to think as Rogers did only in terms of the flow of information to an individual farmer who alone decided whether or not to act on it. In societies such as those of rural Nigeria farmers were subject to group pressures from family, friends, and community norms. It was important to take these into account, and to discover to what extent the adoption of farm practices was a matter of individual or of collective decision.

Ogionwo concluded with a plea for two-way communication, 'downwards' to farmers about government-recommended practices, balanced by an 'upwards' feedback to the government of rural opinion and experience, presupposing a 'degree of mutual confidence between the two'.[3]

David C. McClelland on achievement motivation

In his studies of human motivation, the Harvard psychologist David McClelland's first concern was to establish that a need for achievement or *n* Ach exists, that it is distinguishable from other needs and drives, and that it occurs to a different extent in individuals and also in cultures. His colleague M. R. Winterbottom was then able to show that the development of *n* Ach takes place fairly early in childhood, and depends on parents' expecting of their children a 'self-reliant mastery' at an appropriate age, namely about eight years. This included such things as knowing their way about the neighbourhood, being active and energetic, trying hard to do things for themselves, making their own friends, and doing well in competition with other children. If all this is called for too soon, then children are discouraged and lose self-confidence; if too late, then their *n* Ach remains low. Japanese parents on the average 'hit it right on the nose', expecting these qualities at the right age, while Brazilians demanded them too soon, and Germans too late.

McClelland suggested that these findings were consistent with, and gave a further depth of understanding to, Max Weber's theory linking the Protestant ethic with the spirit of capitalism, since the attitudes and values of puritan Calvinist parents could well have led them to bring up their children in a way likely to engender a high *n* Ach. However, differences in *n* Ach between latter-day Protestants and Catholics were not clear-cut, though Jewish boys clearly showed high *n* Ach.

The general level of *n* Ach in past societies was assessed from achievement themes in popular literature, children's books, and other cultural manifestations, and related to evidence of economic growth. For instance, such a correlation was shown between *n* Ach, derived from English popular literature from 1500 to 1800, and coal shipments to London, with a time-lag of thirty to fifty years. From such studies McClelland concluded that high levels of *n* Ach were followed some time later by a period of economic growth, which subsided after the level of *n* Ach dropped. Presumably the time-lags occurred as the qualities engendered in children's upbringing affected the country's economic performance decades later in their adult working lives.

In more recent societies, McClelland found a close correlation, with a time-lag, between *n* Ach and subsequent economic growth in the period from 1925 to 1950. Per capita GNP was not quite the best measure of economic growth, and McClelland found an even closer correlation with electric power, or both GNP and electrical output combined.[4]

Turning to the implications for development in poor countries: in the long term the number of people with high *n* Ach and the *n* Ach level of the people as a whole presumably depend on the way children are brought up. This is at least partly under governments' control in the schools, and there seems no reason why a government taking these findings seriously should not act directly on, for example, the contents of children's first reading books.

In the short term, however, the poor countries would have to make do with whatever resources of achievement motivation their adult populations already possessed, for instance through motivational training seminars for business managers. Looking further forward, their leaders should promote 'an achievement mystique'. One who had notably done so was President Nyerere of Tanzania, though McClelland demurred slightly over Nyerere's equating 'self-reliance' with 'hard work'. That was not quite the same as the need to achieve; 'many peasants all over the world work very hard without producing rapid economic growth'.

Education for women should be pressed forward. An achievement ideology could hardly be promoted in a society which was 'so to speak "half slave and half free"'. Moreover, women as wives and mothers were the chief source of the achievement motivation among boys and men.[5]

A number of criticisms may be made of McClelland's work. Achievement motivation seems to conflate several different concepts, the relations among which are not clear. The disposition to *set oneself tasks* rather than have tasks set from outside is not self-evidently the same as the search for the satisfaction from *performing a task well* whether it is self-imposed or externally induced. Both should be distinguished from *performing a task better than others*, excelling in competition, or 'winning'. Excelling over others is further to be distinguished from *gaining others' recognition* of work well done, and enjoying the approval of significant others – notably, of course, one's mother in early childhood at least. Recognition is again to be distinguished from *symbolic reward*. As for the desire to *assert oneself over others* in such a way that they *accept one's leadership*, the subject of one of Winterbottom's questions, it may be that these qualities are more highly valued, encouraged, and rewarded in the United States than in other cultures. A certain ethnocentricity, too, is evident in McClelland's handling of the concept of other-directed behaviour, which is first diluted from altruism to 'paying attention to the opinion of others as a way of guiding one's own behaviour', and hence degraded into mere market morality.

Alex Inkeles and David H. Smith on individual modernization

Alex Inkeles (most of whose previous studies had been of Soviet society) and David H. Smith conducted research in the mid-1960s into individual modernization in six developing countries: Argentina, Chile, India, East Pakistan (now Bangladesh), Nigeria, and Israel, where almost all their sample were 'Oriental Jews' of non-European origins. Each national sample consisted of about a thousand men aged 20–30 and included industrial workers both experienced and inexperienced, urban non-industrial workers, and countrymen. Interviews lasting about four hours were carried out by locally recruited field staff, and followed a schedule which, while broadly standard for the whole inquiry to ensure comparability, was suitably adapted to each country's circumstances and carefully translated into the appropriate languages. It was designed primarily to measure the subject's 'overall modernity' (OM) as indicated by such traits as his aspirations, readiness for change, attitude to women's rights and to family limitation, sense of personal efficacy, active public participation, media exposure and how much he had learned from it, religious attitudes and behaviour, and kinship attitudes and behaviour. The initial hypothesis to be tested was that there is a *syndrome* of modernity, a systematic tendency for these traits to occur together, so that for instance a man with a strong sense of personal efficacy also tends to favour birth control, to join voluntary organizations, and to take an interest in world affairs. Early designs of the questionnaire embodied this initial approach, clearly based as it was on the ideas of the modernization school. On testing them it was found that most of the traits did cohere, and the initial hypothesis was to that extent confirmed; some did not, and were dropped. The questionnaire and measurement scale progressed through a series of validating steps to their final form, code-named OM500, to be used in the full-scale national surveys. In the light of the discussion in chapter 8, and of Ogionwo's findings about familism, it is of interest to note that among the questions dropped were those about family attitudes, since it was found that men of high overall modernity were no less likely than others to accept their kinship obligations. The final schedule OM500 consisted of questions addressed to thirty 'sub-themes' that 'had passed a rigorous test proving that they were indeed unmistakably part of the OM syndrome' while also being free of the 'partialling fallacy', that is, they were not the same thing under different names.

A first analysis showed that individual modernity was associated with schooling, and also with father's schooling; factory experience, skill, and income (as evidenced by consumer goods possessed); living in towns; and media exposure. However, some partialling fallacies were suspected at this stage; in particular, working in a factory is almost bound to entail living in town, and the two influences had to be disentangled.

Schooling's pre-eminence was confirmed in a more detailed analysis by means of partial correlation techniques designed to single out each contributory factor in turn. Disregarding all other influences, each year at school put anything from 1.3 to 2.3 on an individual's OM score out of a hundred, so that a full eight years' primary schooling could raise the OM score by 10–18 percentage points. Schooling was therefore a stronger and more consistent influence than any other. Oddly, though, it did not seem to matter whether it was a good or bad school, nor whether it was in town or country.

Exposure to the mass media, measured by a simple index giving equal weights to radio listening and newspaper reading, also proved to be a strong and consistent modernizing influence.

Factory experience too was closely related with modernity, especially for men born in the country. For such men, each year in a factory added 0.5 to 0.9 points to the OM score, while for men born in town it added about 0.4. As a modernizing influence it was second only to schooling, and Inkeles and Smith pointed out that the gain (if it be so regarded) is achieved at no cost in organizations primarily engaged in producing goods or providing services, whereas schooling entails public and private costs; factory experience thus emerges as the most cost-effective. Furthermore, it accords as it were a second chance for those who missed schooling to be exposed to modernizing influences. As with schooling, it did not seem to matter much whether the factory was modern or traditional, large or small, competently managed or not. And the term 'factory' needed to be widely understood in this context. To have a modernizing effect, work experience did not have to be in industry narrowly defined; it could equally well or even better be in a reorganized agriculture. Thus in Israel farmers in the co-operative settlements known as moshavim were about equal to industrial workers in their OM scores; while in the rural development scheme at Comilla set up under government auspices in what was then East Pakistan, the OM scores of members of the village co-operative society actually exceeded those for factory workers, and those of non-member villagers were not much lower. The important thing, it seemed, was to work in a modern organization, whether agricultural or in the narrow sense industrial.

Disentangling work experience from that of town life was the particular reason for including in each national sample some urban non-industrial workers in what later became known as the informal sector (see chapter 7). They included self-employed artisans, taxi drivers and rickshaw pullers, street vendors, and casual labourers, and the findings about their modernity were somewhat equivocal. Their OM scores consistently exceeded those of rural cultivators, but despite their longer experience of town life they mostly scored lower than even new, inexperienced factory workers. It seemed clear that factory work's modernizing effect was direct and independent of the factory's urban setting. When other socializing influences were partialled out, especially schooling, factory experience, and media exposure, the modernizing influence of urban residence alone proved to be little or none in five of the six countries (the exception was Nigeria); and the authors concluded that 'It is not urban experience *per se* which makes men more modern but rather the differential contact with the schools, mass media, and factories which the town contains.'

Comparing early with late socializing experiences in the life of an individual, Inkeles and Smith found that men born in town started with higher OM scores than their country cousins, but once in a factory the latter learned faster. An educated home was an advantage, and father's education was significantly correlated with modernity, but boys from less advantaged homes could and did catch up at school, and boys lacking both an educated home and schooling could and did catch up at work in a modern organization; the latter, indeed, could well be regarded as a second chance for remedial education.

Inkeles and Smith acknowledged that their study was confined to men; that was for practical reasons, since in developing countries at that time there were very few women in the industrial jobs in which they were especially interested. They saw no reason, however, why their findings should not prove equally true of women, since presumably the same forces that had made men modern – schooling, work in modern organizations, and mass-media exposure – would also make women more modern. Rebutting in advance any criticisms of ethnocentricity or a capitalist bias, they cited the 25 years Inkeles had spent studying Soviet society, and pointed to the similarity between most, though not all, of the themes included in the OM scale and the personal qualities officially extolled in the Soviet Union. They concluded that individual modernity could be summed up under four major headings. People who could be characterized as modern were informed participant citizens; they had a marked sense of personal efficacy; they were highly independent and autonomous in their relations to traditional sources of influence, especially when making basic decisions about how to conduct their personal affairs; and they were ready for new experiences and ideas, that is, they were relatively open-minded and cognitively flexible.[6]

12

Politics in post-colonial states

Politics in 'Third World' countries is shaped by influences to some of which attention has been paid in earlier chapters, including low levels of income and low, zero, or negative rates of economic growth; the colonial heritage; cultural diversity, ethnic rivalries or conflicts, and the plural society; language, schooling, the educated elite, and the mass media of communication.

In most societies the most important power source is the state, that unique institution which according to Max Weber's classic definition successfully asserts a monopoly of legitimate force over a defined geographical area; and politics is generally thought of as being 'about' who controls the state and for what purposes it is used.

States are not all-powerful, and indeed a problem for many 'Third World' countries is that of a 'weak' or 'soft' state, not successfully asserting control of important areas of the country's life such as the military and the black-market economy. Indeed, many 'Third World' states hardly come up to Weber's definition by that test. But nor are states quite powerless; and the phrase 'the autonomy of the political' has been coined to counter reductionist explanations of politics in terms of modernization on the one hand or dependence on the other. Thus it has been argued that political structures and processes are to be seen as independent forces, operating in an area (or arena) where there are genuinely open choices among different policy options.[1]

The widely different meanings given to terms such as 'political development' and 'political modernization' have been summarized by C. H. Dodd. Political development has been taken by some to mean a movement towards an end-state regarded as desirable and probably inevitable, depending on one's political convictions, such as a communist utopia, a multi-party electoral democracy, or a theocratic Islamic society. Or it may be understood in functionalist terms such as 'the expansion and centralization of government power, and the differentiation and specialization (and subsequent integration) of political functions and structures'.[2] The slightly different phrase 'the politics of development' can be usefully applied to policies conducive to economic development, or to human development in a wider sense, such as land reform and schooling for girls.

For the modernization school of thought, as seen in chapter 6, an essential part of the whole process of political modernization was the increasing participation of people in politics, including the spread of the right to vote in free elections and equal opportunity to participate and compete for office. However, the experience of 'departicipation' in countries such as Uganda (as detailed by Nelson Kasfir)[3] led to a reassessment, notably by Samuel P. Huntington and Joan M. Nelson. As seen in chapter 6, the prevailing view in the United States in the 1950s and 1960s had been that socio-economic development would lead to greater equality, political stability, and democratic political participation. That 'benign line' of the liberal model of development, however, had been shown to be 'methodologically weak, empirically questionable, and historically irrelevant except under specialized circumstances'; and there were other possibilities. For example, in a 'bourgeois model' political participation might be extended to the urban middle class, the leaders of rapid economic development, resulting in increased inequality and demands for participation from the unenfranchised poor, and political instability. Or a modernizing autocrat might deny political participation to the rising middle class while promoting equality in order to mobilize political support from the masses. Land reform would be a key issue in such a case; could the government muster enough support to overcome opposition from the landed aristocracy despite middle-class indifference and an as yet not very participant 'peasantry'? A 'technocratic model' might achieve faster development with greater inequality, less stability, and less participation, unless there were a 'participation explosion' or revolt and an abrupt switch to another path of development. Or a 'populist model' might result in greater equality and more participation, at the cost of slower economic growth and less stability, unless there were a 'participation implosion' with power taken out of the people's hands and politics superseded by central administration. Huntington and Nelson concluded that 'At least in the short run, the values of the political elite and the policies of government are more decisive than anything else in shaping the participation patterns of a society':[4] an appraisal consonant with that of Myrdal and the other neo-institutionalist economists, and with 'the autonomy of the political' cited above.

Departicipation may occur when a modernizing autocrat finds it impossible to bring about reforms, judged necessary for economic or general development, by democratic means and without force (that is, in so far as such a one is not motivated only by sheer greed and self-aggrandizement). For example, in 1975 Indira Gandhi suspended the constitution and civil liberties, arrested opposition leaders, and introduced a 20-point economic programme including land redistribution, along with the sterilization campaign which, as told in chapter 2, led to her electoral defeat in 1977. As Francine Frankel pointed out, land reform by fiat from above would have depended for its implementation on the very people, the local landowning elites, whom it would have dispossessed. An authoritarian government, therefore, might well be as 'soft' a state as a democracy.[5]

Would-be modernizers, whether an elite or a sole autocrat, have tended to regard traditional cultural patterns, including diverse indigenous languages, religious beliefs and practices, and traditional social structures, as obstacles to economic development and a source of ethnic division and national disunity, as has been seen in chapter 9. This is another factor in departicipation, for as Kasfir found in Uganda, if elections are going to be fought on the ethnic issue that is a strong reason for not holding them. 'Elections mean participation, and participation is likely to lead to ethnic mobilization.'[6] To paraphrase Patrick Chabal's paradox, ethnic politics thrives on democracy yet weakens democratic institutions; and the solution may appear to be a one-party state.[7]

The colonial heritage

Even though the end of colonial rule at various dates – in Latin America in the 1820s, in Asia in the late 1940s especially India and Pakistan's independence in 1947, and 'the year of Africa' 1960 – recedes into the past, some aspects of the colonial heritage have endured.

Nearly all post-colonial states have retained the boundaries which represented either agreements among the colonial powers about the limits of their respective domains, or their own internal administrative divisions. Especially in Africa, many of these states were highly arbitrary and even artificial creations, whose borders parted like from like while including unlike peoples in a single state. Yet a general re-drawing of the map of Africa along ethnic lines would undoubtedly have been an immensely long and contentious task; and it may reasonably be surmised that colonial officials and African political leaders alike shrank from it, and decided that African aspirations for freedom from foreign rule would have to be met within the framework of the former colonies. The leading case may well have been that of the Kingdom of BuGanda, whose unilateral declaration of independence in 1960 failed to achieve international recognition, and the British view prevailed that it must be considered an integral part of Uganda. And if African leaders were reluctant to allow their countries to be fragmented along ethnic lines, they were equally averse to those countries being federated into larger units, like the Central African Federation under British rule, or the project of an East African Federation. Likewise, Kwame Nkrumah's call for a united states of Africa fell on deaf ears.

Thus, as Robert H. Jackson and Carl G. Rosberg pointed out, despite attempted secessions (such as that of 'Biafra' from Nigeria) and terrible civil wars, no African state has been divided as a result, none has been annexed in whole or part, and with few exceptions black African states have not invaded one another. (Invasions of their northern neighbours by the white-dominated regimes in Rhodesia and South Africa occurred when these were pariah states with presumably little to lose by incurring further international disapproval.) According to Jackson and Rosberg, the Organization for African Unity (OAU) has been most effective in behind-the-scenes diplomacy upholding the principles of the sovereign equality of member-states, non-interference, the peaceful settlement of disputes, and the illegitimacy of subversion. This has entailed accepting and endorsing the colonial frontiers and recognizing the sovereignty of the states within them, including some extremely small weak 'micro-states'.[8]

Inheritance elites and 'parties' in the successor states

As noted in chapter 3, the government of colonies was characteristically regarded by those engaged in it as administration rather than politics. The principal legacy of colonial rule, therefore, was an administrative bureaucracy, while political institutions and their articulation with the administration were in most cases much less well developed. These circumstances commonly gave rise to what F. W. Riggs termed the 'interference complex': mutual accusations of interference as the bureaucrats tried to safeguard matters such as appointments, contracts, and allocations from 'political interference', while the politicians complained that they could not carry out their proper function because of 'bureaucratic interference'.[9] And if that led to friction between politicians and civil servants, how much more so with the military will emerge below.

The end of colonial rule was not always foreseen and planned for very long in advance. At best, representative institutions might have been in place, and general elections held, three to five years before independence; at worst, the colonial power might simply withdraw, leaving the leaders of an anti-colonial movement and its guerrilla fighters to take charge as best they could.

In some countries the forms of government adopted, initially at least, were closely modelled on those of the former colonial power. Thus the

'Westminster model' was followed by many former British colonies, and it was indeed a general condition for the grant of self-government by Britain that parliamentary democracy, justified as 'the best we know', should be a working reality. Moreover, some of the political elite in those countries, such as Dr Nnamdi Azikiwe in Nigeria, wanted nothing better than that the rights and freedoms and democratic institutions of the British people should be shared by those of their colonies.[10] Likewise the French political system, similar in many respects to the British, provided the model not only for former French colonies but also for some Latin American countries.[11]

In some countries there was no constitutional decolonization, and independence came with victory in a war of liberation. In Guinea-Bissau, according to Patrick Chabal, the victors faced the problem of creating a modern state out of a clandestine party, half military, half revolutionary, and the remnants of a colonial bureaucracy, highly paid, not much in sympathy with the party's aims, but indispensable. Partisan leaders experienced an abrupt transition almost literally overnight from bush warfare into ministerial office. There was no question of parliamentary democracy, and a one-party state was envisaged from the first, though before his death on the eve of independence in 1973 the revolutionary leader Amilcar Cabral believed he could prevent a slide into a party dictatorship and intended the party to be politically accountable to the people.[12]

However, as Martin Staniland pointed out in relation to Africa, in countries where there was time for a transition from colonial rule to independence the politics of the process could be represented in two ways. One was that independence was granted reluctantly under pressure from mass movements whose leaders were concerned, first to integrate sectional interests into the new nation, then after independence to end colonial exploitation and raise everybody's living standards. Those leaders were characterized as democratic and egalitarian, and they stood for modernization (represented by the national movement, and associated with young people and town life) against an opposed traditionalism (associated with the countryside and represented by the traditional chiefs). The second and perhaps truer interpretation was that colonial development had created an indigenous elite imbued to some extent with the values of the metropolitan country, some of whom were admitted to political participation at the level of the colony or *territoire*. To enlarge that participation, they resorted to a 'tactical politicization' at local and sectional levels, in which 'only the vaguest formulation of general goals was possible or desirable [as] rigid definition would have made it harder to get so much support'. Decolonization then consisted of a bargain between the retiring colonial power and the indigenous 'inheritance elite'

– whose version of events constituted the first interpretation. As already noted, a commitment to parliamentary democracy typically formed part of that bargain.

Despite their pretensions to be the authentic national movements, it is clear from a number of accounts that many of the 'parties' that came to power in the post-colonial states were in fact weak. For example, according to Staniland the Parti Démocratique de Côte d'Ivoire began as an alliance of voluntary associations: a planters' co-operative, ethnic associations, the teachers' union, and intellectuals' societies, with neither organizational coherence nor ideological precision. The actual working of the party was quite at variance with its official structure, committees at district level were as often nominated as elected, and only four annual congresses were held in twenty years, giving little chance to unseat party officials.[13]

Similarly, according to Cherry Gertzel's account of the Kenya African National Union, both before and after independence in 1963 rival leaders whose power was based on local support in their home districts preferred not to have a strong national party which might enable one leader to gain control. Neither the National Executive nor the Governing Council met between 1963 and 1966. KANU headquarters in Nairobi was practically deserted. The telephone was cut off because no one paid the bill. 'Party finances were said to be in disarray, [and at] district level ... membership dues were not collected.'[14]

Central planning and one-party states

In the ideologies of many of the new states, it was taken almost for granted that imperialism was linked with capitalism. If one was condemned, the other was at least suspect, and there was a preference for economic policies that could in the widest sense be identified as socialist. Much-needed economic development was to be furthered by central planning and organized by public corporations rather than by private enterprise, and even the small-scale indigenous private enterprise of the informal sector was not always favoured. Thus several of the new states of Africa professed attachment to 'African socialism', though they interpreted the term in their own ways. The materialist premises of the Marxist-Leninist tradition were widely rejected; Senghor wrote eloquently of the spiritual values he thought were lost to Soviet communism under Stalin, Nkrumah found no contradiction between socialism and Christianity, and Nyerere linked African socialism with an image of traditional kinship solidarity in the evocative word *ujamaa*. And when it came to actual policies when in power, there were wide divergences; for example, the government of Tanzania nationalized large private businesses while that of Kenya refused to do so. In Kenya, indeed, Africanization rather than nationalization soon became the aim; foreign firms were pressed to train and employ Africans at managerial levels, and Africans were encouraged to develop commercial banks, even though such policies could hardly fail to result in the rise of an indigenous business class committed to private enterprise.[15]

Yet while in some of these varieties of socialism it was hoped and intended to avoid the emergence of antagonistic classes like those of nineteenth-century Europe, there was a clear strand of elitism in them. Socialism both in theory and in practice has generally been associated with central planning. Whether that is necessarily so is a question for debate, but it certainly was so in the models available to the new states in the 1960s, most of all the Soviet Union. By its very nature planning tends to be 'from the top down'. Even where, as in Tanzania, there were sincerely meant gestures towards planning 'from the bottom up', it is clear from Leys' account that the government's main aim in setting up local planning committees was to secure local commitment to the plan and co-operation in its implementation. The initiative still came from the centre.[16]

Just as a one-party state seemed to offer a solution to the problem of ethnic division, so central economic planning was another reason why many nationalist leaders saw strong central government as the only way to achieve development, and coined phrases like Sukarno's 'guided democracy', Ayub Khan's 'basic democracy', and Sékou Touré's 'democratic dictatorship' to express and legitimate the leadership which the modernizing elite or autocrat must give the people through the government and ruling party.[17] In these qualified democracies parliamentary institutions soon became a sham before they were formally superseded by one-party autocratic government.

Yet, as already emphasized, many of these would-be strong central governments were in fact weak, exemplifying the discrepancy between formal authority and actual power characteristic of 'soft states'. Among the institutions many governments conspicuously failed to bring under control were the military.

The armed forces in politics

'Third World' countries have in the past proved particularly vulnerable to the take-over of state power by the armed forces. Hardly a week went by without our hearing of yet another *coup* in some state of Asia, Africa, or Latin America. The movement of army vehicles into the capital or its outskirts; the seizure of the radio station; the arrest, flight, or murder of the former prime minister, president or other leading politicians; the dawn broadcast commanding the populace to remain calm. Then the amplified statement of the reasons for the *coup*. The selfish intrigues of small-minded politicians, intolerable against the background of the country's needs, its economic crisis, its humiliation in the eyes of the world. Political interference in the administration of the country and particularly of the armed forces. Corruption (always corruption). The appointment of a military cabinet together with a few civilian leaders worthy of the public's trust. The announcement of a regime of sensible administration at the hands of experienced administrators capable of putting country before party and self. The pledge to restore normal democratic political processes as soon as conditions allow – a constituent assembly dangled as a future possibility – but meanwhile the disband-ment of the now totally discredited former ruling party, control of the press, control of political meetings, a curfew, the temporary suspension of the legislature.[18]

Military intervention in politics is a matter of degree. It is rare indeed for a government to be wholly military, with every ministerial post held by a long-serving regular officer. Almost always some civilians are included for their expertise in fields such as health and foreign relations. As the original *coup* recedes into the past, they may come to be in a majority, and the cabinet may end up almost wholly civilian, yet still owe their tenure of office to their willingness to carry out policies acceptable to the armed forces. Such a government may then seek to legitimate its position by holding elections, usually carefully arranged to secure the desired result; important opposition parties may be suppressed, their leaders jailed or exiled. And there are other possibilities. Military leaders may gain popularity and even become national heroes, like Nasser in Egypt, capable of winning genuinely contested elections. The line between civilians and soldiers may be blurred when civilians appointed to a military government are commissioned as officers and so find themselves under military discipline, including ferocious penalties for disobeying the order of a superior officer, especially the commander-in-chief. And in almost all countries the military have some political influence, if only from making representations about the needs of national defence and the allocation of resources for that purpose.

Thus Ruth Sivard defined military control in terms of 'key political leadership by military officers; the existence of a state of emergency or martial law; extra-judicial authority exercised by security forces; lack of central political control over armed forces; occupation by foreign military forces'. By those criteria, in 1992 61 of the 112 governments of 'Third World' countries with 62 per cent of their total population were military-controlled. (It may be noted that according to Sivard's wide definition Uganda was still to be regarded as military-controlled, since despite the overthrow of Idi Amin and the much improved record on human rights under Museveni's NRM the army were still committing human rights violations in combat areas and attempting to recover the immunities and powers they had possessed under Amin and Obote.) According to Louise Pirouet, 'inadequate domestication' of the army was counter-productive in ending insurgency, and its sheer size a problem rather than a solution.[19]

According to Ruth Sivard, countries currently under military control were more highly militarized than most of those under civilian rule. Nearly twice as high a proportion of their population was in the armed forces. Between 1960 and 1992 they had experienced six times as many years of war, and lost nearly 14 million of their people from deaths in wars compared with 2 million in the other countries. During the same 33-year period countries currently under military control had been so for 22 years, compared with 8 years in the others.

Military governments were characteristically sustained in power by fear and repression. Of the 61 military-controlled governments, all but three were seriously violating human rights with torture, brutality, disappearances, and political killings. While the human rights record of some other 'Third World' countries was not specially good either, in most the abuses were much less flagrant.[20]

Praetorianism

Praetorianism in the strict sense refers to a state of affairs like that in ancient Rome, where the imperial guard were detached from the main body of the army and loyal to, and paid by, the emperor personally rather than the senate representing the public.[21] In such circumstances, the guards soon recognize that the converse is also true: the ruler is the one to whom they choose to give their allegiance. A need then arises for an inner and even more personal guard to protect the ruler against a change of allegiance by the Praetorians. Foreign mercenaries are often preferred for this purpose, lacking as they do local affections and loyalties. And as an alternative or supplement to paying them in money, a ruler may reward the trusted troops with licence to plunder the civilian populace. There are examples of some or all of these tendencies in recent African history. In Ghana, according to William Gutteridge, after an attempt on his life in 1962 Nkrumah turned increasingly to non-Africans for protection. With help from communist countries he formed a President's Own Guard Regiment independently of the regular army at a time when the latter's equipment was becoming run down and its interests neglected. Resentment at this deterioration of the army's national position, and apprehension that before long the only institution capable of resisting Nkrumah would lose its effectiveness, contributed to a 'now or never' feeling that precipitated the *coup* of 1966.[22] In Ethiopia, according to Levine, the imperial bodyguard established as an elite force separately from the army 'specifically to protect the Emperor against *coup* attempts' themselves attempted to overthrow him in December 1960. Antagonism between the two forces contributed to the promptitude with which the army deployed their greatly superior numbers and weapons to thwart the attempted *coup*.[23] But the defeat of the bodyguard left the army in a commanding position in Ethiopian politics, of which they took advantage in their turn in 1974.

However, the term praetorianism is also used in a wider sense to mean military intervention in politics generally, including cases where an apparently civilian government hold office at the will of armed forces who can oust them at any time.

Liability to military rule

It remains to explain why 'Third World' countries have been so vulnerable to army *coups* and military rule, compared with western countries where with rare exceptions the armed forces have long been firmly under civilian control, and also with communist regimes where if anything the party's control was even firmer. This had indeed led to an assumption that civilian control of the armed forces was normal and natural, and that any loss of control represented a temporary disturbance after which things would return to normal. Questioning that assumption, S. E. Finer pointed out that armed forces generally had three advantages over civilian institutions: superior organization; a highly emotionalized symbolic status as the one truly national institution; and a monopoly of arms. What needed explaining was not why the armed forces sometimes rebelled against a civilian government, but why they ever obeyed it. Finer's explanation was in terms of 'levels of political culture'. The sheer technical complexity of a modern society and economy was too great for it to be brought easily under military control. Even more important was the question of legitimacy. Strong public attachment to civilian institutions made successful military intervention in politics less likely. In societies at a lower level of political culture, however, where the society and economy were not too complex, and where public attachment to civilian institutions was weak, the military's political scope would be very wide.[24]

Finer's analysis in terms of levels of political culture, however, did not find general acceptance; as Jacques van Doorn wrote, 'It is not a low political culture as such that permits military intervention, but the impotence of the regime to safeguard the political order.'[25]

According to Morris Janowitz, the armed forces in many new nations were organized as much for internal repression as for defence against external attack. They were 'in essence a form of super-police'. Moreover, in the 1960s and 1970s there had been a worldwide increase in para-military forces including large national police forces living in barracks and armed with light military weapons and vehicles. While such units might have other duties, for instance as frontier guards, clearly their main purpose was internal repression.[26]

Robin Luckham pointed out that because of the client status of most new nations in the international system there were few whose armed forces had much to do with external security, whereas in most such states the army could not avoid being called on to perform internal security duties.[27] Stanislav Andreski gave a specific example: 'The armies of Latin America cannot fight each other, because in virtue of a multilateral treaty the USA would come to the defence of the invaded country'; while the security of the western hemisphere as a whole was also guaranteed by the United States.[28] Military officers' self-image as defenders of the nation against external attack was therefore unrealistic, and in some countries their actual role in internal politics had been openly rationalized in doctrines of 'the enemy within'. Thus according to Bruce Drury the Escuola Superior de Guerra in Brazil taught its students the need to struggle against internal communist aggression capitalizing on misery, hunger, and just nationalist anxieties.[29] Such considerations no doubt help to explain the bold decision of the liberal centrist government of Costa Rica to disband its armed forces entirely in 1948.[30] To adapt a remark of Roberta McKown, among the best advice one could offer 'Third World' politicians would be: if you want to serve out your allotted term in peace, do not have an army.[31]

Democratization

However, in the 1980s and 1990s an opposite trend set in, away from the centralized state and one-party autocratic regimes, with a democratic ferment and a wave of free elections, while instead of news of a successful army *coup* we seemed to hear almost daily of the toppling of another military dictator.

Thus James S. Wunsch and Dele Olowu expressed the growing disillusionment at the failure of the centralized state in Africa. For example, in Ghana the high hopes of independence had faded as GNP had declined every year at an average rate of 1.3 per cent between 1960 and 1982, while there had been five military *coups*, the civil service was demoralized, the economy devastated by inflation, talent 'brain-draining' away. And Ghana was not alone; in most other African states too there had been *coups*, political inefficacy, administrative weakness, and economic decline or stagnation.[32]

Larry Diamond, Juan J. Linz, and Seymour Martin Lipset traced a 'democratic ferment in the developing world' beginning in the 1970s. Besides the end of the last three Western European dictatorships in Greece, Portugal, and Spain, most of the Latin American dictatorships collapsed or withdrew, there was democratic progress in several East Asian countries, and more equivocally so in South Asia, while democracy was 'struggling to emerge' in Uganda and South Africa.[33]

Chris Allen, Carolyn Baylies, and Morris Szefetel identified a general process of political restructuring in Africa beginning in 1989 and accelerating thereafter, involving a shift from authoritarian single- or no-party systems, and leaving few countries untouched. However, 'multi-partyism, rule of law, [and] codification of basic human rights', highly desirable in themselves, were necessary but not sufficient conditions for 'participation, representativeness, accountability, [and] transparency.' Quite commonly, democracy had been a system legitimating and perpetuating class dominance and inequality. Democratization did no more than open a space to continue earlier struggles for greater justice for the mass of the people.

Baylies and Szeftel analysed in particular 'the fall and rise of multi-party politics in Zambia'. General elections in 1991, supervised and monitored by several outside bodies, resulted in victory (overwhelming in votes cast, though in a low poll) for the Movement for Multi-Party Democracy, a coalition of disaffected politicians with some academics and other eminent people, the business bourgeoisie, and trade union leaders, one of whom, Frederick Chiluba, became president. Baylies and Szeftel regarded this as a major achievement for democracy, ending almost twenty years of increasingly unrepresentative and coercive autocratic rule, unleashing public scrutiny of government, and making possible the beginnings of an autonomous civil society, with new independent associations and publications. It remained to be seen whether the MMD government could carry through measures to set an indebted economy in order without losing political support, especially if they involved complying with World Bank conditions; and it was feared that the new government might slip back into an autocratic 'presidentialism' like its predecessor.[34]

Similar reservations were expressed by Michael Bratton and Beatrice Liatto-Katundu. Though ordinary people had played major roles as protesters and voters in the overthrow of Kenneth Kaunda, it could not be taken for granted that they would go on to be active and well-informed citizens. Frederick Chiluba and other MMD leaders had called for a 'new culture', a break from the political deference and economic dependence of one-party rule. But people spoke of '*nyu katcha*' in a sneering tone, conveying cynicism about political leaders taking advantage of liberalization to line their own pockets.[35]

In the first issue of a new journal *Democratization* William Tordoff reviewed 'a wave of free elections in the early 1990s following a growing conviction in the 1980s among urban groups that one-party government and state regulation of the economy were responsible for their countries' decline'.[36] This gave new urgency to long-continuing debates about the very nature of democracy and its applicability to 'Third World' countries, particularly those in Africa with their cultural diversity and ethnic divisions. In particular it was asserted that democracy had failed, not because it was intrinsically unsuitable, but because the wrong model had been adopted. It was argued that the Westminster model in particular was unworkable in plural societies, and that a better model would be one termed 'consociational'.

'Plural' and 'pluralistic' societies

Although the words are very similar, it is necessary to draw a clear distinction between 'plural' and 'pluralistic' societies. For Leo Kuper these terms represented two antithetical traditions. One was the plural society as conceived by Furnivall, held together by domination. The other, well established in American political thought (Kuper cited Kornhauser and Shils), associated pluralism with democracy. It was an equilibrium model, whereas the plural society was a conflict model. In a pluralistic society there were cross-cutting loyalties, multiple affiliations, and a tolerance of diversity, for example among white immigrants to the USA, drawn from different national origins and following different religious traditions. As applied to black Americans, however, the pluralistic model was much more problematic, and their position was more like that in a Furnivall-type plural society.[37] It seems clear that a pluralistic model can apply only where there is a solid basis of equal individual rights and equality before the law.

A choice of models

An early critic of the Westminster model was (Sir) Arthur Lewis in his study of thirteen newly independent West African states, published in 1965. Lewis distinguished 'class societies', primarily Britain, where the main political parties represented the respective interests of the economic classes Capital and Labour, from plural societies. He attributed the failure of democracy and the rise of one-party regimes to the wrong model: Westminster-style, government versus opposition, majority rule, and central-ized government. It was not democracy as such that had failed, but only a particular kind.

Plural societies needed coalition government, not polarization with the opposition excluded for long periods. Following an election, instead of the head of state being required to send for the leader of the biggest single party to form a government, the constitution should require him or her to send for the leaders of all the parties which had received more than a given minimum proportion of the votes (Lewis specified 20 per cent) to divide the cabinet posts among them ('or such of them as will co-operate'). The different segments should be proportionately represented in all decision-making bodies, and the electoral system too should provide for proportional representation through a single transferable vote. And there should be a federal constitution according a considerable degree of autonomy to regions or provinces.[38]

Lewis' analysis and recommendations were not unlike those put forward by Arend Lijphart in 1977. Lijphart believed that, though difficult, it was not impossible to establish stable democratic government in a plural society; European examples were Austria, Belgium, the Netherlands, and Switzerland. His 'consociational' model of democracy rested on four constitutional provisions designed to foster co-operative attitudes and actions among the leaders of the different segments. They were: a permanent coalition; minority veto rights; proportionality; and autonomy for the segments.

Lijphart's 'Grand Coalition' stood in complete contrast to the British adversarial model of government versus opposition, with a bare majority sufficing for even the most important decisions. In such a system elections were exciting events like Cup Final football matches; the interest was in who wins; the winners formed the government, while the losing party, even a large opposition narrowly defeated, were excluded from power till next time round. But in a plural society with ethnically-based parties the outcome was not in doubt, and excitement became anxiety about the outcome for permanent minorities. Even in Britain coalition governments had been formed in extreme emergencies, especially wars. Consociational democracy entailed a 'Grand Coalition' as the normal state of affairs, not a response to a crisis; or, conversely, the plural society itself being seen as constituting a permanent crisis.

Likewise, in a consociational system minorities had veto rights to protect their integrity and vital interests. A rule of proportionality governed the distribution of public funds, civil service appointments, and the like, while the electoral system too provided for some form of proportional representation, the list system rather than the single transferable vote. Like Lewis, Lijphart favoured a federal constitution with a high degree of constitutionally guaranteed internal autonomy for the segments. And he was critical of the Westminster model's fusion of powers, with the cabinet dominating parliament, in contrast to the United States' separation of the powers of the executive, legislature, and judiciary.

Unlike the British system, a consociational democracy did not give rise to a strong opposition, as under the proportionality rule sizeable parties were taken in to the government and only small weak parties were excluded. It could be argued that it did not bring about positive reconciliation but only accommodation; however, that might be judged better than strife. To maintain their distinctive identity and culture, segments might bring oppressive pressure to bear on their individual members to conform to group norms (for instance speaking the group's indigenous language). There might be costly duplication of bureaucracy at the different levels. But even the sheer immobility entailed by ponderous federal machinery and the veto could have its positive aspect if it encouraged segments to circumvent the centre and make decisions for themselves or in bilateral agreements with one another.[39]

Lijphart's analysis could be criticized for blurring the all-important distinction between plural and pluralistic societies, which seemed to be manifest in his choice of European examples: culturally diverse, yes, but pluralistic, surely, not plural? This may have given some colour to the use of consociationalism (not, obviously, by Lijphart himself) as 'a fashionable facade to hide white domination' in South Africa. As noted by Kasfir, the immense inequalities of the apartheid regime precluded the kind of negotiation and accommodation on equal terms among leaders of the different segments that was essential to the consociational model.[40]

Outside influences

It remains briefly to make the obvious point that the government a country gets is not always decided wholly within its borders.

Not all foreign interventions in 'Third World' states have been by Great Powers, and not all have been entirely unhelpful. Thus Tanzania invaded Uganda in 1978–9 to overthrow the Amin regime.

However, during the 'cold war' there were many interventions in 'Third World' countries by the United States and the Soviet Union, concerned as each was not to allow its position to be weakened by a hostile regime anywhere in the world that might threaten its vital interests and serve as a strategic base for the other's forces. Thus United States policy-makers strove to prevent the rise to power of left-wing movements, and above all not to permit another Cuba in the western hemisphere. According to Nordlinger they took economic measures to weaken the Goulart government of Brazil as it became more radical, and the Central Intelligence Agency gave encouragement and support to the *coup* that overthrew the elected socialist government of Allende in Chile in 1973.[41] In the 1980s the USA were in direct confrontation with the Sandinista government of Nicaragua, including support for the anti-Sandinista fighters known as the Contras, with repercussions throughout Central America and in US domestic politics. Among other US interventions, in 1983 a joint US/Caribbean force invaded Grenada (despite its status as a Commonwealth nation) to overthrow its Marxist government and install one more to the United States' liking. In 1994, again as part of a multi-national force, US forces entered Haiti to overthrow a military regime and enable the elected president Aristide to return from exile.

For their part, the Soviet Union supported communist regimes in Vietnam and Cuba; perhaps mistakenly anticipating a US move into Iran, they invaded Afghanistan in December 1979; while in Africa they actively intervened, directly or with Cuba as proxy, in Ethiopia and Angola.

Second only to the 'cold war' were racial conflicts in southern Africa, where the white-dominated regimes in South Africa and the former Rhodesia, with some US involvement, fomented civil wars and otherwise intervened in their northern neighbours, causing great suffering especially in Angola and Mozambique. It remains to be seen whether the end of the 'cold war' and of racist regimes will result in such countries no longer being used as battle-grounds for conflicting ideologies, with correspondingly greater scope for democratization.

Suggestions for further reading

Samuel P. Huntington and Joan M. Nelson, *No Easy Choice: Political Participation in Developing Countries* (Cambridge, Mass., Harvard University Press, 1976)

Nelson Kasfir, *The Shrinking Political Arena* (Berkeley, Calif., University of California Press, 1976)

James C. Scott, *Comparative Political Corruption* (Englewood Cliffs, N.J., Prentice-Hall, 1972)

Eric A. Nordlinger, *Soldiers in Politics* (Englewood Cliffs, N.J., Prentice-Hall, 1977)

Arthur Lewis, *Politics in West Africa* (London, Allen & Unwin, 1965)

Leo Kuper and M. G. Smith (eds.), *Pluralism in Africa* (Berkeley, University of California Press, 1969)

Arend Lijphart, *Democracy in Plural Societies* (New Haven, Conn., Yale University Press, 1977)

Atul Kohli (ed.), *The State and Development in the Third World* (Princeton, N.J., Princeton University Press, 1986)

Patrick Chabal (ed.), *Political Domination in Africa* (Cambridge, Cambridge University Press, 1986)

James S. Wunsch and Dele Olowu (eds.), *The Failure of the Centralized State* (Boulder, Col., Westview Press, 1990)

13

Aid and development

International economic organizations and the idea of aid

In 1944, with victory in the Second World War assured, representatives of the allied nations 'determined to save succeeding generations from the scourge of war' held two important conferences at small places in the United States, at which the leading international institutions of the post-war world took shape.

At Dumbarton Oaks (Washington, DC) they agreed to set up the central political and diplomatic organizations of the United Nations, its General Assembly and Security Council, which were formally constituted in 1945. To them were added specialist organizations, some carried over from the former League of Nations particularly the International Labour Office (ILO) and World Health Organization (WHO); others newly created including the Food and Agriculture Organization (FAO) and Educational Scientific and Cultural Organization (UNESCO); and yet others added later, notably the UN Development Programme (UNDP).

At Bretton Woods, New Hampshire, the prime aim was to stabilize the world economy and remedy the economic causes of war, which were widely associated with currency crises, slumps, and unemployment, leading to mass unrest and extremist political movements especially the rise of the fascist dictators in Europe in the 1930s. With that aim it was decided to set up an International Monetary Fund (IMF) to which each member state made an agreed contribution, nine-tenths in its national currency, one-tenth in gold, and from which each could borrow in case of need. Each member government declared the value of its currency in US dollars, which were pegged to gold by means of a fixed price. With the Fund's agreement, member states could adjust the value of their currency up or down in an orderly manner, quite unlike the hectic speculative trading of the pre-war world; while to help countries stabilize their currencies the Fund could issue loans to member states to tide them over balance-of-payments difficulties, subject to the appropriate adjustment of their financial policies as agreed with the Fund's officials and set out in a letter of intent when applying for the loan. Also at Bretton Woods it was agreed to set up an International Bank for Reconstruction and Development (IBRD, later more generally known as the World Bank), whose first task was to be to finance the rebuilding of Europe's war-shattered economies.

In all these organizations, member states' contributions were proportionate to their resources (as agreed after appropriate consultations). But voting rights differed. In the Dumbarton Oaks organizations, subject to a great powers' veto in the Security Council, the general rule was and is one member state one vote. In the Bretton Woods organizations, however, voting rights were proportionate to contributions, so that initially the United States and Britain together had half the total votes.

The Soviet Union was represented at both conferences. They decided not to join the Bretton Woods organizations. They joined the Dumbarton Oaks organizations, but it often seemed to the West that they did so only to prevent them working as intended by the frequent use of the veto.

In 1947 the United States took a fresh initiative when their Secretary of State, General George C. Marshall, held out the prospect of aid for post-war reconstruction if there were 'some agreement among the countries of Europe as to the requirements of the situation'; and substantial funds were in fact forthcoming for the US's own European Recovery Program, rather than through the IBRD, when Congress passed the Economic Co-Operation Act in 1948.[1] If this was another attempt to draw the Soviet Union into peaceful constructive co-operation, this time in a European setting, then it too failed as the USSR rejected Marshall's plan and would not let Poland and Czechoslovakia accept US aid either.[2] However, it succeeded in promoting the remarkably rapid recovery of western Europe; and it gave a strong impetus to the movement towards co-operation there that led eventually to the Treaty of Rome and the formation of the European Economic Community (EEC), above all ending the deadly quarrels between France and Germany that had caused three wars in 70 years and twice engulfed the world in conflict. So while the recipients of Marshall aid set up the Organization for European Economic Co-Operation (OEEC), the Soviet Union and eastern European states formed their counterpart, the Council for Mutual Economic Assistance (officially CMEA in English, also popularly known as Comecon).

Encouraged by the success of Marshall aid, and in the face of relations with the Soviet Union that deteriorated into a 'cold war', in the early 1950s the United States sought to extend the idea of aid beyond Europe and make use of their ample resources to build bulwarks against communism in Asia and the Far East. Here, though, their activities were seen by their critics as propping up corrupt and repressive regimes for no other reason than that they were anti-communist – a recurrent dilemma for United States foreign policy. After 1956, the Soviet Union began to enter the field of foreign aid, and though they never committed anything like the same resources to it as those of the West they did so in the form of large spectacular projects such as, notably, the Aswan high dam in Egypt, and a steel mill at Bhilai in India. The United States' response was to play down the bulwarks-against-communism argument, which could have been counter-productive, and to link aid more closely to economic development.[3]

In the 1950s, too, there was a great increase in aid from other sources. As Britain and France recovered from the war they extended aid on an unprecedented scale to their colonies and former colonies. For Britain the 1950s were the heyday of the Colonial Development and Welfare scheme which, as noted in chapter 3, was initiated in 1929 and extended in remarkable acts of faith in 1940 and 1945; while France too made much aid available to French African countries, especially for the reconstruction of Algeria after the disastrous civil war there.

In December 1960 the UN General Assembly in Resolution no. 1522 designated the 1960s as a Development Decade, and called upon industrialized countries to contribute 1 per cent of their national incomes as aid for the development of underdeveloped countries. An expert committee subsequently ruled that the term 'national income' should not be interpreted in its strict technical economists' sense, but should be taken to mean Gross National Product – the interpretation more favourable to the developing countries.[4]

In 1961, when the accession of Canada and the United States made it no longer a purely European organization, the OEEC was reconstituted as the Organization for Economic Co-Operation and Development (OECD), and it was in keeping with the spirit of the times that it added development aid to its other aims and set up a Development Assistance Committee (DAC) for that purpose. At that time, too, the United States persuaded West Germany and Japan, former enemy countries now prospering (largely as a result of having been defeated, disarmed, and so relieved of military expenditure), to join the OECD and DAC and to take part in development aid. Other countries, including the neutral Switzerland and Sweden, also entered the field of aid. After 1960, countries such as Britain, France, Holland, and Belgium began to run out of colonies. In particular, the British Colonial Development and Welfare Acts made funds available only for dependencies, yet the needs for development assistance certainly did not lessen as former colonies became independent. Accordingly, as CD & W was wound down, more aid was made available under the Overseas Aid Act of 1966. In Britain as in other donor countries, new government departments were set up for this purpose, adding yet more organizations with their initials and acronyms: the British Department of Technical Co-Operation, later re-named the Overseas Development Ministry (ODM); in the United States the Agency for International Development (AID); in West Germany the Bundes-ministerium für Wirtschaftliche Zusammenarbeit (BMZ).

Meanwhile the IMF and World Bank were established in adjacent buildings in Washington, though with separate staffs and different objectives. The IMF continued to operate the Bretton Woods system for stabilizing currencies; while the World Bank, its prime task of reconstructing Europe taken over by US Marshall aid, became the leading organization for multilateral aid to developing countries.

The Bretton Woods system worked as intended for some 25 years, mainly because the United States' balance-of-payments deficit made ample dollars available as a world currency. It broke down in the early 1970s when, among other reasons, the rest of the world began to lose confidence in the United States' ability to maintain the dollar's value. The dollar was in fact devalued (that is, the price of gold was raised) in December 1971; in partial replacement, since 1968 the IMF has created and issued Special Drawing Rights as a reserve asset for use by member states and multilateral development banks.

In association with the World Bank, the International Finance Corporation (IFC) was set up in 1956 to handle loans to the private sector in developing countries. In 1960 a second affiliate, the International Development Association (IDA), was established to extend credits, derived from surpluses from the Bank's other operations, on the 'softest' or most concessional terms to the poorest countries.

In recent years the World Bank's policy objectives have strongly emphasized poverty reduction, 'the benchmark against which the Bank's performance . . . is judged', together with environmentally sustainable development and investment in health and education, particularly of girls.[5] The Bank has co-operated in conservation projects with other organizations including the World Wildlife Fund and International Union for the Conservation of Nature, and UN agencies including the Food and Agriculture Organization and UNDP.[6] And in the context of investment for health, for example, in 1992 the Bank announced that it did not support projects involving tobacco production, either directly or so far as practicable indirectly.[7]

Notable among the Bank's activities since 1978 has been the collection and publication of data about the world economy and that of individual countries in its annual *World Development Report*. This has been of the utmost value for development studies (as these pages bear ample witness), supplemented and rivalled only since 1990 by the UNDP's annual *Human Development Report.*

Over time the United States and Britain lost their commanding position over the Bank's policies, and in 1993 the five biggest depositors, the USA, Japan, Germany, UK, and France, held some 39 per cent of the votes in the IBRD and 43 per cent in the IDA, and appointed five of the 24 executive directors. The rest were elected to represent groups of countries, and the system of election virtually guaranteed seats to China, India, and Russia.[8]

Also at Bretton Woods, a proposed International Trade Organization was discussed whose aims were to have been the stabilization of world commodity trade and prices. Following further talks a charter was drawn up at Havana in 1948; but the US Senate refused to ratify it, and without US participation it was clearly pointless. Some of its provisions were incorporated in the 1948 General Agreement on Tariffs and Trade (GATT), under which developing countries have taken an increasing part in successive 'rounds' of conferences and consultations to negotiate mutual reductions of import duties, literally by the thousand. Originally regarded as a temporary stop-gap, GATT in fact endured, and in 1995 after nearly half a century became the World Trade Organization.

Meanwhile, following the 1960 'development decade' resolution, the United Nations took to organizing Conferences on Trade and Development (UNCTAD). Since the first at Geneva in 1964 these have been held at roughly three- to four-year intervals, and with a continuing secretariat and board have assumed the character of an organization rather than a succession of *ad hoc* meetings. Like the General Assembly, UNCTAD's membership was 'universal', and the Dumbarton Oaks principle of one member state, one vote made it a congenial forum for the growing number of small 'Third World' states to put their case and pass resolutions, while the effective control of the Bretton Woods institutions and their resources lay overwhelmingly with a dozen or so rich industrial states.

The Pearson commission, 1968–9

When in 1968 Robert McNamara became President of the World Bank, he at once appointed a commission under the veteran Canadian statesman Lester B. Pearson to 'study the consequences of twenty years of development assistance, assess the results, clarify the errors and propose the policies which will work better in the future'. The commission's report, presented in 1969, set out the case for aid as it was understood at the time with arguments directed at that archetypal donor the United States senator.

That case at its simplest rested on a moral imperative: it was only right that those who have should share with those who have not. There was also the appeal of enlightened self-interest: a secure and prosperous future for the world depended on our showing a common concern for common problems, and refusing to tolerate extreme and shameful disparities within and among nations.

The commission linked aid to development by adopting the DAC definition: 'funds made available by governments on concessional terms primarily to promote economic development and the welfare of developing countries'. Aid so defined excluded official funds made available for purposes other than development, for example military assistance; and it also excluded private investment. Not that they saw anything wrong with the latter; on the contrary, they emphasized its positive contribution to economic development. But aid worthy of the name was something that was given, not a transaction that profited both parties. There were needs for which private capital flows were inappropriate and inadequate, such as schools, roads, hospitals, and irrigation. Private capital flowed mostly to better-off countries with rich mineral resources. Echoing Rostow, they believed that aid could be a once-for-all operation which should, if successful, enable developing countries to achieve self-sustaining growth by the end of the century.

The Pearson commissioners were at pains to dispel any suggestion that poor countries were not doing enough to help themselves. Perhaps their most important single finding was that in the 1960s the poor countries had in fact raised most of their own investment capital, as much as 85 per cent of the total, by domestic savings. The commissioners were similarly concerned to defend previous aid programmes against allegations of waste, mismanagement and corruption, which they said were no greater than in other public programmes. More effective use of aid resources, however, could be attained if donor governments would give up 'tying' their aid to their own products and allow recipient countries to shop around for the best bargains.

Tying was a persistent feature of bilateral aid, that is aid from one donor to one recipient country. Most aid was of this kind, and the commission recognized why, for example, Britain had primarily assisted newly independent Commonwealth countries, France had concentrated on French-speaking African countries, Japan had concentrated its aid activities in Asia, and the larger part of the United States' assistance had been to Latin America and countries on the periphery of the communist world. Multilateral aid channelled through international agencies represented little more than one-tenth of all aid in 1967, but it filled the gaps in countries such as Ethiopia with no obvious bilateral links, and it was free from tying; for these reasons the commission recommended that there should be more of it, particularly through the IDA. Endorsing the General Assembly's 1 per cent target, they further recommended that 0.7 of that 1 per cent should be official development assistance (ODA) according to the DAC definition cited above.[9]

How much aid?

As Pearson pointed out, it was ironic that total resource flows did actually exceed 1 per cent of the combined national income of OECD countries in the five years before the DAC adopted that target in 1964, but not after. Likewise, the OECD countries were nearer to devoting Pearson's 0.7 per cent of their combined GNP to official development assistance in 1960 than they have been at any time since; in 1960 the proportion was 0.51 per cent, in 1970 0.34 per cent, and it has remained at about that level.

At first the United States gave far more aid than any other country. Their ODA was more than that of the rest of the OECD countries put together till the late 1960s, and still the biggest till 1992, when for the first time it was over-topped by Japan with 11 billion dollars out of an OECD total of 60 billion. As a proportion of GNP, however, US aid has been below the OECD average since 1970, falling from 0.31 per cent in that year to 0.18 per cent in 1992. British aid has been fairly close to the OECD average, falling from 0.42 to 0.30 per cent of GNP over the same period. Countries whose ODA contributions have much increased include Japan, Germany, and France; while Sweden, Norway, and Denmark were the only OECD countries whose ODA exceeded 1 per cent of their GNP in 1992, followed by the Netherlands with 0.88 per cent.

There have also been substantial though variable aid flows from OPEC (the Organization of Petroleum Exporting Countries), ranging from more than a third as much as the OECD's in 1980 to less than a thirtieth in 1989. By far the biggest donor has been Saudi Arabia, followed by Kuwait and the United Arab Emirates.

As noted above, the Pearson commission found that in 1967 about a tenth of OECD aid was channelled through multilateral agencies such as the World Bank, and recommended that much more should be. In 1992 28.9 per cent of OECD aid was multilateral, including over a third from European countries, led by Britain with 45.2 per cent and the Netherlands with 44.4. According to UNDP, however, only 7 per cent of the OECD's remaining bilateral aid was directed to the 'human priorities' of basic education, primary health care, safe drinking water, adequate sanitation, family planning, and nutrition.

According to UNDP again, private investment flows to developing countries increased from 5 billion dollars in 1970 to 102 billion in 1992.

This has nearly reversed Pearson's recommended ratio, seven-tenths ODA to three-tenths private; now it was more like six-tenths private to four-tenths ODA. What Pearson said about private capital flows remained broadly true, however. They went mostly to a few countries, 72 per cent to just ten: China, Mexico, Malaysia, Argentina, Thailand, Indonesia, Brazil, Nigeria, Venezuela, and South Korea. Very little went to the poorer countries.

Official development assistance, however, made up a substantial part of the GNP of some small poor countries, according to World Bank data for 1991: 69.2 per cent in Mozambique, 47.6 per cent in Nicaragua, 43.4 per cent in Guinea-Bissau, 33.8 per cent in Tanzania, and over 20 per cent in Uganda, Bhutan, Burundi, Malawi, Chad, Rwanda, and Lesotho. China and India received large amounts of ODA, but only a small proportion of their GNPs were from that source (0.4 per cent and 1.1 per cent respectively), and the amounts per head of population were tiny ($1.70 and $3.20 respectively). By contrast, ODA per head of population was over $200 in Nicaragua and over $100 in Guinea-Bissau, Mauritania, and Zambia. But by far the biggest recipient of ODA was Egypt; and, no doubt for related reasons, the one high-income country to figure as a recipient of aid on a big scale was Israel.[10]

It remains to mention, however briefly, the voluntary aid agencies mostly based in western countries. Official aid in billions of dollars makes OXFAM's £87 million in 1993–4 look puny by comparison,[11] but their influence is far wider. While some leading charities contribute much of their limited resources to aid for developing countries, their activities are not confined to the 'Third World' and they operate worldwide for their particular concerns. For example, Save the Children supports projects in the UK as well as overseas. One of the voluntary agencies' advantages, giving their activities special value, is their independence and their willingness to disregard official disapproval, as Save the Children did in the Sudan famine. Likewise Amnesty International has become unpopular with governments of all political hues in rich and poor countries alike for its reports exposing injustice and inhumanity in their countries. In the affluent countries where most of their funds are raised the voluntary agencies' educational and publicity activities keep the issues of disparity and development continually to the fore; while in the field their aid workers, less hampered by official protocol and maintaining a neutral stance between conflicting factions, may be able to take aid straight to where it is most needed.

Criticisms of aid in the 1970s

Pearson epitomized what may without disparagement be termed the conventional wisdom of the 1960s: aid, viewed as a transfer of resources, was manifestly right and desirable for the purpose of promoting the economic development and general welfare of the people of poor countries. If it did not always succeed in doing so, any gap between promise and performance was seen as failure or ineffectiveness; and, to be sure, there was much to be learned about how to make aid more effective. Aid practitioners – men and women who staffed the innumerable national, international, and voluntary agencies that made up a veritable world of aid – saw their task as learning from experience how to do better next time with the resources available. Often it was represented, though, that aid could not be made more effective unless there was much more of it, and that the central problem was to persuade the governments and people of the rich industrial countries to give more.

Clearly it was hard for the world of aid to accommodate radical critics who disputed its fundamental assumption and maintained that aid could be actually harmful to poor countries, not as a matter of failure or ineffectiveness, but systematically so.

For P. T. Bauer (later Lord Bauer) the basic argument was unconvincing because there was nothing wrong with inequality. In effect, it could be both an incentive to and a consequence of economic development. Aid benefited people in poor countries who were already better off: town-dwellers, politicians, civil servants, academics, and some business people; while it was paid for out of taxes levied among others on the poor. It involved a transfer of resources from poor people in rich countries to rich people in poor countries. Aid was not indispensable for development; the rich countries were all (as he put it) underdeveloped two centuries ago, and many later-developing countries had made rapid economic progress without foreign aid. Some aid projects had absorbed domestic inputs greater than the net output, so that the recipient country would have been better off without them. Reliance on food aid had reinforced governments' tendency to invest in prestige industrial projects and neglect agriculture. And aid in general was a 'dole', tending to erode or sap attitudes and beliefs conducive to self-reliance, thrift, effort, and enterprise.[12]

Teresa Hayter worked for some years in the world of aid, but her studies in Latin America led her to conclude that the conventional wisdom constituted 'a complicated edifice of deception' and that aid itself could be explained only as 'an attempt to preserve the capitalist system in the Third World'. Since capitalism was to be identified with exploitation and dependence, it was clearly not in the interest of the people of the Third World that it should succeed. But though she wrote from an ideological position diametrically opposed to that of Bauer, there were distinct similarities in her criticisms of the effects of aid. It could help to sustain a privileged class; it could be used 'directly as a bribe' to secure the adoption of measures favourable to donors and unfavourable to recipients; deliberately or otherwise, it could be used for projects which made people worse off, not better; and it usually added to the indebtedness of recipient countries, 'and hence to their dependence'.[13]

Without rejecting the idea of aid outright, other criticisms indicated reservations and qualifications to the conventional wisdom. Thus Judith Tendler pointed to the paradox that aid practitioners on the one hand maintained that aid funds were pitifully small and much more were needed, yet on the other hand tended to act in practice as if aid funds were abundant and what were really scarce were worthy, viable projects. To safeguard themselves against criticism, aid practitioners could conscientiously recommend only projects that satisfied a number of exacting criteria. They should be practicable and economic, and offer good prospects of contributing to general economic development, preferably with greatest benefits to the poorest people. They should be manageable, and enable the donor organization to monitor their progress and audit their books, with some assurance that donors' money would not be wasted in mismanagement or corruption. Aid organizations often had to move quickly to dispose of their allotted funds before losing them at the end of the financial year. The bigger the project, the more funds could be disposed of with less effort. Capital-intensiveness and import finance made supervision and control possible, whereas many small projects with much local expenditure would be impossible to monitor and audit. Such considerations were important reasons for a bias towards big, capital-intensive projects.[14]

Similarly, John White, a defender of aid, analysed the conditions in which aid might be said to make its recipients worse off. Tying was one, and there had been a number of cases in which the extra cost of an aid project due to tying had exceeded the amount saved by the concessional terms of the associated loan. In such cases it would have been more advantageous to decline aid and carry through the project with money borrowed at commercial terms on the open market. It was simply not true that 'any aid is better than no aid', and there was no excuse for recipients who did not bother to do their sums.

Further, while the conventional wisdom assumed that aid supplemented local resources, left- and right-wing critics alike alleged that it displaced them. Thus Keith Griffin had shown that Latin American countries that received more aid had lower savings rather than those that received less aid. But it could equally well be argued that countries with low domestic savings would naturally seek external aid for their investment programmes, so that such a finding did not invalidate the supplemental view of aid. While it was theoretically possible that aid might displace local resources to such an extent as to make the recipients worse off than they were before, it was hard to find unequivocal evidence of a case in which that had really happened.

White emphasized that while aid could be viewed in economists' terms as a transfer of resources, it was also always a political transaction. Simply by seeking aid, a government – acting for a country as a whole – put itself into a position of dependence which it would see as a set of constraints limiting its freedom of action in domestic policy. Its relations with donor agencies were therefore likely to be fraught. For their part, those agencies would inevitably form judgements about recipients' policies, and find themselves supporting those they judged beneficial and opposing others. Promises of aid on the one hand, and threats to withdraw it on the other, could therefore be used as 'leverage', imposing demands on recipients often with a high political cost. The supplemental view of aid increased the likelihood that the donor would come into conflict with, and try to bring pressure to bear upon, domestic political forces in the recipient country. That would be seen as interference, causing aid to fall into disrepute.[15]

The Brandt commission, 1977–80

In 1977 Robert McNamara again took the initiative in setting up a commission under Willy Brandt, former Chancellor of West Germany, to review aid and development in the widest possible setting of the world economic system. Where the Pearson commission had been appointed by and had reported to the World Bank, a Bretton Woods body dominated by the rich industrial countries, great pains were taken to make the new commission independent not only of the World Bank but also of every other powerful institution, official or non-governmental.

While aid from the rich countries of the 'North' had fallen far short of the UN-Pearson target, their trade with the poor countries of the 'South' was on unequal terms that hindered the latter's development. The South pressed for fairer terms particularly in their chosen forum UNCTAD in which, as already pointed out, they had no difficulty in getting majorities for resolutions; but the North controlled the resources through the IMF and World Bank.

Central to the commission's recommendations was a transfer of resources on a massive scale to developing countries. The industrial countries should commit themselves to reaching the 0.7 per cent target by stages from 1980 to 1985. Other countries also, such as those of Eastern Europe and the better-off developing countries, should contribute according to their national income.

Disarmament was vital, not only for its own sake, but to free resources for development. The sale of arms from 'Northern' industrial countries, both west and east, to the 'South' should be restrained, possibly by means of a special tax, internationally levied, the proceeds of which would be used for development.

A special effort should be made to help the least developed countries of Africa and Asia. Largely humanitarian, this would include water and soil management, health care, and the eradication of diseases such as river-blindness, malaria, sleeping sickness, and bilharzia. There was scope for afforestation, solar energy development, mining, and industrial development. In many countries agrarian reform was important. Increased provision should be made for food aid in emergencies, but without weakening incentives to local food production.

The whole onus of world development did not fall on the North. Governments of countries in the South too needed to take measures, notably making family planning freely available; extending social services to the poor; agrarian reform; and encouraging small-scale enterprises in rural areas and the informal sector in towns.

A world energy policy was required to reduce the dependence of Northern life-styles on abundant energy from non-renewable resources, and to make more use of solar energy which would most benefit the poorer countries.

Urgent action was needed to stabilize commodity prices at levels that were fair to the producers. 'Protectionism by industrialized countries against the exports of developing countries should be rolled back.'

International agreements were needed to regulate the multinational corporations and clarify their position in relation to the issues discussed in chapter 4.

Finally, there should be a thoroughgoing reform of the international monetary system, beginning with the IMF. While the commission praised the IMF's initiative in issuing SDRs following the collapse of the Bretton Woods system, they were sharply critical of many other aspects of the IMF's policies and practices. It had appeared to assume that governments needing short-term financial help 'must have been incompetent or careless', an attitude that some member states had found paternalistic. It had formulated policies on the basis of a monetarist approach that attributed balance-of-payments problems to excessive domestic demand. Accordingly, it had insisted on corrective measures, 'balancing the budget, curbing the money supply, cutting subsidies and setting a realistic exchange rate', in unrealistically short periods. Such measures had been extremely unpopular, 'on occasion leading to "IMF riots" and even the downfall of governments'. The commission urged the IMF not to insist on 'highly deflationary measures as standard adjustment policy', and recommended greater participation by the developing countries in the IMF's decision-making.

Similarly, though the World Bank came in for less stringent criticism, it was urged to modify the conservative regulations that allowed it to lend no more money than it possessed, and to lend out up to twice its capital. To be sure, there were risks; but the commission pointed out that the record of the Bank's borrowers had been excellent, and there had been no case of default in its whole history.[16]

Criticism of the Brandt report came most notably from Gunnar Myrdal and Dudley Seers. Though none had done more in their time to advocate generous aid policies on the part of western countries, they now expressed profound disillusionment, alike with the report, with the whole idea of official development assistance, and above all with the political regimes of many 'Third World' countries.

The Brandt commission had confused countries with governments, and had failed to distinguish between aid to a country's economy and aid to its poor. Together, these confusions had given rise to the assumption that because a country's people were poor, financial transfers were justified to its government. It was further assumed that a government represents a country, acts on behalf of its people, and is the best judge of their problems and needs. Such assumptions needed to be questioned and were in many cases false. 'In many countries the problem precisely is the government.'

Many governments in the 'South' were no longer short of resources; their revenues had grown faster than their populations, and would have grown faster still if taxes had been properly collected (the 'soft state' again). And they had borrowed heavily. But much of the money had been spent on weapons and luxury goods, and trickled away in bribes and administrative salaries. Much aid, too, went to governments who co-operated with United States' policies, though some of these did little about social problems and were among the most repressive.

'The only type [of aid] that deserves a word meaning help' was for 'elementary needs, such as pure water or primary health care, in a really poor country', and that only if the donor was sure it would not be misused. Aid for emergencies such as floods, famines, and earthquakes should be administered by special international agencies, or by non-governmental organizations such as OXFAM, once looked on as 'non-professional "do-gooders"', but whose advantages I have mentioned above.[17]

The Brundtland commission, 1983–7

In 1983 the UN General Assembly set up a World Commission on Environment and Development 'to propose long-term environmental strategies for achieving sustainable development by the year 2000 and beyond', chaired by Mrs Gro Harlem Brundtland, formerly environment minister, then Prime Minister, and currently leader of the Labour Party in Norway. Like its predecessor, this commission was as independent as possible, particularly from great power pressure. Its members were drawn from a wide variety of countries and backgrounds. It was based in Geneva and financially supported by a number of countries and academic foundations, and its meetings and public hearings were held in cities all over the world. It reported to the General Assembly in 1987.

The Brundtland commission was in effect the UN's response to the question posed in chapter 5: 'But is it possible?': 'it' being *sustainable development*, the key phrase. From the first Brundtland resisted limiting the commission's scope to environmental issues only; the very word invited comparison with politically naive campaigns to defend the environment against human activities. Likewise, development alone would have been too narrow a focus, and too easily dismissed as a matter for specialists in development assistance, or how to help poor countries grow richer. 'But the "environment" is where we all live; and "development" is what we all do in attempting to improve our lot within that abode. The two are inseparable.'

It was a principal theme that environmental degradation was linked with poverty and inequality. Economic growth was needed, but only if it was socially and environmentally sustainable. On this the commission's thinking was close to that of the development economists in the world of aid (see next section). The alleviation of poverty, meeting basic needs, and fair shares for the poor were repeatedly endorsed as prime aims of sustainable development.

At the same time, the international economy was not always very favourable to environmental conservation. For example, debtor countries were drawing heavily on non-renewable resources to service their debts.

The commission focussed on six closely inter-linked areas of concern: population, food security, the loss of species and genetic resources, energy, industry, and human settlements. Their analysis was complex and their recommendations numerous; by way of illustration I have chosen, more or less at random, to trace their thinking on just one subject, namely forests.

The conservation of forests was important for a number of reasons; first, as part of species conservation. Wild species contained genetic material of immense commercial benefit to agriculture, medicine, and industry. For example, fungus-resistant maize had been developed from stocks originating in Mexico, while a perennial species of maize, almost extinct, had been discovered in a forest area also in Mexico. Cocoa-growing in West Africa depended on genetic material from the Amazon forests. Brazil supplied genetic material from wild rubber to plantations in south-east Asia, while depending on genetic material for coffee-growing from wild species found mostly in Ethiopia.

Much damage had been done to tropical forests by commercial exploitation on terms which the commission strongly criticized for inducing loggers to over-exploit the resource. They recommended more detailed regulation of revenue systems and concession terms, along with much larger protected areas, so raising the cost of conservation. To be effective, such measures would have to embody financial incentives to protect wild species and eco-systems; and these in turn were more likely to be adopted if developing countries and their governments were ensured an equitable share of the profits from the commercial use of genetic material.

Secondly, as the World Bank had pointed out, fuel-wood was the main source of domestic energy for nearly half of humanity; many were short of it, and their number was growing.[18] As a form of energy it was highly inefficient. Cooking in an earthen pot over an open fire used some eight times more energy than in an aluminium pan on a gas cooker. It was an exact illustration of 'the tragic paradox of poverty': the poor pay more, and have to adopt more environmentally destructive practices.

Fuel-wood included charcoal, a more convenient and cleaner fuel than raw wood, causing less eye irritation and respiratory trouble; but its production by conventional methods was extremely wasteful. Deforestation around cities could be reduced if more efficient techniques were adopted.

In rural areas fuel-wood could be grown as a subsistence crop, using 'agroforestry' methods practised for centuries by traditional farmers. Generally speaking, the rural poor did not fell trees, but rather gathered twigs and fallen dead wood, or lopped branches off the living tree; and to that extent (it was implied) they posed a lesser threat to the forests, certainly less than commercial logging. However, in the Côte d'Ivoire, which had been generous in admitting refugees, and which depended on timber exports for foreign currency, there was rapid deforestation caused in part by land-hunger.

Thirdly, forests protected other environments. Deforestation in the Andes and Himalayas had been followed by increased flooding. Elsewhere, however, conservation of upland forests had protected valley fields from floods and erosion. A particularly striking example was a forest reserve in Sulawesi, which protected large populations of indigenous mammals and birds, while also protecting an irrigation scheme funded by the World Bank to increase rice production on the flat lands downstream.

In sum, the Brundtland commission called for an integration of environmental and development policies, reflecting a closer integration of natural and social science perspectives; and they were largely responsible for bringing into general currency the very phrase sustainable development.[19]

Development thinking and aid policies reviewed

According to the development economist Frances Stewart, from the beginnings of aid and development in the 1950s the main aim was *economic growth* measured by growth in per capita GNP. It was supposed that this would be achieved largely through *industrialization*. *Employment* was seen as a prime objective; and it was further expected that the benefits of development would spread or '*trickle down*' from industrial growth poles.

By about 1970 there had indeed been economic growth in most low-income countries, and to that extent it could be said that the thinking had been correct and the policies based on it had been successful. However, mainstream thinking in the world of aid had come under critical attack from radical writers. Moreover, it had become inescapably clear that 'trickle-down' was simply not happening. Industrial development together with urban bias had created well-paid employment for a few, so increasing average incomes, but leaving many no better off or actually worse off.

In response, some in the world of aid came to see the next objective as that of raising the incomes of the poor ('*poverty-alleviation*') without detriment to growth; hence the '*redistribution with growth*' approach, which found some favour in the 1970s.[20]

However, it was soon swept away by the disasters of the 1980s, a terrible decade for the 'Third World'. Droughts and famines were widespread especially in Africa. The rapid spread of HIV/AIDS, unknown before 1980, occurred mostly in low-income countries. Among purely human-made disasters was the leak from a pesticide factory at Bhopal, India. Mainly as a consequence of wars and political oppression, the number of refugees in the world nearly doubled from 8 million to 14 million between 1980 and 1988, while vast numbers of persons were displaced within their own countries: 10 million in Africa, including 2.7 million in Uganda alone.[21]

And all that in a decade when primary commodity prices declined by almost a half;[22] and while poor countries' export earnings fell, their debt service payments increased. GNP growth-rates fell sharply in low-income countries as a whole apart from China and India, and some experienced negative growth.[23] As a result between 1983 and 1992 the net flow of resources was from poor countries to rich, and in the late 1980s and early 1990s there was even a net flow from low-income countries to the Bretton Woods institutions particularly the IMF.[24] (As the UNDP pointedly remarked in 1992, the IMF had for several years been taking money out of Africa.)[25] Furthermore, in the early 1980s under the influence of monetarist theories the USA and UK raised interest rates and cut aid. True, soon afterwards British aid was increased again somewhat in response to the African famine emergency; but that did not increase the official development assistance available to make up for the loss of export earnings.

In the world of aid it must have seemed as if the whole nature of the problem had changed. The net flow from poor countries to rich constituted negative aid. It was less a question of how to promote growth, more a problem of how best to use existing, even dwindling resources to stop things going from bad to worse. Raising incomes as an end in itself came to be seen as less important than maintaining the availability of essential goods and services to the poor at prices they could afford (and at this point there was a clear convergence on Amartya Sen's 'entitlement' approach).[26] By 1980 there was a renewed emphasis on *Basic Needs*, and on adjusting in such a way as to protect the nutrition and basic health and education services of the poorer and more vulnerable people in low-income countries. This approach was summed up in a new slogan, '*Adjustment with a human face*', adding a poverty-alleviation aspect to adjustment much as 'redistribution with growth' had to growth.

In the early 1980s the governments of many low-income countries found themselves with current account deficits they could not finance, and turned to the IMF and World Bank for help. (The IMF was always involved as the World Bank deferred to its judgement on monetary and exchange rate policy.)[27] When short-term assistance was made available it was conditionally on measures of '*structural adjustment*'. As noted by the Brandt commission, these typically included reducing domestic demand, balancing the budget, and especially eliminating consumer subsidies (but the UNDP commented 'It is short-sighted to balance budgets by unbalancing the lives of the people').[28]

By the end of the 1970s the Basic Needs approach dominated the world of aid. It had the support of bilateral aid donors as well as the ILO, the IMF and World Bank, and other international agencies, as evidenced by a number of policy pronouncements, though it was acknowledged that protecting human needs might take political courage.

However, as the financial crisis deepened, more and more emphasis came to be placed on adjustment, less and less on human needs; and the onus of decision was entirely on the recipient countries' governments. The effects of adjustment measures on income distribution or on particular groups within each country were regarded as matters for political choices by the government concerned, in which international agencies could not interfere.

According to a study carried out for UNICEF by G. A. Cornia, Richard Jolly, and Frances Stewart, in many countries structural adjustment measures had devastating effects on the basic health and education services available to the most vulnerable. 'After nearly three decades of steady progress, child welfare and nutrition sharply deteriorated'. In some countries indiscriminate cuts in government health expenditure resulted in an upsurge of infectious diseases, for instance in Ghana, while an immunization programme in Brazil was delayed. Nutrition deteriorated and improvement in infant and child mortality slowed; for example, the reduction in food subsidies resulted in malnutrition in Sri Lanka, where they had once contributed much to the country's notably low infant mortality rate.[29]

However, the UNICEF team argued that measures to benefit the poor and protect vulnerable groups need cost little or even nothing if existing resources were reallocated. For example, a nationwide immunization programme in Pakistan had been financed by postponing one urban hospital. Indeed, hospitals in general gobbled up resources to the detriment of basic health care, which could be remarkably economical and cost-effective.[30]

If South Korea and Taiwan had been the exemplars of redistribution with growth, those of basic needs and adjustment with a human face were Botswana, South Korea, and above all Zimbabwe. While pursuing conventional expansionary economic policies, all three had protected vulnerable groups during difficult times by maintaining the incomes of the poor and reallocating resources to basic health and education. Botswana in addition had given direct support to nutrition in the most vulnerable groups, and created employment in public works to restore incomes lost by drought, half the cost of the drought relief programme being met by foreign donors. South Korea too had emphasized public works, at a cost of less than one per cent of total government expenditure.

As for Zimbabwe, for much of the 1980s the government could not reach agreement with the IMF and went ahead with their own adjustment policies. Credit and marketing reforms favoured small farmers. Military expenditure was cut, and there were economies in administration. Preventive medicine's share of total health expenditure was increased, and likewise primary schools' share of total spending on education. Despite drought and financial crisis, infant mortality continued to fall, school enrolments rose, and there was no increase in malnutrition.[31]

Global policies for world development

Generalizing from such instances, in 1990 the UNDP pointed out that in many cases policy-makers could decide whether public expenditure cuts should fall on such things as military expenditure and social subsidies for the privileged, or on health, education, and food subsidies for vulnerable groups.

'Special attention should go to reducing military spending in the Third World'. Subject to that overriding priority, other recommended policies involved 'shifting resources:

- from curative medical facilities to primary health care programmes,
- from highly trained doctors to para-medical personnel,
- from urban to rural services,
- from general to vocational education,
- from subsidizing tertiary education to subsidizing primary and secondary education,
- from expensive housing for the privileged groups to sites and services projects for the poor,
- from subsidies for vocal and powerful groups to subsidies for inarticulate and weaker groups, and
- from the formal to the informal sector, and programmes for the unemployed and the underemployed.'[32]

It will be noticed that though they were primarily addressed to 'Third World' issues and problems, some of these recommendations have an even wider application. I hope that this book may help to provide a background against which they can be seen in perspective.

Suggestions for further reading

Partners in Development (the Pearson Report: London, Pall Mall, 1969)
North–South: A Programme for Survival (the Brandt Report: London, Pan, 1980)
Our Common Future (the Brundtland Report: Oxford, Oxford University Press, 1987)
John White, *The Politics of Foreign Aid* (London, Bodley Head, 1974)
Frances Stewart, *Basic Needs in Developing Countries* (Baltimore, Md., Johns Hopkins University Press; published in UK as *Planning to Meet Basic Needs*, London, Macmillan, 1985)
Giovanni Andrea Cornia, Richard Jolly and Frances Stewart, *Adjustment with a Human Face* (2 vols., Oxford, Clarendon Press, 1987)

Notes

1 Introduction and argument

1 Ernest Gellner, *Thought and Change* (London, Weidenfeld and Nicolson, 1964), p. 33n.
2 United Nations Development Programme, *Human Development Report 1990* (New York, Oxford University Press for UNDP, 1990), p. 36.
3 UNDP, *Human Development Report 1992*, pp. 1, 34–7.
4 World Bank, *World Development Report 1993* (New York, Oxford University Press for World Bank, 1993), table 5, pp. 246–7.
5 *Ibid.*, table 3, pp. 242–3.
6 United Nations, *Measures for the Economic Development of Under-Developed Countries*, E/1986 ST/ETA/10 (New York, 3 May 1951).
7 Karl Gunnar Myrdal, *Asian Drama: An Inquiry into the Poverty of Nations* (3 vols., New York and Harmondsworth, Twentieth-Century Fund, Random House, and Penguin, 1968), vol. III, appendix 1, pp. 1839–42.
8 Auguste Comte, *Positive Politics*, vol. IV, appendix, pp. 149–50, quoted by N. S. Timasheff, *Sociological Theory, Its Nature and Growth* (New York, 1955), p. 19; *Positive Philosophy*, transl. Harriet Martineau (London, 1853), esp. vol. II, ch. VI.
9 Herbert Spencer, *Principles of Sociology* (3 vols., London, Williams and Norgate, 1893–7), vol. I, part II, chs. X, XI; vol. II, part V, chs. XVII, XVIII.
10 Sir Henry Sumner Maine, *Ancient Law*, 11th edn (London, John Murray, 1887), p. 170.
11 Emile Durkheim, *The Division of Labour in Society*, transl. G. Simpson (Glencoe, Ill., The Free Press, 1947); *Elementary Forms of the Religious Life*, transl. J. W. Swain (London, Allen and Unwin, 1915).
12 Lewis S. Feuer (ed.), *Marx and Engels: Basic Writings on Politics and Philosophy* (New York, Doubleday, 1959); George Lichtheim, *Marxism: An Historical and Critical Study* (London, Routledge and Kegan Paul, 1961).
13 Max Weber, *The Protestant Ethic and the Spirit of Capitalism*, transl. Talcott Parsons (London, Allen & Unwin, 1930).
14 Ferdinand Tönnies, *Gemeinschaft und Gesellschaft*, 1887, revised 1922; transl. Charles P. Loomis, *Community and Association* (London, Routledge and Kegan Paul, 1955), *Community and Society* (East Lansing, Michigan State University Press, 1957).
15 L. T. Hobhouse, *Social Development* (London, Allen and Unwin, 1924); J. A. Hobson and Morris Ginsberg, *L. T. Hobhouse: His Life and Work* (London, Allen and Unwin, 1931).
16 Bronislaw Malinowski, *A Scientific Theory of Culture* (Chapel Hill, University of North Carolina Press, 1944).

17 Talcott Parsons, *The Structure of Social Action* (New York, McGraw Hill, 1937; 2nd edn, Glencoe, Ill., Free Press, 1949).
18 Talcott Parsons and Edward A. Shils (eds.), *Toward a General Theory of Action* (Cambridge, Mass., Harvard University Press, 1951), pp. 49, 76–7.
19 Talcott Parsons, *Societies: Evolutionary and Comparative Perspectives* (Englewood Cliffs, N.J., Prentice-Hall, 1966), pp. 1, 21–3.
20 W. W. Rostow, *The Stages of Economic Growth: A Non-Communist Manifesto* (Cambridge, Cambridge University Press, 1971).
21 Philip Abrams, *The Origins of British Sociology: 1834–1914* (Chicago, University of Chicago Press, 1968), pp. 88–91.
22 Michael Redclift, *Sustainable Development: Exploring the Contradictions* (London, Methuen, 1987).
23 Marshall Sahlins, *The Use and Abuse of Biology: An Anthropological Critique of Sociobiology* (London, Tavistock, 1977).
24 K. S. Gapp, 'The universal famine under Claudius', *Harvard Theological Review*, 28 (1935), 258–65.
25 Michael Mortimore, *Adapting to Drought: Farmers, Famines, and Desertification in West Africa* (Cambridge, Cambridge University Press, 1989), p. 191.
26 Louis Dumont, *Homo Hierarchicus*, transl. Mark Sainsbury (London, Weidenfeld and Nicolson, 1970).
27 Aidan Foster-Carter, 'From Rostow to Gunder Frank: changing paradigms in the analysis of development', *World Development*, 4 (1976), 167–80.
28 Stephen Howe, *Anticolonialism in British Politics: The Left and the End of Empire* (Oxford, Clarendon Press, 1993), pp. 168, 178–9.
29 Larousse, 1978: 'Tiers état . . . nom donnée en France, sous l'Ancien Régime, à la partie de la population qui n'appartenait ni à la noblesse ni au clergé. Tiers monde, ensemble des pays peu developpés economiquement qui n'appartiennent ni au groupe des Etats industriels d'economie libérale, ni au groupe des Etats de type socialiste.' Dupré, *Encyclopédie de bon français*, 1972: 'Tiers . . . Aujourd'hui, cet adjectif archaïque a connu une fortune nouvelle dans les expressions le tiers monde', etc.
30 Peter Lloyd, 'A new catchphrase for an old problem', *The Times Higher Education Supplement*, 4 Oct. 1974, p. 1.
31 Peter Worsley, *The Third World* (London, Weidenfeld and Nicolson, 1964).
32 Irving Louis Horowitz, *Three Worlds of Development* (New York, Oxford University Press, 1966).

2 Technology, society, and population

1 V. Gordon Childe, *Man Makes Himself* (London, Watts, 1936), ch. 2; Don R. Arthur, *Survival: Man and His Environment* (London, English Universities Press, 1969); S. Lilley, *Men, Machines, and History* (London, Cobbett Press, 1948, revised edn, 1965); Carlo M. Cipolla, *The Economic History of World Population*, 7th edn (Harmondsworth, Penguin, 1978); Colin McEvedy and Richard Jones, *Atlas of World Population History* (Harmondsworth, Penguin, 1978).
2 United Nations, *The Determinants and Consequences of Population Trends* (1953), ST/SDA/Ser. A/17 (New York, 1953); Marshall Sahlins, *Stone Age Economics* (London, Tavistock, 1974).
3 J. V. Grauman, 'Population growth', *International Encyclopaedia of the Social Sciences* (1968).
4 Alexander de Waal, *Famine that Kills: Darfur, Sudan, 1984–1985* (Oxford, Clarendon Press, 1989), p. 175.

5 J. Hajnal, 'European marriage patterns in perspective', in D. V. Glass and D. E. C. Eversley (eds.), *Population in History* (London, Arnold, 1965), pp. 101–43.

6 R. W. Firth, *We the Tikopia* (London, Allen & Unwin, 1936), ch. XI.

7 A. M. Carr-Saunders, *World Population: Past Growth and Present Trends* (Oxford, Oxford University Press, 1936; reprinted by Frank Cass, 1964); United Nations *Demographic Yearbooks* for figures after 1930.

8 Warren S. Thompson, 'Population', *American Journal of Sociology*, 34 (1929), 959–75; J. C. Caldwell, *Theory of Fertility Decline* (London, Academic Press, 1982), ch. 4; Simon Szreter, 'The idea of demographic transition', *Population and Development Review*, 19 (1993), 659–701.

9 C. P. Blacker, *Eugenics, Galton and After* (London, Duckworth, 1952), ch. 8.

10 Michael Drake, *Population and Society in Norway 1735–1865* (Cambridge, Cambridge University Press, 1969); D. V. Glass (ed.), *Introduction to Malthus* (London, Watts, 1953), pp. 30–8.

11 United Nations Development Programme, *Human Development Report 1990*, p. 2.

12 D. M. de Silva, 'Public health and sanitation measures as factors affecting mortality trends in Ceylon', *Proceedings of the World Population Conference, 1954* (UN, 1955), vol. I, pp. 411–38; UN, *Demographic Yearbooks*, 1966 and historical supplement 1979.

13 World Bank, *World Development Report 1993* (New York, Oxford University Press, 1993), table 27.

14 Population Reference Bureau, *World Population Data Sheet, 1991*.

15 Francis X. Murphy, 'Catholic perspectives on population issues II', *Population Bulletin*, vol. 35, no. 6 (Washington, D.C., Population Reference Bureau, February 1981).

16 *Partners in Development* (the Pearson Report; London, Pall Mall, 1969), pp. 55–8, 194–9.

17 Population Reference Bureau, 'China's "one-child" population future', *Intercom*, vol. 9, no. 8 (August 1981); H. Yuan Tien, 'China: Demographic Billionaire', *Population Bulletin*, vol. 38, no. 2 (April 1983), p. 5; Griffith Feeney and Wang Feng, 'Parity progression and birth intervals in China', *Population and Development Review*, 19 (1993), 61–101.

18 Peter J. Donaldson and Amy Ong Tsui, 'The international family planning movement', *Population Bulletin*, vol. 45, no. 3 (November 1990), pp. 6, 14.

19 Lord Blackett, *The Gap Widens* (the Rede Lecture, 1969; London, Cambridge University Press, 1970).

20 Michael Lipton, 'The international diffusion of technology', in Dudley Seers and Leonard Joy (eds.), *Development in a Divided World* (Harmondsworth, Penguin, 1971), pp. 45–50.

21 Georges Tapinos and Phyllis T. Piotrow, *Six Billion People* (New York, McGraw Hill, 1978).

22 Depending on definition, middle-class infant mortality in 1911 was estimated at 55 to 96 per 1,000 live births: R. M. Titmuss, *Birth, Poverty and Wealth* (London, Hamish Hamilton, 1943), pp. 23–31.

23 Etienne van de Walle and John Knodel, 'Europe's fertility transition: new evidence and lessons for today's developing world', *Population Bulletin*, vol. 34, no. 6 (February 1980).

24 Chris Scott and V. C. Chidambaram, 'The World Fertility Survey: origins and achievements', in John Cleland and John Hobcraft (eds.) with Betzy Dinesen, *Reproductive Change in Developing Countries* (Oxford, Oxford University Press, 1985), pp. 7–10.

25 World Fertility Survey, *World Fertility Survey: Major Findings and Implications* (London, WFS, 1984).

26 John Cleland, 'Fertility decline: theories and evidence', in Cleland and Hobcraft, *Reproductive Change*, p. 224.

27 *World Fertility Survey*, pp. 25–30.

28 R. E. Lightbourne, 'Individual preferences and fertility behaviour', in Cleland and Hobcraft, *Reproductive Change*, pp. 165–91.

29 John C. Caldwell, in Cleland and Hobcraft, *Reproductive Change*, pp. 47–58; *Theory of Fertility Decline*, ch. 4.

30 Robert Chambers, *Rural Development* (London, Longman, 1983), pp. 55–6.

31 Lightbourne, in Cleland and Hobcraft, *Reproductive Change*.

32 Scott and Chidambaram, in Cleland and Hobcraft, *Reproductive Change*, p. 21.

33 UNDP, *Human Development Report, 1994*, p. 28.

34 World Bank, *World Development Report, 1993*, pp. 32–3, 99–106.

35 Tony Barnett and Piers Blaikie, *AIDS in Africa: Its Present and Future Impact* (London, Belhaven, 1992), p. 36.

36 *Ibid.*, pp. 46–50.

37 George C. Bond and Joan Vincent, 'Living on the edge: changing social structures in the context of AIDS', ch. 7 of Holger Bernt Hansen and Michael Twaddle (eds.), *Changing Uganda: The Dilemmas of Structural Adjustment and Revolutionary Change* (London, James Currey, 1991), p. 123.

38 World Bank, 1993, p. 104.

39 For a wider assessment see John C. Caldwell and Pat Caldwell, 'The nature and limits of the sub-Saharan African AIDS epidemic', *Population and Development Review*, 19 (1993), 817–48.

Case-study 1: India

1 Kingsley Davis, *The Population of India and Pakistan* (Princeton, N.J., Princeton University Press, 1951).

2 Myrdal, *Asian Drama*, pp. 1489–91, 1518–20, and appendix 12.

3 Quoted in Tapinos and Piotrow, *Six Billion People*, pp. 98–9, 115–16.

4 Pravin Visaria and Leela Visaria, 'India's population: second and growing', *Population Bulletin*, vol. 36, no. 4 (October 1981).

Case-study 2: England and Wales

1 E. A. Wrigley and R. S. Schofield, *The Population History of England, 1541–1871: A Reconstruction* (London, Edward Arnold, 1981).

2 R. A. Lewis, *Edwin Chadwick and the Public Health Movement, 1832–1854* (London, Longmans Green, 1952).

3 J. A. Banks, *Prosperity and Parenthood* (London, Routledge and Kegan Paul, 1954).

4 Graham Wallas, *The Life of Francis Place* (London, Longmans Green, 1898), ch. 6; St John G. Ervine, *Francis Place* (Fabian biographical tract no. 1; London, The Fabian Society, 1912).

5 J. H. Clapham, *An Economic History of Modern Britain, 1850–1866* (Cambridge, Cambridge University Press, 1932), ch. IX; W. W. Rostow, *British Economy of the Nineteenth Century* (Oxford, Clarendon Press, 1948), chs. III, IV, VII.

6 *Royal Commission on Population Report*, Cmd 7695 (London, HMSO, 1949); E. Lewis-Faning, *Family Limitation* (Papers of the Royal Commission on Population; London, HMSO, 1949), p. 7.

Case-study 3: Japan

1 Irene B. Taeuber, *The Population of Japan* (Princeton, N.J., Princeton University Press, 1958).

3 The colonial episode and the race question

1 Morris D. Morris, *Measuring the Condition of the World's Poor: The Physical Quality of Life Index* (Oxford, Pergamon, 1979), pp. 23–4.

2 Carlo M. Cipolla, 'Guns and Sails', *European Culture and Overseas Expansion* (Harmondsworth, Penguin, 1970), pp. 104–5.

3 De Kiewiet, quoted in Pierre L. van den Berghe, *South Africa: A Study in Conflict* (Berkeley, University of California Press, 1970), pp. 13–14.

4 Burton Benedict, *Indians in a Plural Society: A Report on Mauritius* (Colonial Research Studies no. 34; London, 1961), esp. chs. II and III.

5 *The Times Atlas of World History* (London, Times Books, 1979), p. 166.

6 Robert W. Fogel and Stanley L. Engerman, *Time on the Cross: The Economics of American Negro Slavery* (2 vols., Boston, Mass., Little, Brown, 1974), vol. I, ch. 1.

7 Carr-Saunders, *World Population*, pp. 34–5; W. F. Willcox, quoted in *ibid.*; Robert C. Cook, 'How many people have ever lived on earth?', *Population Bulletin*, vol. 18, no. 1 (1962); J. N. Biraben, 'Essai sur l'evolution du nombre des hommes', *Population*, 34 (1979), cited in Massimo Livi-Bacci, *A Concise History of World Population*, transl. Carl Ipsen (Oxford, Blackwell, 1992).

8 McEvedy and Jones, *Atlas of World Population History*, pp. 213–16.

9 Karl Gunnar Myrdal, *An American Dilemma* (New York, Harper, 1944); abridged edition by Arnold M. Rose, *The Negro in America* (New York, Harper, 1948); C. W. Wagley, 'The situation of the Negro in the United States', *International Social Science Bulletin* (later *Journal*), 9 (1957), 427–38; Roger Bastide, 'Race relations in Brazil', *ibid.*, 495–512; Donald Pierson, *Negroes in Brazil* (Chicago, University of Chicago Press, 1944), pp. 30–7.

10 G. M. Trevelyan, *English Social History* (London, Longmans, 1944), pp. 347, 388–9, 495–6; R. Coupland, *The British Anti-Slavery Movement* (London, Thornton Butterworth, 1933); Eric Williams, *Capitalism and Slavery* (Chapel Hill, University of North Carolina Press, 1943; London, Andre Deutsch, 1964).

11 W. E. F. Ward, *The Royal Navy and the Slavers* (London, Allen & Unwin, 1969).

12 Roland Oliver, *The Missionary Factor in East Africa* (London, Longmans, 1952), ch. I.

13 Myrdal, *Asian Drama*, ch. 5, section 1, 'The advance of colonial rule'.

14 Andrew K. H. Boyd and P. van Rensburg, *An Atlas of African Affairs* (London, Methuen, 1962), pp. 24–7; Roland Oliver and J. D. Fage, *A Short History of Africa* (Harmondsworth, Penguin, 1962), ch. 16.

15 Harry Thuku, *An Autobiography* (Nairobi, Oxford University Press, 1970).

16 Oliver, *The Missionary Factor*, pp. 149–62; D. A. Low, 'British public opinion and the Uganda question, October–December 1892', *Uganda Journal*, 18 (1954), 81–100.

17 Elspeth Huxley, *White Man's Country: Lord Delamere and the Making of Kenya* (2 vols., London, Chatto and Windus, 1935); Elspeth Huxley and Margery Perham, *Race and Politics in Kenya* (London, Faber, 1944); L. H. Gann and P. Duignan, *White Settlers in Tropical Africa* (Harmondsworth, Penguin, 1962).

18 A. P. Elkin, *The Australian Aborigines*, 4th edn (Sydney, Angus & Robertson, 1964), ch. XIV; 'Aborigines and Europeans in Australia', *American Anthropologist*, 53 (1951), 164–86.

19 Myrdal, *Asian Drama*, pp. 449–52, 832–3, 839.

20 A. I. Richards, *Land, Labour and Diet in Northern Rhodesia* (London, Oxford University Press for the International African Institute, 1939), pp. 256–62; R. L. Buell, 'Forced labour', *Encyclopaedia of the Social Sciences* (1932).

21 Oliver, *The Missionary Factor*, pp. 247–57.

22 Myrdal, *Asian Drama*, pp. 969–71.

23 Boyd and van Rensburg, *Atlas of African Affairs*, p. 19.

24 Each £100 invested in the company when it began in 1903 earned a first dividend of £2. 10. 0 in 1907. In 1913 it was written down to £50, and no more dividends were declared until 1918. From then till 1925 the company paid dividends at 5^1/₂ to 15%, but that was only 2³/₄ to 7^1/₂% on the original capital. No more dividends were forthcoming till 1937, by which time the original investment had been further written down to £37. 10. 0. Later the company paid bigger and more regular dividends, but even so the average yield over the first fifty years was little more than 3% – C. Ehrlich, *The Uganda Company Limited: The First Fifty Years* (Kampala, The Uganda Company, 1953), pp. 54–5.

25 C. Wagley and M. Harris, *Minorities in the New World* (New York, Columbia University Press, 1958), p. 27.

26 F. B. Welbourn, *East African Rebels* (London, SCM Press, 1961), ch. 7; Carl G. Rosberg and John Nottingham, *The Myth of 'Mau Mau': Nationalism in Kenya* (New York, Praeger, 1966), pp. 112–25.

27 J. E. Goldthorpe, *Outlines of East African Society* (Kampala, Makerere College, 1958), ch. VIII.

28 William Malcolm Hailey (Lord Hailey), *An African Survey* (London, Oxford University Press, 1938), pp. 413ff; Max Gluckman, 'Analysis of a social situation in modern Zululand', *Bantu Studies*, 14 (1940), 1–30, 147–74, reprinted as Rhodes-Livingstone Paper no. 28 (1958); also his 'Inter-hierarchical roles', in Marc J. Swartz (ed.), *Local-Level Politics* (London, University of London Press, 1969), pp. 69–93; L. A. Fallers, *Bantu Bureaucracy* (Cambridge, Heffer, 1956), esp. pp. 196–203; D. A. Low and R. C. Pratt, *Buganda and British Overrule, 1900–1955* (London, Oxford University Press, 1960); David E. Apter, *The Political Kingdom in Uganda* (Princeton, N.J., Princeton University Press, 1961), ch. 13; The Kabaka of Buganda, *Desecration of my Kingdom* (London, Constable, 1967).

29 Goldthorpe, *Outlines of East African Society*, ch. X.

30 Arthur Phillips (ed.), *Survey of African Marriage and Family Life* (London, Oxford University Press for International African Institute, 1953), pp. 179–89.

31 John Iliffe, *The African Poor* (Cambridge, Cambridge University Press, 1987), p. 143.

32 J. E. Goldthorpe, *An African Elite* (Nairobi, Oxford University Press for East African Institute of Social Research, 1965).

33 Iliffe, *The African Poor*, ch. 7.

34 Cyril Sofer and Rhona Ross, 'Some characteristics of an East African European population', *British Journal of Sociology*, 2 (1951), 315–27.

35 Roger Bastide, 'Dusky Venus, black Apollo', *Race*, 3 (1961), 10–18; Carl N. Degler, *Neither Black Nor White* (London, Collier-Macmillan, 1971), pp. 185–95.

36 Wagley and Harris, *Minorities in the New World*, p. 24; Pierson, *Negroes in Brazil*, pp. 321–50.

37 C. Wagley (ed.), *Race and Class in Rural Brazil* (Paris, UNESCO, 1952), pp. 23–4.

38 Bastide, 'Race relations in Brazil'.

39 van den Berghe, *South Africa*, pp. 14–21, 39–42, 55–9; John Dugard, 'Racial legislation and civil rights', ch. 4 of Ellen Hellman and Henry Lever (eds.), *Race Relations in South Africa, 1929–1979* (London, Macmillan, 1980); Sheila T. van der Horst (ed.), *Race Discrimination in South Africa: A Review* (Cape Town, Philip, 1981).

40 J. S. Furnivall, 'The political economy of the tropical Far East', *Journal of the Royal Central Asian Society*, 29 (1942), 195–210; and his *Colonial Policy and Practice* (Cambridge, Cambridge University Press, 1948), pp. 303–12. See also John Rex, 'The plural society in sociological theory', *British Journal of Sociology*, 10 (1959), 114–24.

41 Myrdal, *Asian Drama*, p. 425.

42 F. D. Lugard, *The Dual Mandate in British Tropical Africa* (Edinburgh, Blackwood, 1923), esp. ch. III.

43 *East Africa Royal Commission 1953–1955 Report*, Cmd 9475 (London, HMSO, 1955), esp. map 2.

44 Myrdal, *Asian Drama*, p. 465.

45 *Ibid*, p. 453–7.

46 Sir Charles Dundas, *African Crossroads* (London, Macmillan, 1955), pp. 123–30; Huxley and Perham, *Race and Politics in Kenya*, pp. 98, 100, 107; Rosberg and Nottingham, *The Myth of 'Mau Mau'*, pp. 74, 207, 304.

47 Myrdal, *Asian Drama*, pp. 144–7.

48 Margery Perham, 'African facts and American criticisms', *Foreign Affairs*, 22 (1944), reprinted in her *Colonial Sequence 1930 to 1949* (London, Methuen, 1967), pp. 250–62.

49 World Bank, *World Development Report 1982*, table 24; Morris Janowitz, *Military Institutions and Coercion in Developing Nations* (Chicago, University of Chicago Press, 1977), table 1 on pp. 38–9.

50 *Colonial Development and Welfare Acts 1929–70: A Brief Review*, Cmnd 4677 (London, HMSO, 1977).

51 Paul Streeten, 'Development dichotomies', in Gerald M. Meier and Dudley Seers (eds.), *Pioneers in Development* (New York, Oxford University Press for the World Bank, 1984), p. 338.

52 Sofer and Ross, *British Journal of Sociology*, 2 (1951), 319–21.

53 George de Vos, 'Conflict, dominance and exploitation in human systems of social segregation: some theoretical perspectives from the study of personality in culture', in A. de Reuck and Julie Knight (eds.), *Conflict in Society* (a CIBA symposium; London, Churchill, 1966), pp. 60–81.

54 Jean-Paul Sartre, preface to Frantz Fanon, *The Wretched of the Earth* (Harmondsworth, Penguin, 1967).

55 G. Andrew Maguire, *Toward 'Uhuru' in Tanzania* (Cambridge, Cambridge University Press, 1969).

56 Kwame Nkrumah, *Ghana: An Autobiography* (Edinburgh, Nelson, 1957); Tom Mboya, *Freedom and After* (London, Deutsch, 1963); Kenneth Kaunda, 'Some personal reflections', ch. II of Kaunda *et al.*, *Africa's Freedom* (London, Unwin, 1964); Oginga Odinga, *Not Yet Uhuru* (London, Heinemann, 1967).

57 Jawaharlal Nehru, *Letters from a Father to his Daughter* (Allahabad, The Allahabad Law Journal Press, 1930); *Glimpses of World History* (Allahabad, Kitabistan, 1934); *Jawaharlal Nehru: An Autobiography* (London, John Lane the Bodley Head, 1936); *The Discovery of India* (Calcutta, Signet Press, 1946).

58 Fanon, *The Wretched of the Earth*; also *A Dying Colonialism* and *Toward the African Revolution* (both Harmondsworth, Penguin, 1970).

59 Jomo Kenyatta, *Facing Mount Kenya* (London, Secker & Warburg, 1938).

60 Aimé Césaire, 'Cahier d'un retour au pays natal', transl. Peter Worsley and quoted in his *The Third World*, p. 124.

61 Quoted in Philip Mason, *Patterns of Dominance* (London, Oxford University Press for Institute of Race Relations, 1970), p. 290.

62 Julius Nyerere, Foreword to Chakravarthi Raghavan, *Recolonization: GATT, the Uruguay Round, and the Third World* (London, Zed, 1990).

4 Economic conditions

1 C. F. Carter, *The Science of Wealth* (London, Edward Arnold, 1966), p. 177.

2 World Bank, *World Development Report 1994*, tables 1 and 27, pp. 162–3, 214–15; UNDP, *Human Development Report 1992*, pp. 1, 34–7. Data for Germany refer to the former West Germany.

3 Polly Hill, *Development Economics On Trial: The Anthropological Case for a Prosecution* (Cambridge, Cambridge University Press, 1986), ch. 3; Giovanni Andrea Cornia, Richard Jolly and Frances Stewart, *Adjustment with a Human Face* (2 vols., Oxford, Clarendon Press, 1987), vol. I, ch. 14; UNDP, *Human Development Report 1993*, p. 108.

4 *World Development Report 1993*, table 30 and technical notes on pp. 319–21.

5 UNDP 1993, table 2.

6 Jan Drewnowski, *On Measuring and Planning the Quality of Life* (The Hague, Mouton, 1974).

7 Morris D. Morris, *Measuring the Condition of the World's Poor: The Physical Quality of Life Index* (Oxford, Pergamon, 1979), chapters 4 and 5.

8 UNDP 1993, p. 100.

9 UNDP 1990, p. 3.

10 UNDP 1993, pp. 11–19.

11 UNDP 1992, pp. 59, 61, 67.

12 Christine Obbo, 'Women, children and a "living wage"', and Susan Reynolds Whyte, 'Medicines and self-help: the privatization of health care in eastern Uganda', in Holger Bernt Hansen and Michael Twaddle (eds.), *Changing Uganda* (London, James Currey, 1991), pp. 99–100, 133.

13 UNDP 1992, pp. 45, 51–2; 1993, table 20 on pp. 174–5.

14 K. Sarwar Lateef, 'Structural adjustment in Uganda: the initial experience', in Hansen and Twaddle, *Changing Uganda*, p. 37.

15 UNDP 94, pp. 63–4.

16 *Ibid.*, pp. 47–60.

17 United Nations Centre on Transnational Corporations, *Transnational Corporations in World Development: Trends and Prospects* (New York, United Nations, 1988), p. 16.

18 G. K. Helleiner, 'Transnational corporations and direct foreign investment', ch. 27 of Hollis Chenery and T. N. Srinivasan (eds.), *Handbook of Development Economics* (2 vols., Amsterdam, Elsevier, 1989), vol. II, pp. 1441–75.

19 UNCTNC 1988, pp. 198–9, 203.

20 Helleiner, 'Transnational corporations', pp. 1445–6.

21 UNCTNC, 1985, quoted in World Commission on Environment and Development, *Our Common Future* (the Brundtland Report; Oxford, Oxford University Press, 1987), p. 85.

22 G. L. Beckford, 'The economics of resource use and development in plantation economies', *Social and Economic Studies*, 18 (Jamaica, 1969), pp. 321–47; reprinted in Henry Bernstein (ed.), *Underdevelopment and Development* (Harmondsworth, Penguin, 1973), pp. 115–51.

23 Independent Commission on International Development Issues, *North–South: A Programme for Survival* (the Brandt Report; London, Pan, 1980), pp. 188–90; UNCTNC, 1988, pp. 94–5.

24 Helleiner, 'Transnational corporations', pp. 1464–5.

25 UNCTNC, 1988, pp. 134, 176

26 Michel Ghertman and Margaret Allen, *An Introduction to the Multinationals* (London, Macmillan, 1984), pp. 85–6.

27 UNCTNC, 1974, p. 60.

28 UNCTNC, 1988, pp. 214–16.

29 *Ibid.*, pp. 222–6.

30 Roger Ballard, pers. comm.

31 *Poverty and Landlessness in Rural Asia* (Geneva, International Labour Office, 1977).

32 Arthur Hazlewood *et al.*, *Education, Work, and Pay in East Africa* (Oxford, Clarendon Press, 1989), pp. 34, 38.

33 Gerald M. Meier, 'Development without employment', in his *Leading Issues in Economic Development*, 2nd edn (New York, Oxford University Press, 1970), pp. 430–9.

34 UNDP 1993, pp. 3, 36.

35 W. Arthur Lewis, *Development Planning* (London, Allen & Unwin, 1966), pp. 80–1.

36 G. Arrighi and J. S. Saul, 'Class formation and economic development in tropical Africa', *Journal of Modern African Studies*, 6 (1968), 141–69; reprinted in Bernstein, *Underdevelopment and Development*, pp. 284–97.

37 World Bank, *World Development Report 1987*, p. 123.

38 Rakesh Mohan, *Work, Wages, and Welfare in a Developing Metropolis* (New York, Oxford University Press for The World Bank, 1986).

39 See for instance Godfrey Wilson, *The Economics of Detribalization in Northern Rhodesia* (Livingstone, Rhodes-Livingstone Institute, 1942); Godfrey and Monica Wilson, *The Analysis of Social Change* (Cambridge, Cambridge University Press, 1945); Audrey I. Richards (ed.), *Economic Development and Tribal Change* (Cambridge, Heffer, 1954).

40 J. van Velsen, 'Labour migration as a positive factor in the continuity of Tonga tribal society', in Aidan Southall (ed.), *Social Change in Modern Africa* (London, Oxford University Press for International African Institute, 1961), pp. 230–41.

41 Richards (ed.), *Economic Development and Tribal Change*, pp. 49–50, 151.

42 World Bank, *World Development Report 1994*, tables 13 and 17, pp. 186, 194; see also 1981, p. 51.

43 J. E. Goldthorpe, *An African Elite* (Nairobi, Oxford University Press for East African Institute of Social Research, 1965), p. 76.

44 M. J. Sharpston, 'The economics of corruption', *New Society*, 26 November 1970, 944–6.

45 Peter L. Berger, *Pyramids of Sacrifice* (Harmondsworth, Penguin, 1977), p. 172; Jagdish C. Kapur, *India in the Year 2000* (New Delhi, India International Centre, 1975); Mihir Bose, 'Middle India', *New Society*, 22/29 December 1977, 617–19.

46 World Bank, *World Development Report 1993*, table 30 on pp. 296–7.

47 John Iliffe, *The African Poor* (Cambridge, Cambridge University Press, 1987).

48 Michael Lipton, *Why Poor People Stay Poor: A Study of Urban Bias in World Development* (London, Temple Smith, 1977).

49 Simon Kuznets, 'Quantitative aspects of the economic growth of nations, part VIII: Distribution of income by size', *Economic Development and Cultural Change*, vol. 11, no. 2, part II (1963), pp. 58–60; *Economic Growth and Structure* (London, Heinemann, 1966), pp. 275–9.

50 Hollis Chenery *et al.*, *Redistribution with Growth* (Oxford University Press, 1974); *Patterns of Development, 1950–1970* (Oxford University Press, 1975).

51 Peter T. Knight, 'Brazilian socioeconomic development: issues for the eighties', *World Development*, 9 (1981), 1063–82; World Bank, *World Development Report 1981*, p. 70; *Our Common Future* (the Brundtland Report, 1987), pp. 193–4.

5 Environmental concerns

1 Paul R. Ehrlich and Anne H. Ehrlich, *Population, Resources, Environment: Issues in Human Ecology* (London, Freeman, 1970); Paul R. Ehrlich and Richard L. Harriman, *How to be a Survivor: A Plan to Save Spaceship Earth* (London, Ballantine, 1971), p. 14.

2 John Maddox, *The Doomsday Syndrome* (London, Macmillan, 1972).

3 *Our Common Future*, p. xi.

4 B. Grzimek, quoted in David Anderson and Richard Grove (eds.), *Conservation in Africa: People, Politics, and Practice* (Cambridge, Cambridge University Press, 1987, p. 5). See also D. H. Lawrence's poem 'Mountain Lion' in his *Complete Poems* (London, Heinemann, 1964), vol. I, pp. 401–2.

5 Laurens van der Post, Introduction to Vance G. Martin (ed.), *Wilderness* (Moray, Findhorn Press, 1980).

6 George Stanley, *ibid.*, pp. 159–63.

7 Quoted in Anderson and Grove, Introduction to their *Conservation in Africa*, p. 3.

8 J. G. Mosley, in Martin (ed.), *Wilderness*, pp. 169–72.

9 R. H. V. Bell, 'Conservation with a human face', in Anderson and Grove (eds.), *Conservation in Africa*, ch. 4.

10 Audrey I. Richards, *Land, Labour and Diet in Northern Rhodesia: An Economic Study of the Bemba Tribe* (London, Oxford University Press for International African Institute, 1939), pp. 35–7.

11 Alexander de Waal, *Famine that Kills: Darfur, Sudan, 1984–1985* (Oxford, Clarendon Press, 1989).

12 Paul R. Brass, 'The political uses of crisis: the Bihar famine of 1966–67', *Journal of Asian Studies*, 45 (1986), 245–67.

13 Amartya Sen, *Poverty and Famines: An Essay on Entitlement and Deprivation* (Oxford, Clarendon Press, 1981).

14 K. S. Gapp, 'The universal famine under Claudius', *Harvard Theological Review*, 28 (1935), 258–65.

15 United Nations Department of Economic Information and Policy Analysis, *World Economic Survey 1993*, E/1993/60 ST/ESA/237 (New York, United Nations, 1993), ch. 6.

16 Michael Mortimore, *Adapting to Drought: Farmers, Famines, and Desertification in West Africa* (Cambridge, Cambridge University Press, 1989).

17 Iliffe, *The African Poor*, p. 6.

18 R. R. Kuczynski, *Demographic Survey of the British Colonial Empire* (2 vols., London, Oxford University Press, 1948–9), vol. II, p. 123; J. E. Goldthorpe, 'The African population of East Africa: a summary of its past and present trends', *East Africa Royal Commission 1953–1955 Report*, Cmd 9475 (London, HMSO, 1955), pp. 462–73.

19 Anderson and Grove, Introduction to their *Conservation in Africa*, p. 7.

20 IUCN, quoted in *Our Common Future*, p. 165.

21 R. H. V. Bell in Anderson and Grove, *Conservation in Africa*, ch. 4.

22 David Turton, 'The Mursi and national park development', in *ibid.*, ch. 8.

23 Anderson and Grove, *Conservation in Africa*, p. 7.

24 *OXFAM News* (Oxford, Oxfam), Summer 1992.

6 The social sciences and the 'Third World'

1 Bronislaw Malinowski, *A Scientific Theory of Culture* (Chapel Hill, University of North Carolina Press, 1944).

2 Margaret Mead, *Growing Up in New Guinea* (Harmondsworth, Penguin, 1942), p. 8.

3 J. E. Meade, 'On becoming an economist', *Christ's College Magazine* (Cambridge), May 1970, p. 123.

4 United Nations, *Measures for the Economic Development of Under-Developed Countries*, E/1986 ST/ETA/10 (3 May 1951).

5 W. W. Rostow, *British Economy of the Nineteenth Century* (Oxford, Clarendon Press, 1948); 'The take-off into self-sustained growth', *Economic Journal*, 66 (1956), 25–48; *The Stages of Economic Growth: A Non-Communist Manifesto* (Cambridge, Cambridge University Press, 1960; 2nd edn, 1971).

6 Paul A. Baran and E. J. Hobsbawm, 'The stages of economic growth', *Kyklos*, 14 (1961), 234–42.

7 Everett E. Hagen, *The Economics of Development*, 2nd edn (Homewood, Ill., Irwin, 1975), p. 214.

8 Myrdal, *Asian Drama*, appendix 2, pp. 1852–5.

9 P. N. Rosenstein-Rodan, 'Problems of industrialization of eastern and south-eastern Europe', *Economic Journal*, 53 (1943), 205–11.

10 Ragnar Nurkse, 'The conflict between "balanced growth" and international specialization', *Lectures on Economic Development* (Istanbul, 1958), reprinted in Gerald M. Meier (ed.), *Leading Issues in Economic Development*, 2nd edn (New York, Oxford University Press, 1970), pp. 362–6.

11 Jacob Viner in a paper to the International Economic Association congress, 1956, quoted in Meier, *Leading Issues*, 2nd edn, p. 399.

12 A. J. Youngson, 'Development myths', *Bulletin of the Institute of Development Studies* (University of Sussex), May 1969, 22–3.

13 Albert O. Hirschman, *The Strategy of Economic Development* (New Haven, Conn., Yale University Press, 1958).

14 David Apter, *The Politics of Modernization* (Chicago, University of Chicago Press, 1965), pp. 9–10.

15 Hagen, *The Economics of Development*, 2nd edn (1975), p. 73.

16 Daniel Lerner, *The Passing of Traditional Society* (Glencoe, Ill., Free Press, 1958).

17 Fred W. Riggs, *Administration in Developing Countries: The Theory of Prismatic Society* (Boston, Mass., Houghton Mifflin, 1964), p. 36.

18 See for example Baidya Nath Varma, *The Sociology and Politics of Development* (London, Routledge & Kegan Paul, 1980).

19 Reinhard Bendix, 'Tradition and modernity reconsidered', *Comparative Studies in Society and History*, 9 (April 1967), 292–346; reprinted in his *Embattled Reason* (London, Oxford University Press, 1970), pp. 250–314.

20 J. P. Nettl and Roland Robertson, 'Industrialization, development, or modernization', *British Journal of Sociology*, 17 (1966), 274–91.

21 It is never easy to date an intellectual movement; some regard this as having been initiated by Paul Baran, *The Political Economy of Growth* (New York, Monthly Review Press, 1957).

22 Philip J. O'Brien, 'A critique of Latin American theories of dependency', in Ivar Oxaal, Tony Barnett and David Booth (eds.), *Beyond the Sociology of Development* (London, Routledge & Kegan Paul, 1975), pp. 7–27.

23 Celso Furtado, *Development and Underdevelopment*, transl. R. W. de Aguiar and E. C. Drysdale (Berkeley and Los Angeles, University of California Press, 1964); *Diagnosis of the Brazilian Crisis*, transl. Suzette Macedo (Berkeley and Los Angeles, University of California Press, 1965).

24 Teresa Hayter, *Aid as Imperialism* (Harmondsworth, Penguin, 1971).

25 A. G. Frank, *Capitalism and Underdevelopment in Latin America* (New York, Monthly Review Press, 1967), pp. 9–11, 221–5, 239, 242; 'The sociology of development and the underdevelopment of sociology', *Catalyst* (1967), 20–73; *Latin America: Underdevelopment or Revolution* (New York, Monthly Review Press, 1969), pp. 21–94.

26 Immanuel Wallerstein, *The Modern World System* (2 vols., New York, Academic Press, 1974–80), vol. I, pp. 1, 67, 87–8; vol. II, pp. 5–6, n19.

27 John Taylor, 'Neo-Marxism and underdevelopment', *Journal of Contemporary Asia*, 4 (1974), 9–10.

28 Barry Hindess and Paul Q. Hirst, *Pre-Capitalist Modes of Production* (London, Routledge & Kegan Paul, 1975).

29 Samir Amin, *Unequal Development: An Essay on the Social Formations of Peripheral Capitalism*, transl. Brian Pearce (Hassocks, Harvester Press, 1976).

30 See for instance Robin Jenkins, *Exploitation* (London, McGibbon & Kee, 1970); Hayter, *Aid as Imperialism*; Colin Leys, *Underdevelopment in Kenya* (London, Heinemann, 1975).

31 Aidan Foster-Carter, 'Development', ch. 3 of M. Haralambos (ed.), *Developments in Sociology: An Annual Review*, 6 (Ormskirk, Causeway Press, 1990).

32 P. W. Preston, *Theories of Development* (London, Routledge & Kegan Paul, 1982), ch. 5.

33 Paul Streeten, 'Development dichotomies', in Gerald M. Meier and Dudley Seers (eds.), *Pioneers in Development* (New York, Oxford University Press for the World Bank, 1984), pp. 350–4.

34 Karl Gunnar Myrdal, *An American Dilemma* (New York, Harper & Row, 1944); *Economic Theory and the Underdeveloped Regions* (London, Duckworth, 1957); *Value in Social Theory* (London, Routledge & Kegan Paul, 1958); *Asian Drama* (1968); *Objectivity in Social Research* (London, Duckworth, 1970); 'Underdevelopment and the evolutionary imperative', *Third World Quarterly*, 1, 2 (April 1979), 24–42; 'International inequality and foreign aid in perspective', in Meier and Seers, *Pioneers in Development* (1984), pp. 151–65.

35 Dudley Seers, 'The limitations of the special case', *Bulletin of the Oxford Institute of Economics and Statistics*, 25 (May 1963), 77–98.

36 Paul Streeten, 'The use and abuse of models in development planning', in Meier, *Leading Issues*, 2nd edn, 1970, p. 73. See also his appendix 3 to Myrdal, *Asian Drama*; and his *The Frontiers of Development Studies* (London, Macmillan, 1979).

37 Atul Kohli (ed.), *The State and Development in the Third World* (Princeton, N.J., Princeton University Press, 1986).

38 Polly Hill, *Studies in Rural Capitalism in West Africa* (Cambridge, Cambridge University Press, 1970); *Development Economics on Trial: The Anthropological Case for a Prosecution* (Cambridge, Cambridge University Press, 1986).

39 Robert Chambers, *Rural Development: Putting the Last First* (Harlow, Longman, 1983).

7 The rise of towns

1 Nathan Keyfitz, 'Political-economic aspects of urbanization in South and South-East Asia', in P. M. Hauser and L. F. Schnore (eds.), *The Study of Urbanization* (New York, Wiley, 1964), pp. 265–309.

2 Homer Hoyt, *World Urbanization* (1962), quoted in Gerald Breese, *Urbanization in Newly Developing Countries* (Englewood Cliffs, N.J., Prentice-Hall, 1966), p. 16.

3 E. A. Kracke, 'Sung society: change within tradition', *Far Eastern Quarterly*, 14 (1955), 479–88.

4 R. E. Pahl, *Patterns of Urban Life* (London and Harlow, Longmans, 1970), p. 19; Phyllis Deane and W. A. Cole, *British Economic Growth 1688–1959* (Cambridge, Cambridge University Press, 1962), pp. 7–8.

5 Kingsley Davis, *The Population of India and Pakistan*, p. 127; World Bank, *World Development Report 1994*, table 31, p. 222.

6 Kingsley Davis, 'The urbanization of the human population', *Scientific American*, 213 (September 1965), 40–53, reprinted in Gerald Breese (ed.), *The City in Newly Developing Countries* (Englewood Cliffs, N.J., Prentice-Hall, 1969), pp. 5–20.

7 Breese, *Urbanization*, p. 19.

8 World Bank, *World Development Report 1994*, table 31.

9 *World Fertility Survey* (1984), p. 37.

10 Samuel H. Preston, 'Mortality in childhood: lessons from the World Fertility Survey', ch. 11 of Cleland and Hobcraft (eds.), *Reproductive Change in Developing Countries*, p. 263.

11 UNDP, *Human Development Report 1990*, pp. 86–9.

12 Michael Lipton, *Why Poor People Stay Poor: A Study of Urban Bias in World Development* (London, Temple Smith, 1977); quotations from pp. 13, 19. See also John Harriss and Mick Moore (eds.), *Development and the Rural–Urban Divide* (London, Frank Cass, 1984).

13 Patrick Chabal, 'Revolutionary democracy in Africa: The case of Guinea-Bissau', ch. 5 of Chabal (ed.), *Political Domination in Africa* (Cambridge, Cambridge University Press, 1986), pp. 88–90.

14 Josef Gugler, in Alan Gilbert and Josef Gugler, *Cities, Poverty, and Development: Urbanization in the Third World* (London, Oxford University Press, 1982), ch. 4; Peter Lloyd, *Slums of Hope? Shanty Towns of the Third World* (Harmondsworth, Penguin, 1979).

15 Robert McNamara, 'Urban poverty' (Extract from World Bank President Robert McNamara's address at 1975 Annual Meeting, mimeographed).

16 Gilbert, in Gilbert and Gugler, *Cities*, ch. 5.

17 David Drakakis-Smith, *The Third World City* (London, Methuen, 1987).

8 Family life in a changing world: two studies

1 W. J. Goode, *World Revolution and Family Patterns* (New York, Free Press, 1963; paperback edition with a new preface, 1970).

2 Clark Kerr *et al.*, *Industrialism and Industrial Man* (Cambridge, Mass., Harvard University Press, 1960; Harmondsworth, Penguin, 1973).

3 John C. Caldwell, *Theory of Fertility Decline* (London, Academic Press, 1982), esp. chs. 5, 7, 10 and 12.

4 John C. Caldwell and Pat Caldwell, 'Family systems: their viability and vulnerability', ch. 5 of Elza Berquó and Peter Xenos (eds.), *Family Systems and Social Change* (Oxford, Clarendon Press, 1992).

5 See also Peter McDonald, 'Social organization and nuptiality in developing societies', in Cleland and Hobcraft (eds.), *Reproductive Change*, pp. 87–109; Christine Oppong, 'Traditional family systems in rural settings in Africa', ch. 6 of Berquó and Xenos (eds.), *Family Systems*, pp. 69–80.

9 Cultural diversity, language, education and communications

1 H. Kloss and G. D. McConnell, *Linguistic Composition of the Nations of the World* (5 vols., Quebec, Laval University Press, 1974–84), vol. III, 'Central and South America', pp. 83–102, 443–9.

2 On the peoples and cultures of Uganda see the appropriate volumes in the International African Institute's Ethnographic Survey of Africa series; also J. E. Goldthorpe, *Outlines of East African Society* (Kampala, Makerere University College, 1959); J. E. Goldthorpe and F. B. Wilson, *Tribal Maps of East Africa and Zanzibar* (Kampala, East African Institute of Social Research, 1960); Audrey I. Richards, *The Multicultural States of East Africa* (Montreal, McGill-Queen's University Press, 1969); L. P. Mair, *Primitive Government* (Harmondsworth, Penguin, 1962); P. H. Gulliver, *Tradition and Transition in East Africa* (London, Routledge & Kegan Paul, 1969); W. H. Whiteley (ed.), *Language Use and Social Change* (London, Oxford University Press for International African Institute, 1971), esp. ch. 7; P. Ladefoged, R. Glick, and C. Criper, *Language in Uganda* (London, Oxford University Press, 1972).

3 Christine Obbo, *African Women: Their Struggle for Independence* (London, Zed, 1980), ch. 3. 'Interlacustrine' refers to the land bordered by Lakes Victoria, Edward, Albert and Kyoga.

4 Audrey I. Richards (ed.), *Economic Development and Tribal Change* (Cambridge, Heffer, 1954), frontispiece and pp. 184, 194–7.

5 Dennis Pain, 'The Nubians: their perceived stratification system and its relation to the Asian issue', in Michael Twaddle (ed.), *Expulsion of a Minority: Essays on Uganda Asians* (London, Athlone Press, 1975), pp. 177–9.

6 D. A. Low and R. C. Pratt, *Buganda and British Overrule* (London, Oxford University Press, 1960); David E. Apter, *The Political Kingdom in Uganda* (Princeton, N.J., Princeton University Press, 1961); L. A. Fallers (ed.), *The King's Men: Leadership and Status in Buganda on the Eve of Independence* (London, Oxford University Press, 1964).

7 J. S. La Fontaine, 'Tribalism among the Gisu: An anthropological approach', in Gulliver (ed.), *Tradition and Transition*, pp. 177–92; E. E. Evans-Pritchard, 'The Nuer of the southern Sudan', in M. Fortes and E. E. Evans-Pritchard (eds.), *African Political Systems* (London, Oxford University Press for International African Institute, 1940), pp. 292–6; P. H. Gulliver, in his *Tradition and Transition*, p. 24.

8 Julius K. Nyerere, *Education for Self-Reliance* (Dar es Salaam, The Government Printer, 1967), p. 2.

9 See for instance S. H. Ominde, *Land and Population Movements in Kenya* (London, Heinemann, 1968).

10 J. E. Goldthorpe, *An African Elite* (Nairobi, Oxford University Press for the East African Institute of Social Research, 1965).

11 David Parkin, *Neighbours and Nationals in an African City Ward* (London, Routledge & Kegan Paul, 1969).

12 R. D. Grillo, *African Railwaymen* (Cambridge, Cambridge University Press, 1973).

13 Gulliver (ed.), *Tradition and Transition*, p. 37.

14 Richards, *The Multicultural States of East Africa*, pp. 102, 107–8.

15 Nelson Kasfir, 'Explaining ethnic political participation', in Atul Kohli (ed.), *The State and Development in the Third World* (Princeton, N.J., Princeton University Press, 1986), pp. 88–111.

16 W. J. Argyle, 'European nationalism and African tribalism', in Gulliver (ed.), *Tradition and Transition*, pp. 41–57.

17 Christopher Moseley and R. E. Asher, *Atlas of the World's Languages* (London, Routledge, 1994).

18 Diana Crampton, 'Language and social structure: a case study of the tourism industry in Kenya' (PhD thesis, University of Leeds, 1983), pp. 347–86.

19 Ladefoged *et al.*, *Language in Uganda*, p. 25.

20 W. H. Whiteley, 'Language choice and language planning in East Africa', in Gulliver (ed.), *Tradition and Transition*, pp. 105–25; *Swahili: The Rise of a National Language* (London, Methuen, 1969); B. Heine, *Status and Use of African Lingua Francas* (Munich, Weltforum Verlag, 1970), pp. 80–105.

21 Ruth G. Mukama, 'Getting Ugandans to speak a common language: Recent developments in the language situation and prospects for the future', ch. 23 of Holger Bernt Hansen and Michael Twaddle (eds.), *Changing Uganda* (London, James Currey, 1991).

22 I. M. Lewis, *The Modern History of Somaliland* (London, Weidenfeld & Nicolson, 1965); 'Integration in the Somali Republic', in A. Hazlewood (ed.), *African Integration and Disintegration* (London, Oxford University Press, 1967), pp. 251–84; 'Nationalism and particularism in Somalia', in Gulliver (ed.), *Tradition and Transition*, pp. 339–61.

23 Nigel Grant, 'Education and language', in J. Lowe, N. Grant, and T. D. Williams (eds.), *Education and Nation-Building in the Third World* (Edinburgh, Scottish Academic Press, 1971), pp. 189–200.

24 Myrdal, *Asian Drama*, pp. 81–9, 1639–50, 1742–3.

25 Eugene A. Nida and William Wonderly, 'Communication roles of language in national societies', in Whiteley (ed.), *Language Use*, pp. 62–3.

26 Robert Chambers, *Rural Development* (Harlow, Longman, 1983), p. 92.

27 John Ziman, *Public Knowledge* (Cambridge, Cambridge University Press, 1968), p. 10; *The Force of Knowledge: The Scientific Dimension of Society* (Cambridge, Cambridge University Press, 1976), ch. 11.

28 Christopher Freeman, 'The international science race', in D. O. Edge and J. N. Wolfe (eds.), *Meaning and Control: Essays in Social Aspects of Science and Technology* (London, Tavistock, 1973), p. 233.

29 Jonathan R. Cole and Stephen Cole, *Social Stratification in Science* (Chicago, University of Chicago Press, 1973); Leo Moulin, 'The Nobel prizes for the sciences, 1901–1950', *British Journal of Sociology*, 6 (1955), 246–63, esp. p. 260.

30 Robin Clarke, *Science and Technology in World Development* (Oxford, Oxford University Press for UNESCO, 1985), esp. p. 50; Robert Chambers, *Rural Development*, pp. 76–7; Martin Fransman and Kenneth King (eds.), *Technological Capability in the Third World* (London, Macmillan, 1984), pp. 33–44.

31 World Bank, *World Development Report 1994*, tables 10 and 28; UNDP, *Human Development Report 1994*, table 4.

32 E. M. K. Mulira, *The Vernacular in African Education* (London, Longmans, 1951).

33 John Simmons (ed.), *The Education Dilemma: Policy Issues for Developing Countries in the 1980s* (Oxford, Pergamon, 1980), ch. 2.

34 Edwin Smith, 'Indigenous education in Africa', in E. E. Evans-Pritchard *et al.* (eds.), *Essays Presented to C. G. Seligman* (London, Kegan Paul, 1934), pp. 319–34.

35 Hugh Ashton, *The Basuto*, 2nd edn (London, Oxford University Press, 1967), pp. 46–61; Austin Coates, *Basutoland* (London, HMSO, 1966), pp. 75–80, 109–11.

36 P. T. W. Baxter in A. I. Richards (ed.), *East African Chiefs* (London, Faber, 1960), p. 194.

37 R. D. Matthews and M. Akrawi, *Education in Arab Countries of the Near East* (Washington, D.C., American Council on Education, 1949), pp. 24, 40, 540.

38 Ruth Sloan and Helen Kitchen (eds.), *The Educated African* (London, Heinemann, 1962), ch. 3, pp. 45–6.

39 Humayun Kabir, *Indian Philosophy of Education* (Bombay, Asia Publishing House, 1961), p. 209.

40 *World Fertility Survey* (1984), pp. 22, 37.

41 Anna Maria Turner Lamperis, 'Teaching mothers to read', *Journal of Developing Areas*, 26, 1 (October 1991), 25–52.

42 Frances Stewart, *Basic Needs in Developing Countries* (Baltimore, Md., Johns Hopkins University Press, 1985), p. 121.

43 John Simmons, *The Education Dilemma*, pp. 58–9.

44 World Bank, *World Development Report 1982*, pp. 29, 81.

45 Udo Bude, 'Primary schools and rural development: the African experience', ch. 8 of Roger M. Garrett (ed.), *Education and Development* (London, Croom Helm, 1984).

46 World Bank, *World Development Report 1988*, p. 135; UNDP, *Human Development Report 1994*, table 15.

47 UNDP 1990, p. 4.

48 R. P. Dore, *The Diploma Disease* (London, Allen and Unwin, 1976), p. 61; John Oxenham (ed.), *Education versus Qualifications* (London, Allen and Unwin, 1984).

49 Roy Clarke, 'Schooling as obstacle to development in Zambia', ch. 11 of Roger Garrett (ed.), *Education and Development* (London, Croom Helm, 1984).

50 Arthur Hazlewood *et al.*, *Education, Work, and Pay in East Africa* (Oxford, Clarendon Press, 1989), ch. 2.

51 Nyerere, *Education for Self-Reliance*, pp. 15, 17.
52 Kevin M. Lillis, 'Vocational education in less-developed countries', ch. 7 of Garrett (ed.), *Education and Development*; Joel Samoff, 'Tanzania', ch. 7 of Martin Carnoy and Joel Samoff (eds.), *Education and Social Transition in the Third World* (Princeton, N.J., Princeton University Press, 1990).
53 Ivan Illich, *De-Schooling Society* (London, Calder and Boyars, 1971); *Celebration of Awareness* (London, Calder and Boyars, 1971), chs. 8 and 9; 'Eco-pedagogics and the Commons', ch. 1 of Garrett (ed.), *Education and Development*.
54 Dore, *The Diploma Disease*, ch. 12 and p. 141.
55 T. H. Marshall, *Citizenship and Social Class* (Cambridge, Cambridge University Press, 1950), pp. 25–6.
56 UNDP 1994, table 16.
57 *Ibid.*, table 7.
58 R. L. Stevenson, *Communication, Development, and the Third World: The Global Politics of Information* (New York, University Press of America, 1988), p. 64 and ch. 6.
59 Wilbur Schramm, *Mass Media and National Development* (Stanford, Calif., Stanford University Press, and Paris UNESCO, 1964), p. 60.
60 *Clockwork Radio*, BBC1 television programme, 8 August 1995.
61 Elihu Katz and E. George Wedell, *Broadcasting in the Third World: Promise and Performance* (Cambridge, Mass., Harvard University Press, 1977, and London, Macmillan, 1978).
62 Jeremy Tunstall, *The Media are American: Anglo-American Media in the World* (London, Constable, 1977), pp. 204ff.
63 Stevenson, *Communication*, p. xiii and chs. 1 and 8.
64 Donald S. E. Taylor, 'The Mass Media and National Development with special reference to Broadcasting in Sierra Leone' (M.Phil. thesis, University of Leeds, 1980).
65 Stevenson, *Communication*, p. 170.

10   Religion and development

1 Parts of Max Weber's posthumous *Gesammelte Aufsätze zur Religions-sociologie* (Tubingen, Mohr, 1921) have appeared in English translations as follows: *The Protestant Ethic and the Spirit of Capitalism*, transl. Talcott Parsons (London, Allen & Unwin, 1930); *The Religion of China*, transl. Hans H. Gerth (Glencoe, Ill., Free Press, 1951); *The Religion of India*, transl. Gerth and Don Martindale (Glencoe, Ill., Free Press, 1958); *Ancient Judaism*, transl. Gerth and Martindale (Glencoe, Ill., Free Press, 1952).
2 *The Religion of China*, chs. 1 and 4, pp. 173–95, 227–9, 243.
3 *The Religion of India*, pp. 111–12.
4 Edmund Gosse, *Father and Son: A Study of Two Temperaments* (London, Heinemann, 1907).
5 Robert W. Green (ed.), *Protestantism and Capitalism: The Weber Thesis and its Critics* (Lexington, Mass., D. C. Heath, 1959).
6 Hugh Trevor-Roper, *Religion, the Reformation, and Social Change* (London, Macmillan, 1967).
7 T. O. Ling, 'Max Weber in India', inaugural lecture at the University of Leeds, 11 December 1972.
8 Brien K. Parkinson, 'Non-economic factors in the economic retardation of the rural Malays', *Modern Asian Studies*, 1 (1967), 31–46.
9 William Wilder, 'Islam, other factors and Malay backwardness: comments on an argument', *Modern Asian Studies*, 2 (1968), 155–64.

10 Brien K. Parkinson, 'The economic retardation of the Malays – a rejoinder', *Modern Asian Studies* 2 (1968), 267–72.

11 Mya Maung, 'Socialism and economic development of Burma', *Asian Survey*, 4 (1964), 1182–90.

12 Melford E. Spiro, *Buddhism and Society: A Great Tradition and its Burmese Vicissitudes* (London, Allen & Unwin, 1971), pp. 12, 453–4, 463–7.

13 Robert J. Bocock, 'The Ismailis in Tanzania', *British Journal of Sociology*, 22 (1971), 365–80.

14 H. S. Morris, *The Indians in Uganda* (London, Weidenfeld & Nicolson, 1968); Goldthorpe, *Outlines of East African Society*, pp. 125–6.

15 Cynthia Taft Morris and Irma Adelman, 'The religious factor in economic development', *World Development*, 8 (1980), 491–501.

16 Morris, *The Indians in Uganda*, pp. 51–4.

17 Norman Cohn, *The Pursuit of the Millennium* (London, Secker & Warburg, 1957).

18 Norman Cohn, 'Medieval millenarism: its bearing on the comparative study of millenarian movements', *Comparative Studies in Society and History*, supp. 2 (1962), 31–43; reprinted in Louis Schneider (ed.), *Religion, Culture, and Society* (New York, Wiley, 1964), pp. 168–78.

19 Peter Worsley, *The Trumpet Shall Sound* (London, Macgibbon & Kee, 1957), pp. 20–2, 144.

20 Peter Lawrence, *Road Belong Cargo* (Manchester, Manchester University Press, 1964), pp. 2–3, 116–221.

21 Vittorio Lanternari, *The Religions of the Oppressed*, transl. Lisa Sergio (London, Macgibbon & Kee, 1963).

22 Weston La Barre, *The Peyote Cult*, enlarged edition (Hamden, Conn., Shoestring Press, 1964), pp. 205–6, 227–37.

23 David Barrett, *Schism and Renewal in Africa* (Nairobi, Oxford University Press, 1968), esp. ch. 6.

24 Paul Gifford, 'Some recent developments in African Christianity', *African Affairs*, 93 (1994), 513–34.

25 B. G. M. Sundkler, *Bantu Prophets in South Africa* (London, Lutterworth Press, 1948).

26 F. B. Welbourn, *East African Rebels: A Study of some Independent Churches* (London, SCM Press, 1961), p. 81.

27 Carl G. Rosberg, Jr. and John Nottingham, *The Myth of 'Mau Mau': Nationalism in Kenya* (New York, Praeger, 1966).

28 Walter H. Sangree, *Age, Prayer and Politics in Tiriki, Kenya* (London, Oxford University Press for East African Institute of Social Research, 1966), esp. chs. 6 and 7.

29 Geoffrey Parrinder, *Religion in an African City* (London, Oxford University Press, 1953), ch. 6.

30 M. J. Field, *Search for Security: An Ethno-Psychiatric Study of Rural Ghana* (London, Faber, 1960), part 1.

31 Georges Balandier, *Sociologie Actuelle de l'Afrique Noire* (Paris, Presses Universitaires de France, 1955), transl. Douglas Garman, *The Sociology of Black Africa* (London, Deutsch, 1970); Marie-Louise Martin, *Kimbangu* (Oxford, Blackwell, 1975).

32 George Shepperson, 'The politics of African church separatist movements in British Central Africa, 1892–1916', *Africa*, 24 (1954), 233–45; George Shepperson and T. Price, *Independent African: John Chilembwe and the Nyasaland Rising of 1915* (Edinburgh, Edinburgh University Press, 1958); R. L. Wishlade, *Sectarianism in Southern Nyasaland* (London, Oxford University Press, 1965).

33 David Barrett, *Schism and Renewal in Africa*, pp. 25, 60, 114, 139.

34 Heike Behrend, 'Is Alice Lakwena a witch? The Holy Spirit Movement and its fight against evil in the north', ch. 10 of Hansen and Twaddle, *Changing Uganda*.

35 C. K. Yang, *Religion in Chinese Society* (1961), pp. 218–29, reprinted in Franz Schurmann and Orville Schell, *Imperial China* (Harmondsworth, Penguin, 1967), pp. 157–68.

36 Wolfgang Franke, 'The Taiping rebellion', translated from the German and reprinted in Schurmann and Schell, *Imperial China*, pp. 170–82.

37 Sundkler, *Bantu Prophets*, p. 37.

38 Barrett, *Schism and Renewal*, p. 71.

39 Lawrence, *Road Belong Cargo*, pp. 225–6.

40 J. M. Yinger, 'Religion and social change: functions and dysfunctions of sects and cults among the disprivileged', *Review of Religious Research*, 4, 2 (1963); reprinted (abridged) in Richard D. Knudten (ed.), *The Sociology of Religion: An Anthology* (New York, Appleton, 1967), pp. 482–95.

41 Bruce B. Lawrence, *Defenders of God: The Fundamentalist Revolt Against the Modern Age* (San Francisco, Harper & Row, 1989), esp. pp. 100–1.

42 Martin E. Marty and R. Scott Appleby (eds.), *Fundamentalisms Observed* (Chicago, University of Chicago Press, 1991), esp. Introduction and ch. 15.

43 James Piscatori (ed.), *Islamic Fundamentalism and the Gulf Crisis* (Chicago, The Fundamentalism Project, American Academy of Arts and Sciences, 1991).

11 Individual modernization: some psychological studies

1 Leonard W. Doob, *Becoming More Civilized: A Psychological Exploration* (New Haven, Conn., Yale University Press, 1960).

2 Everett M. Rogers, *Diffusion of Innovations* (New York, Free Press, 1962).

3 W. W. Ogionwo, 'The adoption of technological innovations in Nigeria: A study of factors associated with adoption of farm practices' (PhD thesis, University of Leeds, 1969).

4 David C. McClelland, *The Achieving Society* (Princeton, N.J., Van Nostrand, 1961).

5 David C. McClelland, 'A psychological path to rapid economic development', *Mawazo* (Makerere Journal of the Arts and Social Sciences, Kampala), 1, 4 (December 1968), 9–15.

6 Alex Inkeles and David H. Smith, *Becoming Modern: Individual Change in Six Developing Countries* (London, Heinemann, 1974).

12 Politics in post-colonial states

1 Atul Kohli, Introduction to Kohli (ed.), *The State and Development in the Third World* (Princeton, N.J., Princeton University Press, 1986), pp. 3, 17.

2 C. H. Dodd, *Political Development* (London, Macmillan, 1972), pp. 9–15.

3 Nelson Kasfir, *The Shrinking Political Arena: Participation and Ethnicity in African Politics, with a Case Study of Uganda* (Berkeley, University of California Press, 1976).

4 Samuel P. Huntington and Joan M. Nelson, *No Easy Choice: Political Participation in Developing Countries* (Cambridge, Mass., Harvard University Press, 1976).

5 Francine Frankel, 'Compulsion and social change: is authoritarianism the solution to India's development problems?' in Kohli (ed.), *The State and Development*, pp. 143–7.

6 Kasfir, *The Shrinking Political Arena*, p. 206.

7 Patrick Chabal, Introduction to Chabal (ed.), *Political Domination in Africa* (Cambridge, Cambridge University Press, 1986), p. 8.

8 Robert H. Jackson and Carl G. Rosberg, 'Why Africa's weak states persist: the empirical and the judicial in statehood', in Kohli (ed.), *The State and Development*, pp. 259–82.

9 Riggs, *Administration in Developing Countries*, p. 236.

10 *Zik: A Selection from the Speeches of Nnamdi Azikiwe* (1961), quoted in Paul E. Sigmund, *The Ideologies of the Developing Nations* (New York, Praeger, 1963), pp. 212, 215.

11 George I. Blanksten, 'The politics of Latin America', in Gabriel A. Almond and James S. Coleman (eds.), *The Politics of Developing Areas* (Princeton, N.J., Princeton University Press, 1960), p. 521.

12 Patrick Chabal, 'Revolutionary democracy in Africa: the case of Guinea-Bissau', ch. 5 of Chabal (ed.), *Political Domination in Africa*.

13 Martin Staniland, 'Single-party regimes and political change: the PDCI and Ivory Coast politics', in Colin Leys (ed.), *Politics and Change in Developing Countries* (Cambridge, Cambridge University Press, 1969), pp. 139, 147, 152

14 Cherry Gertzel, *The Politics of Independent Kenya 1963–68* (Nairobi, East African Publishing House, 1970), p. 58.

15 William H. Friedland and Carl G. Rosberg, Jr (eds.), *African Socialism* (Stanford, Calif., Stanford University Press, 1964).

16 Leys, *Politics and Change in Developing Countries*, pp. 272–3.

17 Sigmund, *The Ideologies of Developing Nations*, pp. 18–24.

18 Edward Luttwak, *Coup d'Etat: A Practical Handbook* (London, Allen Lane, 1968).

19 M. Louise Pirouet, 'Human rights issues in Museveni's Uganda', ch. 13 of Hansen and Twaddle, *Changing Uganda*, pp. 14, 197–209.

20 Ruth Leger Sivard, *World Military and Social Expenditures 1993* (Washington, D.C., World Priorities, 15th edn, 1993), pp. 22–3.

21 Edward Gibbon, *The History of the Decline and Fall of the Roman Empire* (1776–88, and many subsequent editions), chs. III–V.

22 William F. Gutteridge, *The Military in African Politics* (London, Methuen, 1969), pp. 104–7.

23 Donald N. Levine, 'The military in Ethiopian politics', in Henry Bienen (ed.), *The Military Intervenes: Case Studies in Political Development* (New York, Russell Sage Foundation, 1968), pp. 28–33.

24 S. E. Finer, *The Man on Horseback: The Role of the Military in Politics* (London, Pall Mall, 1962), pp. 6, 16, 21.

25 Jacques van Doorn, *The Soldier and Social Change* (Beverly Hills, Calif., Sage, 1975), p. 83.

26 Morris Janowitz, *Military Institutions and Coercion in the Developing Nations* (Chicago, University of Chicago Press, 1977, incorporating *The Military in the Political Development of New Nations*, 1964).

27 Robin Luckham, *The Nigerian Military: A Sociological Analysis of Authority and Revolt 1960–67* (Cambridge, Cambridge University Press, 1971), p. 202.

28 Stanislav Andreski (formerly Andrzejewski), *Military Organization and Society*, 2nd edn (London, Routledge & Kegan Paul, 1968), p. 214.

29 Bruce R. Drury, 'Civil–military relations and military rule: Brazil since 1964', in George A. Kourvetaris and Betty A Dobratz (eds.), *World Perspectives in the Sociology of the Military* (New Brunswick, N.J., Transaction Books, 1977), pp. 239–41.

30 G. Pope Atkins, 'The armed forces in Latin American politics', in Charles L. Cochran (ed.), *Civil–Military Relations: Changing Concepts in the Seventies* (New York, Free Press, 1974), pp. 229, 237.

31 Roberta E. McKown, 'Domestic correlates of military intervention in African politics', in Kourvetaris and Dobratz, *World Perspectives in the Sociology of the Military*, p. 196.

32 James S. Wunsch and Dele Olowu (eds.), *The Failure of the Centralized State: Institutions and Self-Governance in Africa* (Boulder, Col., Westview Press, 1990), pp. 1–3.

33 Larry Diamond, Juan J. Linz, and Seymour Martin Lipset, *Democracy in Developing Countries* (4 vols., Boulder, Col., Lynne Reisner, 1988–9), vol. III, pp. ix–x.

34 Chris Allen, Carolyn Baylies and Morris Szeftel, 'Surviving democracy?'; Baylies and Szeftel, 'The fall and rise of multi-party politics in Zambia', *Review of African Political Economy*, 54 (July 1992), 3–10 and 75–91.

35 Michael Bratton and Beatrice Liatto-Katundu, 'A focus group assessment of political attitudes in Zambia', *African Affairs*, 93, 373 (October 1994), 535–63.

36 William Tordoff, 'Political liberalization and economic reform in Africa', *Democratization*, 1 (1994), 100–15.

37 Leo Kuper, ch. 1 of Leo Kuper and M. G. Smith (eds.), *Pluralism in Africa* (Berkeley, University of California Press, 1969). See also M. G. Smith, 'Pluralism, violence, and the modern state', ch. 9 of Ali Kazancigil (ed.), *The State in Global Perspective* (Paris, UNESCO, 1966).

38 Arthur Lewis, *Politics in West Africa* (London, Allen & Unwin, 1965).

39 Arend Lijphart, *Democracy in Plural Societies* (New Haven, Yale University Press, 1977). For a more detailed criticism of the Westminster model, see also Lijphart, *Democracies: Patterns of Majoritarian and Consensus Government in Twenty-One Countries* (New Haven, Yale University Press, 1984).

40 Kasfir, in Kohli (ed.), *The State and Development*, pp. 108–10.

41 Eric A. Nordlinger, *Soldiers in Politics: Military Coups and Governments* (Englewood Cliffs, N.J., Prentice-Hall, 1977), pp. 9–10.

13 Aid and development

1 W. G. Zeylstra, *Aid or Development* (Leyden, Sijthoff, 1977), p. 33.

2 George C. Herring, *Aid to Russia, 1941–1946* (New York, Columbia University Press, 1973), pp. 271–2; Thomas G. Paterson, *Soviet–American Confrontation: Postwar Reconstruction and the Origins of the Cold War* (Baltimore, Md., Johns Hopkins University Press, 1973), pp. 208–21.

3 John White, *The Politics of Foreign Aid* (London, Bodley Head, 1974), pp. 130, 215.

4 United Nations, *Measurement of the Flow of Resources to Developing Countries*, E/4327 ST/ECA/98 (1967); *Partners in Development* (the Pearson Report), p. 144.

5 *World Bank Annual Report 1993*, pp. 9, 11, 37, 45.

6 *Our Common Future* (the Brundtland Report), p. 161.

7 World Bank, *World Development Report 1993*, pp. 89, 165–6.

8 *World Bank Annual Report 1993*, p. 17.

9 Commission on International Development, *Partners in Development* (the Pearson Report) (London, Pall Mall, 1969), esp. pp. vii, 9, 30, 136, 144.

10 World Bank, *World Development Reports 1979*, table 16, pp. 156–7, and *1994*, table 18, pp. 196–7; UNDP 1994, pp. 61–2 and table 41, p. 197.

11 OXFAM, *Annual Review 1993–94*, p. 16.

12 P. T. Bauer, *Dissent on Development* (London, Weidenfeld & Nicolson, 1971).

13 Teresa Hayter, *Aid as Imperialism* (Harmondsworth, Penguin, 1971); see also Cheryl Payer, *The Debt Trap: The IMF and the Third World* (Harmondsworth, Penguin, 1974).

14 Judith Tendler, *Inside Foreign Aid* (Baltimore, Md., Johns Hopkins University Press, 1975).

15 John White, *The Politics of Foreign Aid*, pp. 78–81, 121–5, 161–3.

16 Independent Commission on International Development Issues, *North–South: A Programme for Survival* (London, Pan, 1980), pp. 14, 67–8, 78, 117, 119, 209, 216, 219, 225, 241–2, 249, 278, 282–90, 293–304. See also *Handbook of World Development: The Guide to the Brandt Report* (Harlow, Longman, 1981); *Common Crisis North–South: Co-Operation for World Recovery* (London, Pan, 1983).

17 *The Guardian*, 2 July 1982; Gunnar Myrdal, 'International inequality and foreign aid in perspective', in Meier and Seers, *Pioneers in Development* (1984), pp. 151, 159–65.

18 World Bank, *World Development Report 1981*, pp. 40–1.

19 World Commission on Environment and Development, *Our Common Future* (the Brundtland Report) (Oxford, Oxford University Press, 1987), pp. xi, xii, 7–18, 51, 55, 68, 69, 137, 155, 159–66, 179–80, 189–92, 196–7, 291.

20 Frances Stewart, *Basic Needs in Developing Countries* (Baltimore, Md., Johns Hopkins University Press, 1985) (published in UK as *Planning to Meet Basic Needs*, London, Macmillan, 1985), ch. 1. See also Hollis Chenery *et al.*, *Redistribution with Growth* and *Patterns of Development*.

21 UNDP 1990, pp. 9, 38–9.

22 UNDP 1992, p. 59.

23 World Bank, *World Development Report 1989*, table 2, p. 166.

24 UNDP 1994, pp. 64–5.

25 UNDP 1992, p. 46.

26 Stewart, *Basic needs*, p. 11.

27 World Bank, *World Development Report 1987*, p. 34.

28 UNDP 1990, p. 34.

29 Giovanni Andrea Cornia, Richard Jolly, and Frances Stewart, *Adjustment with a Human Face* (2 vols., Oxford, Clarendon Press, 1987), vol. I, pp. 11–14, 66–7.

30 *Ibid.*, vol. I, pp. 222–3.

31 *Ibid.*, vol. I, pp. 124–7, 164; vol. II, p. 298; UNDP 1990, p. 35.

32 UNDP 1990, p. 4.

Index